OMNIVM LVX CIVIVM

BOSTON
PUBLIC
LIBRARY

TWENTIETH CENTURY VIEWS

The aim of this series is to present the best in contemporary critical opinion on major authors, providing a twentieth century perspective on their changing status in an era of profound revaluation.

Maynard Mack, *Series Editor*
Yale University

THE WESTERN

THE WESTERN

A COLLECTION OF CRITICAL ESSAYS

Edited by
James K. Folsom

Prentice-Hall, Inc. A SPECTRUM BOOK *Englewood Cliffs, N.J.*

Library of Congress Cataloging in Publication Data
MAIN ENTRY UNDER TITLE:
The Western: a collection of critical essays.

(Twentieth century views) (A Spectrum Book)
Bibliography: p.
CONTENTS: Davis, D. B. Ten-gallon hero.—
Hutchinson, W. H. Virgins, villains, and varmints.—
Dobie, J. F. Andy Adams, cowboy chronicler, [etc.]
  1. American fiction—History and criticism—
Addresses, essays, lectures.   2. Western stories—
History and criticism—Addresses, essays, lectures.
3. The West in literature—Addresses, essays,
lectures. I. Folsom, James K.
PS374.W4W4   813'.0874   78-21663
ISBN 0-13-950717-5
ISBN 0-13-950709-4 pbk.

10   9   8   7   6   5   4   3   2   1

PRENTICE-HALL INTERNATIONAL, INC. (London)
PRENTICE-HALL OF AUSTRALIA PTY. LIMITED (Sydney)
PRENTICE-HALL OF CANADA, LTD. (Toronto)
PRENTICE-HALL OF INDIA PRIVATE LIMITED (New Delhi)
PRENTICE-HALL OF JAPAN, INC. (Tokyo)
PRENTICE-HALL OF SOUTHEAST ASIA PTE. LTD. (Singapore)
WHITEHALL BOOKS LIMITED (Wellington, New Zealand)

Contents

IV. Intrepretations

Acknowledgments

Quotations from *The Ox-Bow Incident* by Walter Van Tilburg Clark © 1940 and renewed 1968 by Walter Van Tilburg Clark. Reprinted by permission of Random House, Inc.

The quotation from *Suicide or Murder? The Strange Death of Governor Meriwether Lewis* by Vardis Fisher is used by permission of Opal Fisher.

THE WESTERN

Introduction

by James K. Folsom

Far before the foundation of the Republic, indeed almost as long ago as the establishment of the infant settlements along the Atlantic coastline of what was later to become the United States of America, the presence of the Western frontier was thought to be the most visible symbol of that intangible but very real difference that was early felt to set America off from its European progenitors. The presumed uniqueness of the American spirit, whatever in fact this may have been, was interpreted from the beginning as in large measure a function of the inescapable presence of a fact both moral and geographical with which European civilization was not confronted — the American frontier. How to deal with this frontier became, then, a symbolic statement of the trials, the triumphs, the failures of the American experiment: For the frontier might be subjugated, as in part it was; it might be assimilated, as in part was also the case; it might be dominated, subdued, incorporated, or exploited; but in no case could it be ignored or left alone.

Although the historian Frederick Jackson Turner, writing "The Significance of the Frontier in American History" in 1893, was the first to state baldly that "the true point of view in the history of this nation is not the Atlantic coast, it is the Great West," his idea had been implicit in American thought much earlier than this. In 1837 Ralph Waldo Emerson, in his famous and influential Phi Beta Kappa address, "The American Scholar," had deplored the fact that "the spirit of the American freeman is already suspected to be timid, imitative, tame." The reason, he said, may be attributed among other things to the fact that "we have listened too long to the courtly muses of Europe." His conclusion is hopeful: "We will walk on our own feet; we will work with our own hands; we will speak our own minds." To the question of how exactly we should speak our own minds, Emerson addresses himself some seven years later in his essay, "The Poet" (1844). There he urges the American poet to turn

1

attention to "our incomparable [native] materials," among which, with other neglected elements, he specifically includes "the western clearing, Oregon and Texas."

Nor was Emerson here, as he was in many another case, a solitary voice crying out in the wilderness. Rather, his was perhaps the most memorable articulation of what was already by that time something of a commonplace. That the American West lacked, not heroes and heroism, but poets to celebrate them had been the earlier somber conclusion of Timothy Flint in his first published book, *Recollections of the Last Ten Years* (1826)—years that, parenthetically, had been passed in the West of the Mississippi Valley, for which Flint was later to become a self-appointed spokesman. Speaking of Daniel Boone, Flint remarks in his melancholy fashion that "this Achilles of the West wants a Homer," who, up to that time at least, had not been forthcoming. Flint was later to attempt to rectify this wrong by himself composing a biography of Boone, the *Biographical Memoir of Daniel Boone* (1833), probably the most widely read popular biography in nineteenth-century America. In the same year with his *Recollections,* Flint expressed his own Homeric longings in a first novel, *Francis Berrian, or the Mexican Patriot,* remembered today primarily as a literary curiosity: It is the first novel in English set in the American Southwest. *The Romance of Western History,* as Timothy Flint's Ohio literary rival, James Hall, was to term it in an 1857 volume of anecdotes, remained not unaccomplished but unsung. This was despite "an abundance of fine materials, endowed with capabilities of being wrought by the hand of genius into an original, a rich, and various literature," according to the winner of a prize essay in the *Western Monthly Magazine* for 1833. My point is merely that America's literary chroniclers have, from the first, been accused of not doing justice to the incomparable materials of the settlement of the West with which they have been surrounded.

This is perhaps not so surprising as it first appears when we remember that although the West has been universally assumed to be important since at least as early as the latter part of the seventeenth century, there has been singularly little agreement as to the exact nature of its importance. Nor should it astound us that our cultural hesitation over the precise significance of our Western experience has carried over into one of the chief imaginative records of that experience, the American "Western." So perhaps it is inevitable that any given work within this area has been felt to be deficient by readers who bring to it different predispositions from the author's own. The very diversity of the demands on Western literature is clear evidence that they cannot all be satisfied. Hence, the chorus of commentary surrounding Western literature has turned, perhaps inevitably, certainly unfortunately, into a litany of blame: To adapt Eliot's "Prufrock," "This is not what we meant at all."

It is the editor's hope that this volume of essays, by emphasizing the sophistication of theoretical approaches to the imaginative expression of the American literary West, will serve a contrary purpose. The essays chosen undertake to demonstrate the rich variety of interpretations that the American Western has elicited and, as a literary genre, rewards. The short introductions to the successive groups of selections emphasize different interpretations of the significance of this Western experience. Before considering specific areas of disagreement, however, let us take a general overview of the principal differences of opinion—an overview admittedly simplified in the interests of clarity.

Our unthinking attitudes today toward the West and the Western experience tend to be in general antiprogressive. The staggering environmental problems we face, our growing realization of the necessity of preserving—if only for recreational purposes—the rapidly dwindling store of natural wonders that Americans have for far too long taken for granted, our growing ecological awareness: All have issued in a habitual (if too often unexamined) cultural attitude that the benefits of progress are not worth their price. A literary reflection of this cultural attitude is the rebirth of a perennial European literary ideal, the "primitivist" myth—the notion, baldly stated, that life is better in a state of nature than in society. This idea is by no means limited to Western writing. It has a long and honorable history in American thought, notably in the Transcendentalist movement of the nineteenth century. Indeed, it is remarkable how that bible of American Transcendentalism, Henry David Thoreau's *Walden* (1854), has picked up resonances in late twentieth-century thought that hitherto had been almost totally lacking. Thoreau would be amazed, and perhaps not altogether pleased, to discover himself quoted on wall posters and in books of an ecological bent as a kind of godfather to the present conservationist movement. Yet whatever Thoreau himself might think of his present canonization, there is a certain logic to it; for he did generally affirm the superiority of the values of nature to those of society, however much he might differ with any given conservationist group about the practical ramifications of his position. Another prophet, not strictly speaking a Transcendentalist, is America's first major novelist, James Fenimore Cooper, whose Leatherstocking tales—most notably *The Pioneers* (1823)—aré now read sympathetically (in a way they have not been read in this country for generations, if at all) as a somber study of the propensity of society to lay waste the wilderness and, in so doing, to destroy itself.

Our habitual present-day view of the West—that it represents a kind of paradise irretrievably lost—seems now so self-evidently right to us that we fail to consider that other views are possible and that up until comparatively recent times, the opposite interpretation was habitually offered to explain the significance of our frontier. Until well into the twentieth century, in fact, the quite contrary metaphor of "progress" was generally presumed to be a more satisfactory rubric under which to marshal the Western experience than the antiprogressive "primitivist" notion. From the perspective of progress, the West improved in desirability as it became more like the East, as its savagery and roughness were tamed to meet Eastern standards.

The most striking statement of this view and one of the earliest is by the French traveler to America, J. Hector St. John de Crèvecoeur. In the third letter of his famous *Letters from an American Farmer* (1782), he thoughtfully considers the question: "What is an American?" The type of the successful American, as Crèvecoeur interprets him, is a mythical character named Andrew the Hebridean, a poor emigrant from Scotland to Pennsylvania. Andrew, forced to leave Scotland because of poverty, is befriended by a number of benevolent Americans, taught the art of farming, and finally is successfully established as a comfortable Pennsylvania freeholder. Crèvecoeur's story is prototypical of the later American success stories popularized by Benjamin Franklin and incorporated into the official American mythology by Horatio Alger. But for our purposes, the most interesting facet of this homiletic story is not to be found in Andrew himself, but in those whose failure to make good affords explicit contrast to his success. Among these are many whose life-styles would be applauded by an uncompromising primitivist. Crèvecoeur is both explicit and emphatic: "Our bad people," he says, "are those who are half cultivators and half hunters; and the worst of them are those who have degenerated altogether into the hunting state." The contrasting implications of the primitivist myth and the myth of progress could scarcely be more clearly drawn.

Crèvecoeur is not unique. The first expanded treatment of Daniel Boone in American letters (in an appendix to John Filson's *Kentucke,* 1784), treats him in precisely the same fashion as Crèvecoeur treats his imaginary Andrew. At the end of his "Adventures," Boone reflects with some satisfaction on the course of history. "Thus we behold Kentucke," he tells us, "lately an howling wilderness, the habitation of savages and wild beasts, become a fruitful field; this region, so favorably distinguished by nature, now become the habitation of civilization." It is not accidental that "civilization" in this passage is seen as a set of values that improve and complete "nature" rather than as a set of values opposed and inferior. Boone himself is delighted with this state of affairs. "I now live in peace and safety," he says, "in this delightful country,…delighting in the prospect of its being, in a short time, one of the most opulent and powerful states on the continent of North-America." The contrast with the aged Natty Bumppo—himself a figure based closely on the historic Daniel Boone—leaving New York for the West at the end of *The Pioneers* could not be more telling. "I'm weary of living in clearings," Natty tells the would-be benefactors who would restrain him, "and where the hammer is sounding in my ears from sunrise to sundown.…I crave to go into the woods ag'in, I do."

It is not to the point, even if it were possible, to settle here the relative merits of these two myths. Whether progress is a more or less satisfactory metaphor than primitivism for resolving the ambiguities of our Western experience is not so important as the fact that Americans are themselves of two minds about the issue. Is the American West—as Cooper would have it—"the Garden of the Lord," or is it—as the contrary view holds—"the Great American Desert?" Americans are themselves uncertain, and as a result these deeply ambivalent attitudes are reflected both in debates about the American West itself as a historic and geographical area and in the imaginative reflection of these debates in the American Western. In a brilliant essay entitled, "Errand into the Wilderness," the Puritan historian Perry Miller notes the contradictions inherent in the word "errand" as at once a task important in its own right and as a mission upon which one is sent for someone else. In either case, the problem of whether the American has gone astray on this errand into the wilderness becomes the great fictional question with which the American Western continually grapples.

How then do Westerns attempt to deal with this question? There are, broadly speaking, two general approaches. The more obvious, and by and large the less successful in literary terms, is to choose one of these opposed myths as true and write a novel incorporating it. So Timothy Flint, for example, in *The Shoshonee Valley* (1830), a novel about life among the Western Indians, specifically mounts an attack upon "the wild and pernicious sophism of Rousseau, that the savage is happier, than the social state"; and Robert Montgomery Bird, in a later preface to his nearly contemporary novel, *Nick of the Woods* (1837), takes James Fenimore Cooper to task on almost identical grounds. *Nick of the Woods,* he says in effect, is the kind of history that in the late twentieth century we call revisionist; it is written in refutation of Cooper's "poetical illusion" that the "red men were...nature's nobles, the chivalry of the forest." They are not. "In his natural barbaric state," Bird flatly writes, the Indian "is a barbarian."

The difficulty with such stories as these, of which there are many examples, is that in them the temptation to handle fictional materials didactically on behalf of the chosen thesis wins out. As a result, the stories shrink to the level of moral platitude and metaphysical cliché. They lack, generally speaking, emotional validity.

A more viable literary strategy has been one analogous to the frontier notion of "growing up with the country." This strategy, pioneered and successfully practiced by James Fenimore Cooper, enables the American reader of these stories to have things both ways. When properly handled, the notion of literary hierarchies does not set "good" primitivists against "bad" exponents of progress but instead visualizes the primitive social state of the frontier as something admirable in itself, but incomplete: Progress is interpreted, not as destroying the frontier, but as fulfilling it. Cooper's method of managing this effect is to offer us an admirable character with whom we can identify and who is associated with the past state of the frontier. At the same time, Cooper suggests an admirable future state of society toward which the frontier society of his novels moves.

Cooper's Natty Bumppo, the "Leatherstocking" of his Leatherstocking tales,, resists with the help of his Indian companion Chingachgook, the dastardly French and their evil Iroquois allies in a romantically conceived New York at the time of the French and Indian War. For the French and Iroquois, Cooper has nothing but the most profound contempt. The English, as the reader knows, beat them, and the victory is hailed by Cooper (somewhat, it should be remarked parenthetically, to the historic detriment of his story) as a clear statement of the triumph of civilization over barbarism. At the same time, the result of this English victory over the forces of darkness is, from the limited perspective of Natty himself, no cause for unmixed rejoicing. Its price, ultimately, is a civilized world of farms and towns—"clearings," as Natty contemptuously calls them —in which Natty can himself no longer live. The good and faithful servant of a society that is itself viewed positively finds himself constantly in the position of aiding a future order that has no place for him. The resulting irony is profound. From Natty's point of view, the plot of the Leatherstocking tales is the story of a man who wins every battle but loses the war. Constantly displaced, he is forced ever more westward, leaving behind in the final tale the forests of New York state, which to him are "the Garden of the Lord," to take up residence on the prairie, where he finally dies, sad emblem of a way of life and a value code that no longer have relevance in the modern world.

The emotional effect of the Leatherstocking tales, as of much later Western writing, is primarily to be found in the fact that we as readers identify—illogically, perhaps, but humanly—with both positions. We cheer the English victories over the French and hence implicitly go along with the notion of progress that is inherent in the success of English arms. At the same time, we realize that this success entails putting behind us something of ourselves that we also find dear. Cooper has anticipated the remark of William Faulkner in his 1950 speech accepting the Nobel Prize: "the problems of the human heart in conflict with itself...alone can make good writing."

Both primitivism and progress ask of us a relatively simple response: If the course of history is ultimately seen to be positive, as the metaphor of progress would have us believe, then our emotional response to it should be positive; if, however, as the primitivist myth tells us, the course of history has been a disaster, then our response can be an equally simple negative. Yet human life is not this simple. As Santayana reminds us, "the necessity of rejecting and destroying some things that are beautiful is the deepest curse of existence." Nor are the best Westerns simple. Though rarely tragic in terms of traditional definitions, they feature the quasi-tragic theme that one cannot have everything, that inherent in life itself is the necessity for choice—followed by the consequences of choice.

Understanding of this fact removes a good deal of force from the objection that Westerns are immature, that they deal with concerns beneath the notice of adults, and encourage an escapism of the most insidious kind. From one perspective, and especially when pulp Western writing alone is considered, there is justice in such criticisms. Yet if we assume that the world of the Western is pre-eminently the world of inevitable and often unwelcome choice, something may be said for its "adolescent" stance. From a psychological point of view, the world of adolescence is that point in life when a human being "chooses against" childhood in favor of an unknown, and faintly terrifying, adulthood, toward which his or her attraction is by no means unmixed. The individual becomes an unlikely Everyman who appeals to that part in all of us that insists that childhood is not necessarily a paradise well lost. On balance, the adult world may well be judged better; but it cannot be overemphasized that the judgment is *on balance.*

This in turn explains another ambivalence in serious Westerns— the often ironic, though not unsympathetic, treatment of the hero. This point is often overlooked and, when admitted, underemphasized. Much good criticism has been damaged by the illusion that the Western hero is intended to be admired without qualification, and therefore, if his values leave something to be desired, so must the values of the world he expresses. Yet this is often precisely the Western writer's point. Natty Bumppo, striking out for an always new and uncharted world, leaves behind him adulthood and, generally speaking, a young couple who are to inherit that world and grow up in it. Jack Schaefer's much admired novel, *Shane* (1949), makes an analogous point. In this story, Shane is the projection of the fantasies of the little boy who, as a grown man, narrates the story about everything a man should be. He is gunfighter, horseman, aristocrat. Yet at the novel's conclusion, Shane rides away, leaving the child to inherit an adult world that Shane has made safe for him. The world, the point is clear, belongs not to Shane but to the little boy.

Perhaps the clearest statement of this obsessive Western theme is found in Stephen Crane's short story, "The Bride Comes to Yellow Sky" (1898). This richly comic tale tells of a gunfight between one Scratchy Wilson, the last of an old gang of gunfighters who had once terrified the metropolis of Yellow Sky, and Jack Potter, the sheriff. Wilson is fond of a kind of ritualized combat in which he and the sheriff fight things out. No one is ever hurt during Scratchy Wilson's occasional rampages, and the townspeople have learned to put up with his peculiarities with good grace. Unbeknownst to Wilson, however, Potter has stolen away to get married, and when the story begins, he is on the way home to Yellow Sky with his new bride. Scratchy is at once perceived as a comic projection of the typical Western "heavy" and at the same time as a child (fond of boots with "red tops with gilded imprints, of the kind beloved in winter by little sledding boys"). When Wilson faces Potter down in the streets of Yellow Sky, he cannot come to terms with the "foreign condition" of matrimony. "It's all off now," he says, and turns away. The world clearly belongs, not to Scratchy, but to Jack Potter and his bride, and the moral of the story, as in so much Western writing, is: "Grow up."

At this point, the individual world of the Western hero and the social world of the Western novel coincide. For, as David B. Davis indicates in the essay that follows, the personal myth of adolescence is closely bound, in Western story, with the myth of the golden age of the antebellum South. This myth is without doubt the clearest statement in American thought of our nagging cultural worry that our errand into the wilderness has led us astray. Have we not sold our birthright for some kind of cultural mess of pottage? Did not, from this perspective, our cultural childhood contain values that we chose against in precisely the same manner as our personal childhood contained values that we as individuals chose against? The concern is again a romantic one and deeply ambiguous. If childhood is innocent and therefore presumably upright, is it not also naive and gullible? There are no simple answers to such questions, which are, at bottom, restatements of a personal and cultural dilemma: the dilemma, as Richard Hofstadter puts it, of a society that, though founded in perfection, aspired to progress.

The essays in this volume have been divided into parts organized according to their general subject matter. In the first of these parts, "Making the Hero," Professor David B. Davis addresses the following question: Why has the brief historic period of the opening of the West, relatively unimportant in its own right and certainly no more colorful or romantic than many other eras in American history, become *the* great vehicle for American cultural myth?

In his article, David B. Davis suggests that most of the usually offered answers to this question are, if not wrong, at least superficial. In his view, the "ten-gallon hero" serves primarily as a catalyst for views that American society holds about itself. He sees in the Western a synthesis of two apparently very different elements, the figure of the Western scout as pioneered by James Fenimore Cooper and the myth of the antebellum South. The Western story, he says, is ultimately "antiutilitarian" in thrust, directed as much against the peculiar institution of modern finance capitalism as it is against Indians or other traditional "heavies"—gamblers, corrupt law officers, evil cattlemen, hired gunfighters, and the like—who provide the ostensible conflicts.

One may disagree with some of Davis's interpretations of specific phenomena in Western writing. At the same time, one can only admire a general approach that attempts to explain the popularity of the Western in terms of American cultural myth and of the paradoxes inherent in the American view of America's destiny. Davis's most striking literary insight is almost a Jungian one: that the cowboy hero, far from being a grotesque, is a shadow of ourselves.

The essays in the next part, "Fidelity to What?," directly address the most vexing problem in criticism of the Western story. Obviously some relationship exists between the actual historical American West and the literary West of the Western, but what precisely this relationship should be has been and is the subject of much disagreement. The disagreement concerns first of all Cooper, whose presentation of the West has always been faulted for owing too much to romantic invention and too little to observation and research. In an 1827 review of *The Prairie,* which had appeared earlier the same year, Timothy Flint sets the tone for much subsequent criticism. "Of all natural scenery," he sniffs, "one would think, a prairie the most easy to imagine, without having seen it": The point of the jibe is that Flint has seen a prairie, while Cooper has not. "We shall read him," Flint pompously concludes, "with pleasure only, when he selects scenery and subjects, with which he is familiarly conversant." In the preceding year Flint himself had published *Francis Berrian,* mentioned earlier as the first American novel set in the American Southwest, an area with which Flint himself was "familiarly conversant." The implication was clear. Flint's firsthand knowledge of his setting guarantees that *Francis Berrian* is superior to *The Prairie.* Few other readers have been inclined to agree.

Flint's attack on Cooper for lack of realism was only the first of many. Bret Harte, in his delightful—and regrettably not well known—parody of the Leatherstocking tales, *Muck-a-Muck,* also takes Cooper to task. At one point, in a clever exaggeration of a scene from *The Pioneers,* Harte's hero saves a young lady by killing with one shot a grizzly bear, mountain lion, wildcat, bull, and buffalo—all of which are simultaneously threatening her life. Similar violations of plausibility are canvassed, somewhat less good-humoredly, by Mark Twain in "Fenimore Cooper's Literary Offenses." These offenses include a scene in *The Deerslayer* in which five out of six Indians miss an easy jump into a passing boat—a jump, Twain unsympathetically points out, into a boat that is 140 feet long traveling at no more than one mile an hour. They also include an impossible shooting match in *The Pathfinder* in which the contestants fire at a nail embedded in a target 100 yards away—twice the distance, Twain remarks, at which they could possibly have seen it.

This ground of criticism of the Western has a good bit of validity, as any reader of pulp Westerns or devotee of "B" Western films will agree. Western horsemen do tend to cover ground, hour after hour, always at an extended gallop and to fire off guns that never need reloading. Although no one would pretend that these faults are really virtues, many critics have felt uneasy with the implicit value judgment that factual accuracy is all that matters. Aesthetic success, they argue, may presuppose a degree of realism but need not depend on it.

The first of the articles in this section, W. H. Hutchinson's "Virgins, Villains, and Varmints," sets up an extremely useful distinction between Westerns written from the "outside-in" and those written from the "inside-out." Westerns written from the "outside-in" are judged to be a type of escape literature whose hallmark is irresponsibility to the world of fact. Westerns written from the "inside-out," in contrast, hon the world of fact and are faithful to it. Although we may quarrel with some of Hutchinson's particular assignments (Professors Dobie and Mogen, for example, place Wister with writers from the "outside-in" instead of the reverse), the distinction may be seen to have its merits in his discussion of Eugene Manlove Rhodes, one of the relatively few working cowboys to have turned his experiences into fiction, and in J. Frank Dobie's discussion of Andy Adams from the same perspective as a "cowboy chronicler." Both incline to the point of view expressed in Dobie's remark about Adams, that his "great virtue...is fidelity."

The next two articles in this section take the position that fidelity is a *prerequisite* for good Westerns, but not their *justification*. For Professor Mogen, Owen Wister's heroes gain significance chiefly as they transcend the limitations of their cowboy environment, both within the stories themselves and in terms of what they represent to American culture at large. Professor Westbrook's discussion of *The*

Ox-Bow Incident makes the same point yet more decisively. In his view, the two usual explications of this novel—that it is about the terrible ironies inherent in lynch law or that it represents a warning against Nazi tyranny—are not so much wrong as incomplete. The most important dimension of *The Ox-Bow Incident* is for him a psychological one, the novel's ultimate concern being "man's... failures to get beyond the narrow images of his own ego."

The last two essays in this part suggest a different approach. For the late Vardis Fisher, a Western novelist of note as well as a distinguished scholar and literary critic, the quality of a fictional performance depends less on some kind of "truth to fact" than on a clear realization that the world of "fact" and the world of "fiction" are not really separable although they may be talked about for certain purposes as though they were. The "blend" of fact and fiction is what is important. It is fruitless, moreover, beyond a certain point, to argue that something is fiction, or is fact, since this argument, to extend Fisher's line of reasoning, leads one at last no further than "revisionist" history. The ultimate thrust of the argument in both Fisher essays is to leave us with a question: Should the imaginative chronicle of the West tell us primarily how private persons have shaped the outer world, or should it tell instead how we have projected our inner concerns upon it? There is, of course, no simple answer.

Important to the world of biology is the notion of parallel or convergent evolution—the idea that similar environments produce similar adaptations. Thus African deserts grow plants much like our cactuses, although not in fact botanically related; and, more bizarrely, they supply the habitat of a poisonous serpent almost indistinguishable in locomotion from the American sidewinder, though the African version is not a rattler. It is tempting to assume, by analogy, that similar literary environments will produce similar literary adaptations. The two articles included in Part Three, "The Foreigner's Western," indicate that such is not the case.

Everyone knows that "the hired man on horseback" is not peculiar to our West. In Central and South America the vaquero and the gaucho represent Spanish equivalents. Indeed, as Professor Morley points out in the following article, the culture of the American cowboy derives from the vaquero of Mexico and Spanish California. Even the American name, *buckaroo,* is a corruption of the Spanish *vaquero,* and similarities in occupational terminology, equestrian equipment, techniques of horsemanship, and the like have long been recognized. Yet the imaginative world of gaucho fiction is almost diametrically opposed to that of cowboy fiction, reflecting not so much the similar environments of the two cattle kingdoms as the diverse cultural expectations of Spanish American and North American cultures. For the gaucho is a grown-up—flawed, often victimized, sometimes even tragic in his self-knowledge. A similar conclusion emerges from the second article in this section. During the late nineteenth century, the British were nearly as fascinated with the American West as their American cousins and created a considerable literature about it, now mostly\forgotten, which for a time enjoyed popularity. Yet British cultural expectations imposed on the great bulk of English Western writings a juvenile and moralistic bias that, though not totally absent from the American Western, is nonetheless of far less significance to it.

Study of either English Westerns or gaucho fiction reminds us salutarily that "the West" is not so much a geographical locality as a symbolic place, a landscape of the mind.

When Emerson remarked in 1837 that each age must write its own books, he was addressing the Phi Beta Kappa society of Harvard University, and his reference was primarily to works of scholarship rather than fiction. Emerson rightly apprehended that criticism is itself a form of art and that interpretation is an activity inseparable from creation. In this final section, "Interpretations," Professor Richard Etulain exhaustively traces the course of Western American literary scholarship in the twentieth century. Although his study is an admirable example of the art of bibliography, the student of Western American literature will find its enduring significances elsewhere. For Professor Etulain's ultimate purpose is not to list scholarly volumes dealing with Western writing—but to chart the development of a new "historiography," that is, to interpret the methodology of history as well as to narrate its achievements.

As one of the most remarkable aspects of Western literary scholarship, Etulain notes that it was practically nonexistent until the 1920's. Since then, its growth has been swift. Historical and critical approaches to American Western writing have not only increased greatly in number, Etulain points out, but have multiplied in sophistication. The astonishing growth and improvement in literary studies of Western writing clearly indicate, if nothing else, a significant shift in American cultural attitudes: For Western writing is now acknowledged to be worthy of serious study, whereas up to comparatively recent times it was viewed as an embarrassment to American letters and a sign of American cultural immaturity. Perhaps, Etulain concludes, Western American literature and the study of it have both come of age.

PART ONE

Making the Hero

Ten-Gallon Hero

by David B. Davis

In 1900 it seemed that the significance of the cowboy era would decline along with other brief but romantic episodes in American history. The Long Drive lingered only in the memories and imaginations of old cowhands. The "hoe-men" occupied former range land while Mennonites and professional dry farmers had sown their Turkey Red winter wheat on the Kansas prairies. To be sure, a cattle industry still flourished, but the cowboy was more like an employee of a corporation than the free-lance cowboy of old.[1] The myth of the cowboy lived on in the Beadle and Adams paper-back novels, with the followers of Ned Buntline and the prolific Colonel Prentiss Ingraham. But this seemed merely a substitution of the more up-to-date cowboy in a tradition which began with Leatherstocking and Daniel Boone.[2] If the mountain man had replaced Boone and the forest scouts, if the cowboy had succeeded the mountain man, and if the legends of Mike Fink and Crockett were slipping into the past, it would seem probable that the cowboy would follow, to become a quaint character of antiquity, overshadowed by newer heroes.

Yet more than a half-century after the passing of the actual wild and woolly cowboy, we find a unique phenomenon in American mythology. Gaudy-covered Western or cowboy magazines decorate stands, windows, and shelves in "drug" stores, bookstores, grocery stores and supermarkets from Miami to Seattle. Hundreds of cowboy movies and television shows are watched and lived through by

"Ten-Gallon Hero" by David B. Davis. From *American Quarterly*, 6 (Summer 1954), 111-25. Copyright, 1954, Trustees of the University of Pennsylvania. Reprinted by permission of the author, *American Quarterly,* and the University of Pennsylvania.

[1] Edward Douglas Branch, *The Cowboy and His Interpreters* (New York: D. Appleton & Company, 1926), p. 69.

[2] Henry Nash Smith, *Virgin Land* (Cambridge: Harvard University Press, 1950), pp. v, vi.

millions of Americans. Nearly every little boy demands a cowboy suit and a Western six-shooter cap pistol. Cowboys gaze out at you with steely eye and cocked revolver from cereal packages and television screens. Jukeboxes in Bennington, Vermont, as well as Globe, Arizona, moan and warble the latest cowboy songs. Middle-age folk who had once thought of William S. Hart, Harry Carey, and Tom Mix as a passing phase have lived to see several Hopalong Cassidy revivals, the Lone Ranger, Tim McCoy, Gene Autry, and Roy Rogers. Adolescents and even grown men in Maine and Florida can be seen affecting cowboy, or at least modified cowboy garb, while in the new airplane plants in Kansas, workers don their cowboy boots and wide-brimmed hats, go to work whistling a cowboy song, and are defiantly proud that they live in the land of lassos and sixguns.

When recognized at all, this remarkable cowboy complex is usually defined as the distortion of once-colorful legends by a commercial society. The obvious divergence between the real West and the idealized version, the standardization of plot and characters, and the ridiculous incongruities of cowboys with automobiles and airplanes, all go to substantiate this conclusion.

However, there is more than the cowboy costume and stage setting in even the wildest of these adventures. Despite the incongruities, the cowboy myth exists in fact, and as such is probably a more influential social force than the actual cowboy ever was. It provides the framework for an expression of common ideals of morality and behaviour. And while a commercial success, the cowboy hero must satisfy some basic want in American culture, or there could never be such a tremendous market. It is true that the market has been exploited by magazine, song, and scenario writers, but it is important to ask why similar myths have not been equally profitable, such as the lumbermen of the early northwest, the whale fishermen of New Bedford, the early railroad builders, or the fur traders. There have been romances written and movies produced idealizing these phases of American history, but little boys do not dress up like Paul Bunyan and you do not see harpooners on cereal packages. Yet America has had many episodes fully as colorful and of longer duration than the actual cowboy era.

The cowboy hero and his setting are a unique synthesis of two American traditions, and echoes of this past can be discerned in even the wildest of the modern horse operas. On the one hand, the line of descent is a direct evolution from the Western scout of Cooper and the Dime Novel;³ on the other, there has been a recasting of the golden myth of the anᵗe-bellum South.⁴ The two were fused sometime in the 1890's. Perhaps there was actually some basis for such a union. While the West was economically tied to the North as soon as the early canals and railroads broke the river-centered traffic, social ties endured longer. Many Southerners emigrated West and went into the cattle business, and of course, the Long Drive originated in Texas.⁵ The literary synthesis of two traditions only followed the two social movements. It was on the Great Plains that the decendants of Daniel Boone met the drawling Texas cowboy.

Henry Nash Smith has described two paradoxical aspects of the legendary Western scout, typified in Boone himself.⁶ This woodsman, this buckskin-clad wilderness hunter is a pioneer, breaking trails for his countrymen to follow, reducing the savage wilderness for civilization. Nevertheless, he is also represented as escaping civilization, turning his back on the petty materialism of the world, on the hypocritical and self-conscious manners of community life, and seeking the unsullied, true values of nature.

These seemingly conflicting points of view have counterparts in the woodsman's descendant, the cowboy. The ideal cowboy fights for justice, risks his life to make the dismal little cowtown safe for law-abiding, respectable citizens, but in so doing he destroys the very environment which made him a heroic figure. This paradox is common with all ideals, and the cowboy legend is certainly the embodiment of a social ideal. Thus the minister or social reformer who rises to heroism in his fight against a sin-infested community, would logically become a mere figurehead once the community is reformed. There can be no true ideal or hero in a utopia. And the civilization for which the cowboy or trailblazer struggles is utopian in character.

But there is a further consideration in the case of the cowboy. In our mythology, the cowboy era is timeless. The ranch may own a modern station wagon, but the distinguishing attributes of cowboy and environment remain. There is, it is true, a nostalgic sense that

³Smith, *Virgin Land*, p. 111.

⁴Emerson Hough, *The Story of the Cowboy* (New York: D). Appleton & Company, 1901), p. 200.

⁵Edward E. Dale, *Cow Country* (Norman, Okla.: University of Oklahoma Press, 1942), p. 15.

⁶Smith, *Virgin Land*, p. v.

this is the last great drama, a sad knowledge that the cowboy is passing and that civilization is approaching. But it never comes. This strange, wistful sense of the coming end of an epoch is not something outside our experience. It is a faithful reflection of the sense of approaching adulthood. The appeal of the cowboy, in this sense, is similar to the appeal of Boone, Leatherstocking, and the later Mountain Man. We know that adulthood, civilization, is inevitable, but we are living toward the end of childhood, and at that point "childness" seems eternal; it is a whole lifetime. But suddenly we find it is not eternal, the forests disappear, the mountains are settled, and we have new responsibilities. When we shut our eyes and try to remember, the last image of a carefree life appears. For the nation, this last image is the cowboy.

The reborn myth of the ante-bellum South also involves nostalgia; not so much nostalgia for something that actually existed as for dreams and ideals. When the Southern myth reappeared on the rolling prairies, it was purified and regenerated by the casting off of apologies for slavery. It could focus all energies on its former role of opposing the peculiar social and economic philosophy of the Northeast. This took the form of something more fundamental than mere agrarianism or primitivism. Asserting the importance of values beyond the utilitarian and material, this transplanted Southern philosophy challenged the doctrine of enlightened self-interest and the belief that leisure time is sin.

Like the barons and knights of Southern feudalism, the large ranch owners and itinerant cowboys knew how to have a good time. If there was a time for work, there was a time for play, and the early rodeos, horse races, and wild nights at a cowtown were not occasions for reserve. In this respect, the cowboy West was more in the tradition of fun-loving New Orleans than of the Northeast. Furthermore, the ranch was a remarkable duplication of the plantation, minus slaves. It was a hospitable social unit, where travelers were welcome even when the owner was absent. As opposed to the hard-working, thrifty, and sober ideal of the East, the actual cowboy was overly cheerful at times, generous to the point of waste, and inclined to value friendly comradeship above prestige.[7]

The mythical New England Yankee developed a code of action which always triumphed over the more sophisticated city slicker, because the Yankee's down-to-earth shrewdness, common sense, and

[7]Alfred Henry Lewis, *Wolfville Days* (New York: Stokes, 1902), p. 24.

reserved humor embodied values which Americans considered as pragmatically effective. The ideal cowboy also had a code of action, but it involved neither material nor social success. The cowboy avoided actions which "just weren't done" because he placed a value on doing things "right," on managing difficult problems and situations with ease, skill, and modesty. The cowboy's code was a Western and democratic version of the Southern gentleman's "honor."

In the early years of the twentieth century, a Philadelphia lawyer who affected a careless, loose-tied bow instead of the traditional black ribbon and who liked to appear in his shirt sleeves, wrote: "The nomadic bachelor west is over, the housed, married west is established."[8] In a book published in 1902 he had, more than any other man, established an idealized version of the former, unifying the Southern and Western hero myths in a formula which was not to be forgotten. Owen Wister had, in fact, liberated the cowboy hero from the Dime Novels and provided a synthetic tradition suitable for a new century. *The Virginian* became a key document in popular American culture, a romance which defined the cowboy character and thus the ideal American character, in terms of courage, sex, religion, and humor. The novel served as a model for hundreds of Western books and movies for half a century. In the recent popular movie, "High Noon," a Hollywood star who won his fame dramatizing Wister's novel, reenacted the same basic plot of hero rejecting heroine's pleas and threats, to uphold his honor against the villain Trampas. While this theme is probably at least a thousand years old, it was Owen Wister who gave it a specifically American content and thus explicated and popularized the modern cowboy ideal, with its traditions, informality, and all-important code.

Of course, Wister's West is not the realistic, boisterous, sometimes monotonous West of Charlie Siringo and Andy Adams. The cowboy, after all, drove cattle. He worked. There was much loneliness and monotony on the range, which has faded like mist under a desert sun in the reminiscences of old cowhands and the fiction of idealizers. The Virginian runs some errands now and then, but there are no cattle-driving scenes, no monotony, no hard work. Fictional cowboys are never bored. Real cowboys were often so bored that they memorized the labels on tin cans and then played games to see how well they could recite them.[9] The cowboys in books and movies are

[8]Branch, *The Cowboy and His Interpreters*, pp. 190 ff.

[9]Philip Ashton Rollins, *The Cowboy* (New York: Charles Scribner's Sons, 1922), p. 185.

far too busy making love and chasing bandits to work at such a dreary task as driving cattle. But then the Southern plantation owner did no work. The befringed hero of the forests did not work. And if any ideal is to be accepted by adolescent America, monotonous work must be subordinated to more exciting pastimes. The fact that the cowboy hero has more important things to do is only in keeping with his tradition and audience. He is only a natural reaction against a civilization which demands increasingly monotonous work, against the approaching adulthood when playtime ends.

And if the cowboy romance banishes work and monotony, their very opposites are found in the immensity of the Western environment. To be sure, the deserts and prairies can be bleak, but they are never dull when used as setting for the cowboy myth. There is always an element of the unexpected, of surprise, of variety. The tremendous distances either seclude or elevate the particular and significant. There are mirages, hidden springs,. dust storms, hidden identities, and secret ranches. In one of his early Western novels William MacLeod Raine used both devices of a secret ranch and hidden identity, while Hoffman Birney combined a hidden ranch, a secret trail, and two hidden identities.[10] In such an environment of uncertainty and change men of true genius stand out from the rest. The evil or good in an individual is quickly revealed in cowboy land. A man familiar with the actual cowboy wrote that "brains, moral and physical courage, strength of character, native gentlemanliness, proficiency in riding or shooting—every quality of leadership tended to raise its owner from the common level."[11]

The hazing which cowboys gave the tenderfoot was only preliminary. It was a symbol of the true test which anyone must undergo in the West. After the final winnowing of men, there emerge the heroes, the villains, and the clowns. The latter live in a purgatory and usually attach themselves to the hero group. Often, after the stress of an extreme emergency, they burst out of their caste and are accepted in the elite.

While the Western environment, according to the myth, sorts men into their true places, it does not determine men. It brings out the best in heroes and the worst in villains, but it does not add qualities to the man who has none. The cowboy is a superman and is adorable for his own sake. It is here that he is the descendant of

---

[10]William MacLeod Raine, *Bucky O'Connor* (New York: Grosset & Dunlap, 1907); Hoffman Birney, *The Masked Rider* (New York: Penn, 1928).

[11]Rollins, *The Cowboy*, p. 352.

supernatural folk heroes. Harry Hawkeye, the creator of an early cowboy hero, Calvin Yancey, described him as:

> ...straight as an arrow, fair and ruddy as a Viking, with long, flowing golden hair, which rippled over his massive shoulders, falling nearly to his waist; a high, broad forehead beneath which sparkled a pair of violet blue eyes, tender and soulful in repose, but firm and determined under excitement. His entire face was a study for a sculptor with its delicate aquiline nose, straight in outline as though chiselled from Parian marble, and its generous manly mouth, with full crimson and arched lips, surmounted by a long, silken blonde mustache, through which a beautiful set of even white teeth gleamed like rows of lustrous pearls.[12]

While the Virginian is not quite the blond, Nordic hero, he is just as beautiful to behold. His black, curly locks, his lean, athletic figure, his quiet, unassuming manner, all go to make him the most physically attractive man Owen Wister could describe. Later cowboy heroes have shaved their mustaches, but the great majority have beautiful curly hair, usually blond or red, square jaws, cleft chins, broad shoulders, deep chests, and wasp-like waists. Like the Virginian, they are perfect men, absolutely incapable of doing the wrong thing unless deceived.[13]

Many writers familiar with the real cowboy have criticized Wister for his concentration on the Virginian's love interest and, of course, they deplore the present degeneration of the cowboy plot, where love is supreme. There were few women in the West in the Chisholm Trail days and those few in Dodge City, Abilene, and Wichita were of dubious morality. The cowboy's sex life was intermittent, to say the least. He had to carry his thirst long distances, like a camel, and in the oases the orgies were hardly on a spiritual plane.[14] Since earlier heroes, like the woodsman, led celibate lives, it is important to ask why the cowboy depends on love interest.

At first glance, there would seem to be an inconsistency here. The cowboy is happiest with a group of buddies, playing poker, chasing horse thieves, riding in masculine company. He is contemptuous of farmers, has no interest in children, and considers men who have lived among women as effete. Usually he left his own family at a

[12]Branch, *The Cowboy and His Interpreters*, p. 191.
[13]A Zane Grey hero is typical and is also seen through the eyes of a woman: "She saw a bronzed, strong-jawed, eagle-eyed man, stalwart, superb of height." Zane Grey, *The Light of Western Stars* (New York: Harper & Brothers, 1914), pp. 29-30.
[14]Charles A. Siringo, *A Lone Star Cowboy* (Santa Fe: C. A. Siringo, 1919), p. 64.

tender age and rebelled against the restrictions of mothers and older sisters. Neither the Virginian nor the actual cowboys were family men, nor did they have much interest in the homes they left behind. Thus it would seem that courting a young schoolteacher from Vermont would be self-destruction. At no place is the idealized cowboy further from reality than in his love for the tender woman from the East. Like the law and order he fights for, she will destroy his way of life.

But this paradox is solved when one considers the hero cowboy, not the plot, as the center of all attention. Molly Wood in *The Virginian*, like all her successors, is a literary device, a *dea ex machina* with a special purpose. Along with the Western environment, she serves to throw a stronger light on the hero, to make him stand out in relief, to complete the picture of an ideal. In the first place, she brings out qualities in him which we could not see otherwise. Without her, he would be too much the brute for a real folk hero, at least in a modern age. If Molly Wood were not in *The Virginian*, the hero might seem too raucous, too wild. Of course, his affair with a blonde in town is handled genteelly; his boyish pranks such as mixing up the babies at a party are treated as good, clean fun. But still, there is nothing to bring out his qualities of masculine tenderness, there is nothing to show his conscience until Molly Wood arrives. A cowboy's tenderness is usually revealed through his kindness to horses, and in this sense, the Eastern belle's role is that of a glorified horse. A woman in the Western drama is somebody to rescue, somebody to protect. In her presence, the cowboy shows that, in his own way, he is a cultural ideal. The nomadic, bachelor cowboys described by Andy Adams and Charles Siringo are a little too masculine, a little too isolated from civilization to become the ideal for a settled community.

While the Western heroine brings out a new aspect of the cowboy's character, she also serves the external purpose of registering our attitudes toward him. The cowboy ideal is an adorable figure and the heroine is the vehicle of adoration. Female characters enable the author to make observations about cowboys which would be impossible with an all-male cast.[15] This role would lose its value if the heroine surrendered to the cowboy immediately. So the more she struggles with herself, the more she conquers her Eastern reserva-

---

[15]No male character could observe that, "'Cowboys play like they work or fight,' she added. 'They give their whole souls to it. They are great big simple boys.'" Grey, *The Light of Western Stars*, p. 187.

tions and surmounts difficulties before capitulating, the more it enhances the hero.

Again, *The Virginian* is the perfect example. We do not meet Molly Wood in the first part of the book. Instead, the author, the I, who is an Easterner, goes to Wyoming and meets the Virginian. It is love at first sight, not in the sexual sense, of course (this was 1902), but there is no mistaking it for anything other than love. This young man's love for the Virginian is not important in itself; it heightens our worship of the hero. The sex of the worshiper is irrelevant. At first the young man is disconsolate, because he cannot win the Virginian's friendship. He must go through the ordeal of not knowing the Virginian's opinion of him. But as he learns the ways of the West, the Virginian's sublime goodness is unveiled. Though increasing knowledge of the hero's character only serves to widen the impossible gulf between the finite Easterner and the infinite, pure virtue of the cowboy, the latter, out of his own free grace and goodness recognizes the lowly visitor, who adores him all the more for it. But this little episode is only a preface, a symbol of the drama to come. As soon as the Virginian bestows his grace on the male adorer, Molly Wood arrives. The same passion is reenacted, though on a much larger frame. In this role, the sex of Molly *is* important, and the traditional romance plot is only superficial form. Molly's coyness, her reserve, her involved heritage of Vermont tradition, all go to build an insurmountable barrier. Yet she loves the Virginian. And Owen Wister and his audience love the Virginian through Molly Wood's love. With the male adorer, they had gone about as far as they could go. But Molly offers a new height from which to love the Virginian. There are many exciting possibilities. Molly can save his life and nurse him back to health. She can threaten to break off their wedding if he goes out to fight his rival, and then forgive him when he disobeys her plea. The Virginian marries Molly in the end and most of his descendants either marry or are about to marry their lovely ladies. But this does not mean a physical marriage, children, and a home. That would be building up a hero only to destroy him. The love climax at the end of the cowboy drama raises the hero to a supreme height, the audience achieves an emotional union with its ideal. In the next book or movie the cowboy will be the carefree bachelor again.

The classic hero, Hopalong Cassidy, has saved hundreds of heroines, protected them, and has been adored by them. But in 1910 Hopalong, "remembering a former experience of his own, smiled in knowing cynicism when told that he again would fall under the feminine spell."[16] In 1950 he expressed the same resistance to actual marriage:

"But you can't always move on, Hoppy!" Lenny protested. "Someday you must settle down! Don't you ever think of marriage?" "Uh-huh, and whenever I think of it I saddle Topper and ride. I'm not a marrying man, Lenny. Sometimes I get to thinkin' about that poem a feller wrote, about how a woman is only a woman but—" "The open road is my Fate!" she finished. "That's it. But can you imagine any woman raised outside a tepee livin' in the same house with a restless man?"[17]

The cowboy hero is the hero of the pre-adolescent, either chronologically or mentally. It is the stage of revolt against femininity and feminine standards. It is also the age of hero worship. If the cowboy romance were sexual, if it implied settling down with a real *girl*, there would be little interest. One recent cowboy hero summarized this attitude in terms which should appeal strongly to any ten-year-old: "I'd as soon fight a she-lion barehanded as have any truck with a gal."[18] The usual cowboy movie idol has about as much social presence in front of the leading lady as a very bashful boy. He is most certainly not the lover-type. That makes him lovable to both male and female Americans. There can be no doubt that Owen Wister identified himself, not with the Virginian, but with Molly Wood.

While some glorifiers of the actual cowboy have maintained that his closeness to nature made him a deeply religious being, thus echoing the devoutness of the earlier woodsman hero who found God in nature, this tradition has never carried over to the heroic cowboy. Undoubtedly some of the real cowboys were religious, though the consensus of most of the writers on the subject seems to indicate that indifference was more common.[19] Intellectualized religion obviously had no appeal and though the cowboy was often deeply sentimental, he did not seem prone to the emotional and frenzied religion of backwoods farmers and squatters. Perhaps his freedom from family conflicts, from smoldering hatreds and en-

[16]Clarence E. Mulford, *Hopalong Cassidy* (Chicago: A. C. McClurg & Company, 1910), p. 11.

[17]Tex Burns, pseud. (Louis L'Amour), *Hopalong Cassidy and the Trail to Seven Pines* (New York: Doubleday, 1951), p. 187.

[18]Davis Dresser, *The Hangmen of Sleepy Valley* (New York: Jefferson House, 1950), p. 77.

[19]Hough, *The Story of the Cowboy*, p. 199; Branch, *The Cowboy and His Interpreters*, p. 160; Rollins, *The Cowboy*, p. 84; Lewis, *Wolfville Days*, p. 216.

tangled jealousies and loves, had something to do with this. Despite the hard work, the violent physical conflicts, and the occasional debaucheries, the cowboy's life must have had a certain innocent, Homeric quality. Even when witnessing a lynching or murder, the cowboy must have felt further removed from total depravity or original sin than the farmer in a squalid frontier town, with his nagging wife and thirteen children.

At any rate, the cowboy hero of our mythology is too much of a god himself to feel humility. His very creation is a denial of any kind of sin. The cowboy is an enunciation of the goodness of man and the glory which he can achieve by himself. The Western environment strips off the artifice, the social veneer, and instead of a cringing sinner, we behold a dazzling superman. He is a figure of friendly justice, full of self-reliance, a very tower of strength. What need has he of a god?

Of course, the cowboy is not positively anti-religious. He is a respecter of traditions as long as they do not threaten his freedom. The Virginian is polite enough to the orthodox minister who visits his employer's ranch. He listens respectfully to the long sermon, but the ranting and raving about his evil nature are more than he can stand. He knows that his cowboy friends are good men. He loves the beauty of the natural world and feels that the Creator of such a world must be a good and just God. Beyond that, the most ignorant cowboy knows as much as this sinister-voiced preacher. So like a young Greek god leaving Mount Olympus for a practical joke in the interest of justice, the Virginian leaves his role of calm and straightforward dignity, and engages in some humorous guile and deceit. The minister is sleeping in the next room and the Virginian calls him and complains that the devil is clutching him. After numerous sessions of wrestling with his conscience, the sleepy minister acting as referee, morning comes before the divine finds he has been tricked. He leaves the ranch in a rage, much to the delight of all the cowboys. The moral, observes Wister, is that men who are obsessed with evil and morbid ideas of human nature, had better stay away from the cowboy West. As Alfred Henry Lewis put it, describing a Western town the year *The Virginian* was published, "Wolfville's a hard practical outfit, what you might call a heap obdurate, an' it's goin' to take more than them fitful an' o'casional sermons I aloodes to,—to reach the roots of its soul."[20] The cowboy is too good and has

[20]Lewis, *Wolfville Days*, p. 216.

too much horse sense to be deluded by such brooding theology. Tex
Burns could have been describing the Virginian when he wrote
that his characters "had the cow hand's rough sense of humor and a
zest for practical jokes no cow hand ever outgrows."[21]
Coming as it did at the end of the nineteenth century, the cowboy
ideal registered both a protest against orthodox creeds and a faith
that man needs no formal religion, once he finds a pure and natural
environment. It is the extreme end of a long evolution of individualism. Even the individualistic forest scout was dependent on his
surroundings, and he exhibited a sort of pantheistic piety when he
beheld the wilderness. The mighty captain of industry, while not
accountable to anyone in this world, gave lip-service to the generous God who had made him a steward of wealth. But the cowboy
hero stood out on the lonely prairie, dependent on neither man nor
God. He was willing to take whatever risks lay along his road and
would gladly make fun of any man who took life too seriously.
Speaking of his mother's death, a real cowboy is supposed to have
said:

> With almost her last breath, she begged me to make my peace with
> God, while the making was good. I have been too busy to heed her last
> advice. Being a just God, I feel that He will overlook my neglect. If
> not, I will have to take my medicine, with Satan holding the spoon.[22]

While the cowboy hero has a respect for property, he does not seek
personal wealth and is generous to the point of carelessness. He
gives money to his friends, to people in distress, and blows the rest
when he hits town on Saturday night. He owns no land and, in fact,
has only contempt for farmers, with their ploughed fields and
weather-beaten buildings. He hates the slick professional gambler,
the grasping Eastern speculator, and railroad man. How are these
traits to be reconciled with his regard for property rights? The
answer lies in a single possession—his horse. The cowboy's horse
is what separates him from vagabondage and migratory labor. It is
his link with the cavalier and plumed knight. More and more, in
our increasingly property-conscious society, the cowboy's horse
has gained in importance. A horse thief becomes a symbol of con-
centrated evil, a projection of all crime against property and concomitantly, against social status. Zane Grey was adhering to this

[21]Burns, *Hopalong Cassidy*, p. 130.
[22]Siringo, *A Lone Star Cowboy*, p. 37.

tradition when he wrote, "in those days, a horse meant all the world to a man. A lucky strike of grassy upland and good water...made him rich in all that he cared to own." On the other hand, "a horse thief was meaner than a poisoned coyote."[23]

When a cowboy is willing to sell his horse, as one actually does in *The Virginian,* he has sold his dignity and self-identity. It is the tragic mistake which will inevitably bring its nemesis. His love for and close relationship with his horse not only make a cowboy seem more human, they also show his respect for propriety and order. He may drift from ranch to ranch, but his horse ties him down to respectability. Yet the cowboy hero is not an ambitious man. He lacks the concern for hard work and practical results which typifies the Horatio Alger ideal. Despite his fine horse and expensive saddle and boots, he values his code of honor and his friends more than possessions. Because the cowboy era is timeless, the hero has little drive or push toward a new and better life. He fights for law and order and this implies civilization, but the cowboy has no visions of empires, industrial or agrarian.

One of the American traits which foreign visitors most frequently described was the inability to have a good time. Americans constantly appear in European journals as ill-at-ease socially, as feeling they must work every spare moment. Certainly it was part of the American Protestant capitalistic ethic, the Poor Richard, Horatio Alger ideal, that spare time, frivolous play, and relaxation were sins which would bring only poverty, disease, and other misfortunes. If a youth would study the wise sayings of great men, if he worked hard and made valuable friends but no really confidential ones, if he never let his hair down or became too intimate with any person, wife included, if he stolidly kept his emotions to himself and watched for his chance in the world, then he would be sure to succeed. But the cowboy hero is mainly concerned with doing things skillfully and conforming to his moral code for its own sake. When he plays poker, treats the town to a drink, or raises a thousand dollars to buy off the evil mortgage, he is not aiming at personal success. Most cowboy heroes have at least one friend who knows them intimately, and they are seldom reserved, except in the presence of a villain or nosey stranger.

Both the hero and real cowboy appear to be easy-going and in-

[23]Zane Grey, *Wildfire* (New York: Harper & Brothers, 1917), pp. 10, 7.

formal. In dress, speech, and social manner, the cowboy sets a new ideal. Every cowboy knows how to relax. If the villains are sometimes tense and nervous, the hero sits placidly at a card game, never ruffled, never disturbed, even when his arch rival is behind him at the bar, hot with rage and whisky. The ideal cowboy is the kind of man who turns around slowly when a pistol goes off and drawls, "Ah'd put thet up, if Ah were yew." William MacLeod Raine's Sheriff Collins chats humorously with some train robbers and maintains a calm, unconcerned air which amuses the passengers, though he is actually pumping the bandits for useful information.[24] Previously, he had displayed typical cowboy individualism by flagging the train down and climbing aboard, despite the protests of the conductor. Instead of the eager, aspiring youth, the cowboy hero is like a young tomcat, calm and relaxed, but always ready to spring into action. An early description of one of the most persistent of the cowboy heroes summarizes the ideal characteristics which appeal to a wide audience:

> Hopalong Cassidy had the most striking personality of all the men in his outfit; humorous, courageous to the point of foolishness, eager for fight or frolic, nonchalant when one would expect him to be quite otherwise, curious, loyal to a fault, and the best man with a Colt in the Southwest, he was a paradox, and a puzzle even to his most intimate friends. With him life was a humorous recurrence of sensations, a huge pleasant joke instinctively tolerated, but not worth the price cowards pay to keep it. He had come onto the range when a boy and since that time he had laughingly carried his life in his open hand, and...still carried it there, and just as recklessly.[25]

Of course, most cowboy books and movies bristle with violence. Wild fist fights, brawls with chairs and bottles, gun play and mass battles with crashing windows, fires, and the final racing skirmish on horseback, are all as much a part of the cowboy drama as the boots and spurs. These bloody escapades are necessary and are simply explained. They provide the stage for the hero to show his heroism, and since the cowboy is the hero of the pre-adolescent, he must prove himself by their standards. Physical prowess is the most important thing for the ten- or twelve-year-old mind. They are constantly plagued by fear, doubt, and insecurity, in short, by evil, and they lack the power to crush it. The cowboy provides the instrument for

[24] Raine, *Bucky O'Connor,* p. 22.
[25] Mulford, *Hopalong Cassiay,* p. 65.

ethics of the cowboy band are the ethics of the boy's gang, where each member has a role determined by his physical skills and his their aggressive impulses, while the villain symbolizes all evil. The past performance. As with any group of boys, an individual cowboy who had been "taken down a peg," was forever ridiculed and teased about his loss in status.[26] The volume of cowboy magazines, radio programs and motion pictures, would indicate a national hero for at least a certain age group, a national hero who could hardly help but reflect specific attitudes. The cowboy myth has been chosen by this audience because it combines a complex of traits, a way of life, which they consider the proper ideal for America. The actual drama and setting are subordinate to the grand figure of the cowboy hero, and the love affairs, the exciting plots, and the climactic physical struggles, present opportunities for the definition of the cowboy code and character. Through the superficial action, the heroism of the cowboy is revealed, and each repetition of the drama, like the repetition of a sacrament, reaffirms the cowboy public's faith in their ideal.

Perhaps the outstanding cowboy trait, above even honor, courage, and generosity, is the relaxed, calm attitude toward life. Though he lives intensely, he has a calm self-assurance, a knowledge that he can handle anything. He is good-humored and jovial.[27] He never takes women too seriously. He can take a joke or laugh at himself. Yet the cowboy is usually anti-intellectual and anti-school, another attitude which appeals to a younger audience.[28]

Above all, the cowboy is a "good joe." He personifies a code of personal dignity, personal liberty, and personal honesty. Most writers on the actual cowboy represented him as having these traits.[29] While many of these men obviously glorify him as much as any fiction writers, there must have been some basis for their judgment. As far as his light-hearted, calm attitude is concerned, it is amazing

[26]Sam P. Ridings, *The Chisholm Trail* (Medford, Okla.: S. P. Ridings, 1936), p. 297.

[27]The cowboy hero was judged to be "out of sorts when he could not vent his peculiar humor on somebody or something." Grey, *The Light of Western Stars,* pp. 118-19.

[28]This anti-intellectualism in the Western myth is at least as old as Cooper's parody of the scientist, Obed Bat, in *The Prairie.* More recently, Will James took pride in his son's poor attitude and performance in school. Will James, *The American Cowboy* (New York: Charles Scribner's Sons, 1942), p. 107.

[29]Ridings, *The Chisholm Trail,* pp. 278-94; Rollins, *The Cowboy,* p. 67; Dale, *Cow Country,* pp. 122, 153.

how similar cowboys appear, both in romances and non-fiction.[30] Millions of American youth subscribed to the new ideal and yearned for the clear, Western atmosphere of "unswerving loyalty, the true, deep affection, and good-natured banter that left no sting."[31] For a few thrilling hours they could roughly toss conventions aside and share the fellowship of ranch life and adore the kind of hero who was never bored and never afraid.

Whether these traits of self-confidence, a relaxed attitude toward life, and good humor, have actually increased in the United States during the past fifty years, is like asking whether men love their wives more now than in 1900. Certainly the effective influence of the cowboy myth can never be determined. It is significant, however, that the cowboy ideal has emerged above all 'others. And while the standardization of plot and character seems to follow other commercial conventions, the very popularity of this standard cowboy is important and is an overlooked aspect of the American character. It is true that this hero is infantile, that he is silly, overdone, and unreal. But when we think of many past ideals and heroes, myths and ethics; when we compare our placid cowboy with, say, the eager, cold, serious hero of Nazi Germany (the high-cheekboned, blond lad who appeared on the Reichsmarks); or if we compare the cowboy with the gangster heroes of the thirties, or with the serious, self-righteous and brutal series of Supermen, Batmen, and Human Torches; when in an age of violence and questioned public and private morality, if we think of the many possible heroes we might have had—then we can be thankful for our silly cowboy. We could have chosen worse.

---

[30]According to Alfred Henry Lewis, surly and contentious people were just as unpopular in Wolfville as they appear to be in fiction. Lewis, *Wolfville Days*, p. 217.

[31] Mulford, *Hopalong Cassidy*, p. 155.

Virgins, Villains, and Varmints

by W. H. Hutchinson

A man who had punched cows in the Raft River country and then in the Sand Hills as a youth opened an essay in *Harper's* with this sentence: "A literary critic can discuss detective stories without being called before the board of governors, but the even more popular form of packaged fiction called the Western appears to be off limits." It is considered possible that Bernard DeVoto knew somewhat of what he wrote.[1] Behind his simple statement is the solid fact that the "western" has been dismissed by literary critics, sociologists, and certificated historians of the American scene as an error of popular taste. No claim is made to any Brahmin caste-mark in what follows.

The basis for this venture is the same as the basis for a backraise on two small pair after the draw—personal opinion. This opinion has been formed over a lively lifetime as the writer has read "westerns," first as an avocation and for the last decade as vocational guidance. The difference is the same as that between keeping a mistress and being married.

In the first instance, you read for the *what* of the story, thus helping the author to sustain the illusion of reality. In the second, you read for the *how* of the story, that you may learn what the author can teach you about "grabbing the reader by the throat and giving it to him while his eyes pop."[2] This may seem a peculiar exercise. It is essential if we are to comprehend one reason why the "western"

[1]"Phaëthon on Gunsmoke Trail," December, 1954.
[2]Attributed to Jack Lait, New York *Daily Mirror.*

has been the bar sinister on any American literary escutcheon for some years past.[3]

Hand in hand with this exercise goes a study of the title of this piece, the same title that was used to announce the seminar on which it is based.[4] It seems highly probable that the title, of itself, induced a larger attendance at that seminar than would have been the case had it been announced as a study of "Vulgar Caricatures of Hegelian World Historical Personalities in a Genre of American Popular Fiction."

The basic fact about the "western" has been overlooked consistently, perhaps deliberately, by those who overlook it. It was and is written for the same reason that all other popular fiction—Dickens, Stevenson, Conrad, Hemingway, and Faulkner not excepted—was and is written: to provide entertainment for the reader and economic well-being, or a facsimile thereof, for the writer. The "western" was and is a commercial product, a standard brand of merchandise for which the customers ask by name—Brand, Drago, Ernenwein, Fox, Foreman, Grey, Haycox, McDonald, Raine, Short. And when the customers—first editors, then readers—ask for a "western," what do they mean?

Depending upon the capillary attraction of the individual, the western-label may encompass anything from John Ledyard's influence upon Thomas Jefferson down to the latest issue of *Powdersmoke Yarns* in the local newsstand. The Fur Trade, Gold Rushes, Overlanders, Indians, Cavalry, the whole complex of Bernard DeVoto's "theme of wonder" can be lumped as "westerns." For our purposes here, the epithet covers but one segment of this complex, the last one in time—the Cowboy—Free Range—Horseback era— told in fiction form in its primary colors of black-and-white and blood-on-the-saddle; "horse opera," the "oater" of Hollywood.

[3]The Western Writers of America have as their goal the improvement of the literary caliber of the "western" and its acceptance on the same plane as other forms of native writing.

[4]The first draft of this essay was an oral seminar by the author during his work in the Rhodes Collection at the Huntington Library. A prose version appeared in the Huntington Library *Quarterly*, August, 1953, and my thanks are due that inspiriting workplace and Dr. French Fogle, editor, for permission to revise, expand and improve that version for inclusion here.

A certain vestigial honesty compels the admission that the title is not mine own creation. Mr. Thomas B. Clark used it first in *American Heritage*, Spring, 1952, for his article on Beadle's dime novels.

Other than this conveyance, the essay is mine own save where footnotes indicate my obligations.

The parents of this stylized art form can be limned with broad strokes of an opinionated brush. Maternal genes and chromosomes came from the timeless womb that has produced the sun god for all ages and all peoples; a blood link to El Cid, Taras Bulba, Robin Hood, and, more recently, Davy Crockett, *redivivus*. The American line of descent can be traced from the writings and editings of Timothy Flint, specifically in the narrative of James Ohio Pattie, through the frontier-Gothic romances of Fenimore Cooper and Mayne Reid to the "yellowbacks"—Col. Prentiss Ingraham and Ned Buntline for ready references—that took over about the time of Fort Sumter and held the field until the turn of the century. This ancestral strain received an incestuous infusion from the buckskin extravaganzas of Buffalo Bill Cody, and this infusion is sustained today by innumerable arena performances by professional *road-eeo* cowboys who could not unroll their beds in an old-time cow camp and would not want to.

The paternity of the "western" may seem as obscure as the sire of a bastard calf on the open range, but such is not the case. Humor is the father of the "western" as we know it: the half-horse and half-alligator tall tales of the *Davy Crockett Almanacs* which the grotesqueries and conventions of Bret Harte fixed in our literary tapestry. Mark Twain, too, had a part in this, as did O. Henry, while Henry Wallace Phillips and Alfred Henry Lewis brought it to its full and fleeting peak.[5] The most recent manifestations of this unalloyed ancestral strain have been the "Painting Pistoleer" yarns by Walker Tompkins in *Zane Grey's Western Magazine,* recently deceased, and the "Buffalo Bend" stories by Michael Fessier [Foster] in *Saturday Evening Post.*[6]

The offspring of these parents made its first faltering steps as a respectable member of the "outdoor-action" story that made a fair share of the contents of such magazines as *Munsey's, McClure's, Everybody's* and *Scribner's* during the late 1890's with writers like Jack London, Stewart Edward White, Joseph Conrad, Rex Emerson Beach, J. Olivier Curwood, and Will Levington Comfort.[7] The discernible "westerns" in this period, by Phillips, Owen Wister,

[5]Take the word *which* in Harte's "Truthful James" and compare it with the same word usage in Lewis's *Wolfville* by his "Old Cattleman." Like finding a drowned cat in the cream jug.

[6]Michael Foster died while this was being written. S. Omar Barker is the only major writer in the field today who consistently uses humor in its olden application and its primeval style.

[7]Beach and Curwood are shown as their by-lines of that period.

White, and O.Henry, were not yet tinged with the tar brush. They were treated as just another face in the "outdoor-action" school, and, as such, they received a fair amount of both space and attention in the current literary journals and supplements. This meed of recognition, this inclusion in the fold of American letters, continued for the first decade of this century as the "western" began to take its final, fatal shape—*The Virginian*, 1902; *Chip of the Flying U*, 1905; *Whispering Smith*, 1906; *Bar-20*, 1907; *Hopalong Cassidy* and *Bucky O'Connor*, 1910.[8] For an opinion, the demarcation comes in 1912 with a book whose closing and most memorable phrase was "Roll the stone!...Lassiter I love you!"

Riders of the Purple Sage not only gave Zane Grey his first taste of success after four unremunerative novels, it ushered in the "western" as we know it. It should be pointed out that, in this book, Grey was ahead of himself, far ahead of the art form he did so much to implant in the consciousness of generations of readers, in the significance of his closing phrase above. When Lassiter did roll that rock, he and the beauteous heroine were sealed in a hidden valley, presumably for all time, with no clergyman in their past, present, or foreseeable future. This was a daring departure from the morals of the current "outdoor-action" school. It was made palatable by the dread alternative in the plot that the heroine otherwise would wind up as a Mormon plural. This, in itself, affords a striking comment on the polygamy propaganda residue in the national psyche, but as a literary convention it did not take. The basic ingredients that Grey borrowed bodily from *The Virginian*, rejecting Wister's still discernible humor, and beat to a froth in *Riders of the Purple Sage* have remained unchanged in essence ever since—virgins, villains, and varmints.

Woman in the "western" was a sawdust doll, and the tags used to depict her character were obvious. If she wore calico or gingham, had hair to her waist when the braids "accidentally" came unwound, possessed a clear complexion and lustrous eyes, she was *good*—lineal descendant of Ouida's idealized English maidens genteelly skirting the whirlpool of life—and the hero would get his just reward in the end by claiming her hand. If she wore tights, or spangles, and worked in a saloon, she was *bad* and was doomed to a miserable end—either as an accomplice of the villain or as a lone figure stumbling off into scorching sun or numbing blizzard, with only her

[8]Wister, Bower, Spearman, Mulford, and Raine in order of titles. Harold Bell Wright probably belongs in here, but enough is enough.

thoughts of what might have been for protection. Occasionally, she was given the chance to lead a better life—Hereafter. Women are not that simple, as any fool or fictioneer should know by experience. In a sense, however, there were only two classes of women in the free range days and everybody knew where they stood, which made for an unembarrassed social life all around. Women in the "western" were not typical of their sex at large any more than the libidinous neurotics or man-eating viragos who populate today's fiction are typical. Their appearances in the "western" made it easier for the reader to concentrate on the action-plot without getting petticoats in his mind and thus complicating the author's task.

If the "western" villain leered and drooled, he was a *heavy* villain, whose slavering approach to the heroine, or to the material crux of the plot, was easily predictable. His end was a matter of physical violence, honorable on the hero's part, generally fatal. If he dressed like a parson or gambler, he was a *sneaky* villain to be dealt with after unmasking, even as the sidewinder who rattles not or if he does cannot be heard. Along with these two categories of Anglo-Saxon menace there was the Mexican or anyone with swarthy skin, flashing teeth, and silver-studded costume. These characters were *always* cast as villains, major or minor, until the rise of the Good Neighbor Policy, and even the hint of one such in a story line was an automatic signal for the reader to mark him well for justice. This type-casting of the *hombre del pais* can be attributed to the Texas influence on the folk-ways of the free range, or it can be traced to a residual fear of the Spanish Armada and the Inquisition. In either case, *Westward Ho* presages the role the Spaniard and his New World descendants were foreordained to play in the "western" story.

As to the varmints in the "western," they were largely incidental props. Coyote, lion, bear, deer, antelope, snake, sheep, sheepherder, Indian, *cañon, malpais, mesquite,* blizzard, drought, and desert were inserted as needed by the demands of the plot. Properly classed among these varmints, for an opinion, was the *hero.* No breed of men ever won the West or lifted a mortgage against such odds and to such little purpose. Not even Francis X. Aubry ever rode so far so fast without saddle boils or a played-out horse. They could fast like a *fakir,* water-out like a camel, win the *good* girl, spurn the *bad* girl, destroy the villain, absorb punishment like a Marine Corps legend, and do it all while overburdened with forty pounds of as-

sorted hardware, mostly lethal. It would be nice to be like that—
which is what the author intended you to feel.[9]

Despite the obvious literary defects of two-dimensional characters, of insistence on action-plot, of exaggerated use of horses, hard-
ship, idiom, and costume, the "western" grabbed an audience from
the start. *Riders of the Purple Sage* sold over one million copies;
When a Man's a Man sold eight hundred thousand copies; during
World War I, His Majesty's Government purchased half a million
copies of William MacLeod Raine's novels for distribution to the
troops. When that war ended, the rising tide of *chili con carnage*
became a flood, even as the spate of so-called magazines for men,
Male, Saga, Mr. America, ad nauseam, afflicts us today.

On the crest of this tidal wave were the pulp paper magazines—
looked down upon by any and every right-thinking literary person,
carrying little advertising and that of the truss-and-goitre type, but
serving the reading needs of millions and requiring more original
material at better rates than is the case today, unfortunately. This
was the golden age for writers of "westerns"—*Argosy* was a weekly,
consuming some six million words of new material a year, *Adventure* appeared thrice-monthly, needing four million words of fuel
per annum, while *Short Story* and *Blue Book,* among others, were in
this bracket. These *books* were balanced as to contents, but they used
a goodly proportion of "westerns" both in their 60/90,000-word lead
stories and in their shorts and fillers. Over and above these were the
strictly "western story" magazines, apparently limited only by the
press capacity of the nation and their editors' ability to find
material.

Added to these predominantly masculine books in the mid-
twenties was *Ranch Romances,* pioneer in the "western love" story
where the formula "western" was told from the heroine's point of
view to provide self-identification for women readers with the story
line and plot. Additional demand for "westerns" swelled from Hollywood, where box-office float had been discovered with Broncho
Billy Anderson and then traced to the mother lode with Fred
Thompson, William S. Hart, Harry Carey, Tom Mix, Jack Hoxie,
Hoot Gibson, *et al., et seq.*

With demand established, supply came posthaste as in any com-

[9]One further stylization is worth noting. The sheep *vs.* cattle animosity provides
the plot for many a yarn. Yet, it is extremely hard to find an authentic portrayal of
the sheer, animalistic brutality involved in a sheep slaughter. Such deeds do not sort
with the *caballero's* way.

modity market. Using either the peak-and-valley technique or the steadily rising curve, depending on story length desired and the prospective editor's known foibles, using very basic plots with only the skill of the wordsmith to make dialog, character tags, costumes, and settings appear untarnished, the production of "westerns" became a lucrative business. William MacLeod Raine produced two novels a year for twenty-five years, besides short stories and articles. His popularity was so great that his English publishers bought his manuscripts sight unseen and, so Raine purportedly believed, did not bother to read them before printing. But Raine was a volumetric piker in the "western" game.

There were many men riding the typewriter range who could produce half a million to a million words a year, all salable. One of the best of them, nameless here because of friendship, had a blackboard in his office on which he kept four story outlines going simultaneously, using two secretaries and a dictating machine because he was conducting a successful advertising agency on the side. Harry Sinclair Drago used several aliases, "Bliss Lomax" and "Will Ermine," and it was not unusual for a writer to make the same issue of a magazine with two stories or more, by this judicious use of his aliases, which, also, came in handy to spread his output among several hard-cover publishers. For the classical example, there can be no better choice than the "Old Master of Thud and Blunder," the twentieth century's Sir Walter Scott, Frederick Schiller Faust, who wanted to be a quill-pen poet.[10] In his writing career, 1917-44, he produced over thirty million words under a baker's dozen of names, three of which, at least, were reserved for his "western" output— "Evan Evans," "Peter Dawson," and "Max Brand." This productive tradition has not suffered. A current practitioner in the field is reputed by *Publishers' Weekly* to bypass conventional methods and compose his "westerns" directly for the press by means of a linotype.

This variant of automation is one of the few major changes in the "western" since *Riders of the Purple Sage.* This statement is made with full benefit of Seth M. Agnew's opinion *(Saturday Review,* March 14, 1953) that "...throughout the field, there is an undoubted trend away from the pattern. There is more attention paid to historical accuracy and mood. There is a realization, as one author put it, that the gun that could fire and does not has more suspense than a dozen corpses. The standard western, however, has

[10]Faust was killed on the Italian front as a war correspondent in 1944.

not been abandoned entirely. But it has been upgraded." The major changes in the "western" since Grey poured the mould have concerned women. If this be upgrading, let us make the most of it.

One significant change was the rise in the pulp field of the "western love" magazines for which *Ranch Romances* showed the way and, thus, kept many a writer of "westerns" from direct starvation. These books made possible a story element which Alan Bosworth calls "Sally's Sweater." The story opening introduces the heroine galloping across the range, or swaying to the motion of a buckboard, with ample verbiage devoted to the inevitable movement of her second-skin sateen blouse. The story problem, setting, and characters are quickly introduced, and then back to Sally's Sweater. Whenever the action lags, this handy *divertissement* flogs it up again. By and large, it is as close as the formula "western" has come towards permitting raw sex to get in the way of action.

The other change has occurred in the slick-paper magazines, where, it should be noted, the writer can expect more help than in the pulps from both editors and readers in closing the gap between what he means when he writes and what they get when they read. Ernest Haycox pioneered this change and Luke Short is now its ablest exponent.[11] This departure from the norm involves the use of two women: one *good* but suspect of either evil or primitive passion, the other *bad* but so suspect of do-to-ride-the-river-with-virtues that the hero spends a lot of his time and the readers' time trying to suppress his hormones and get his sense of values back on the *good* standard. The use of the two-woman angle introduced something of the psychological suspense narrative into the "western" formula which, heretofore, depended upon simple issues and direct decisions with conclusive consequences—all stemming from direct action, generally physical, by the protagonist.

It is easy to dismiss the "western" as escape trash, and it has been dismissed in this wise ever since it engulfed literary people in the twenties. It is not so easy to dismiss the fact that for some forty-five years the "western" has held and enhanced the audience it grabbed. The Council of Books in Wartime published over 1,300 titles in Editions for the Armed Services; 160 of these, the largest identifiable bloc, were "westerns." The last count at my local newsstand

[11] Frederick D. Glidden uses the name "Luke Short"; another skillful exponent of this school, Jonathan Glidden, uses the old Faust pseudonym, "Peter Dawson."

showed thirty-odd exclusively "western" pulps together with five
"western love" magazines. Cursory notes indicate that 200 "westerns"
appeared in book form in 1951, 213 in 1952, and at least 114 original
"westerns" in 1953. The "western" accounted for 16 per cent of all
the varnish-covered paperback reprints in 1951, and a personal
count of the nearest revolving wire-rack emporium will prove
there has been no diminution. In point of fact, the paperback book,
in both original and reprint editions, has been a massive shot in the
arm for the "western."

Other evidence as to the sustained appeal of the "western" comes
from a count of the "comic" books that are built around past or current heroes of the Hollywood "western." This leads logically to
the number of "westerns" released, or re-released annually by Hollywood. It invites tabulation of the number of "western" radio scripts
aired annually and leads, inevitably, to the ubiquitous presence of
"Cheyenne," "Wyatt," "Wild Bill Hickok," "Hop-along," *et al.*, in
the bat-cave called television.

Other evidence concerning the "western" comes from a highly
improbable source. M. Jean Paul Sartre's existentialist monthly, *Les
Temps Modernes,* has dubbed *Shane* "...that nostalgic outlaw of
a Racine-like modesty." And a body of serious French appraisal of
the "western" in film form apparently has equated it with *le jazz hot*
as our finest native flowering. A Swedish critic, Harry Schein, writing in *The American Scholar,* has termed *High Noon* "...the most
convincing and, likewise, certainly the most honest explanation of
American foreign policy." He says, too, "The pistol in westerns is
by now accepted as a phallic symbol." *"Methinks yon Cassius,"* etc.,
but if there be reason with this foreign accolade for the "western
movie," some of it must rub off on the "western story" from which
the horse-operas were and are derived. It is worth noting, too, that
the "western" story long has been one of our most stable and staple
exports, with foreign editions in tongues amounting to Babel.[12]

The popular appeal of the "western" seems destined to endure
until the last fragmentary memory of our last, wholly-owned frontier, "the Cattle Kingdom" defined by Walter Prescott Webb, has
been obliterated from our national consciousness. The question naturally arises as to what legacy of letters the "western" has caused to
bloom amidst the piled compost of its millions of words. The ques-

[12]German editions of Zane Grey are found in the Lenin Library, Moscow.

tion is not easy to answer.[13] Any arrogation of omnipotence brings to mind the advice given by an old-timer to a cow camp button: "Son, I wouldn't set that kerosene on the stove. It ain't judicious." Some of the best of it has been preserved by anthologists, which is another way of saying by personal opinion, the same criterion that has governed that which follows.

The surest craftsmanship, the most assimilable prose, has been achieved by men who did with words what Frederick Remington did for the western scene with another medium—capture it from the "outside-in." They combined a surpassing mastery of craft with extraordinarily detailed knowledge to produce "westerns" that are exercises in intellectual analysis rather than immediacies of human experience. Ernest Haycox, Luke Short, Peter Dawson the Latter, T. T. Flynn, L. L. Foreman, Les Savage, Jr., and Norman Fox, for examples, all unquestionably are fine craftsmen writing fine fiction —giving their readers the meat in the coconut without the labor of husking it. They know more about what their audience wants than that audience knows or wants to know about the same. If they did not know this, they would be wasting their time, their agents' time, and the time of many editors, which leads to an inconvenient short-ness of tempers all around and brings the writer down with creeping poliomyelitis of the exchequer. In this knowledge of market wants, needs, or preconceptions, they are doing precisely what Bret Harte did when he wrote his stories amidst the urbanities of San Francisco for the Eastern readers of whom he had been one. That these men wrote, are still writing, "westerns" from the "outside-in" cannot cause their work to be dismissed—there comes to mind no *good* book about the North Pole written by an Eskimo. That some of these authors, like Haycox, disliked horses and most things Western, that others, like Max Brand, actively loathed them, cannot mitigate the fact that the "outside-inners" have written the best entertainment and employed the finest craftsmanship in the "western" field.

The truest legacies in the "western" field have been left by men who did with prose what Charles M. Russell did with another me-dium—capture the free range days from the "inside-out." Several of these men were outsiders who knew their craft before they ab-sorbed the West by a process of mental and spiritual osmosis that

[13]Jeff C. Dykes tried it in *The Brand Book* (Chicago "Westerners," September, 1955), for the period 1902-52. He covered a great deal more of the Western scene than just the "western" of this opinionated piece. The longest attempt was made by Joe B. Frantz and Julian E. Choate, Jr., in *The American Cowboy* (Norman, 1955).

vitally affected the stature of their work. Others were insiders-born who learned their trade and used it to give their birthright meaning. Owen Wister, "a Pennsylvanian writing about a Virginian in Montana," seems to have made the first genuine contribution to American literature with *The Virginian.* It seems from here that Wister started out to write another story of humor in a Western setting and suffered a range-change that produced the strong, silent "When-you-call-me-that—smile!" hero. There are skeletal remains of the Johnson County War, which Wister learned about from first-hand participants, in this book, and the evolution of *The Virginian* from *Lin McLean* and *The Jimmy John Boss* may rest on this excavated evidence. It has been ably shown by DeVoto, J. Frank Dobie, and Walter Prescott Webb that Wister was the first to distill certain essential oils from the free range days and bottle them for market in fiction form. Coming off the presses in April, 1902, *The Virginian* went through six printings in six weeks, sixteen printings inside its first year. The stage version ran for ten years, in New York and on the road, and at least three versions have been perpetrated by Hollywood.[14]

Andy Adams must be included on any list, although applying the term fiction to Adams's solid narratives seems pure courtesy. His books are constructed of the minutiae of daily working life on the range and up the trail, all artifacts and properties included, as meticulously as Luis Ortega braids *la reata* from strings that he has prepared himself. You have only to read *The Log of a Cowboy* in comparison with Emerson Hough's *North of 36* to taste the difference.

Stewart Edward White has certain short stories, most of them in *Arizona Nights* and the best of them involving Señor Buck Clark, that deserve to live in any critical appraisal of the "western."

W. C. Tuttle, a volumetric producer for many years, created three characters, Sad Sontag, Hashknife Hartley, and Sleepy Stephens, around whom he built some hundreds of yarns, the best of which are in the great tradition of salty humor and credible action. The radio series that Tuttle, himself, adapted from his stories afforded what one set of ears considers the finest audio or video "western" ever offered an undiscerning public.

George Patullo, who went up like a skyrocket in the "western"

[14]It made money for its author, a new and wholly agreeable Wisterian experience, thus meeting the test of certain moderns that if your "westerns" don't make money, you ain't writing "westerns."

hierarchy and then exploded with inherited affluence, left some short stories to mark his passage and keep his name alive. His "Off the Trail" (*McClure's*, March 3, 1912) will grab your guts and twist them tight today, and his 1911 collection, *The Untamed*, has preserved "Corazón," which may well be the finest story about a horse ever written.

Eugene Cunningham, one of the finest literary mechanics to work the "western" field, has set down the West Texas—Mexican border country of his raising in novels that possess but one flaw—his lapidary skill at preparing a piece of merchandise for the market place. His latest, *Riding Gun*, appearing in 1956 after an absence from print of some fifteen years, can be used as a text for comparison with the contemporary school of the "western." The difference is that between a vigorous and genuine *ocotillo* and an equally vigorous but hybridized and cultivated flat-leaf succulent. It is quite probable, however, that the nuances and subtleties of shading in Cunningham's characterizations will be lost on a generation conditioned to having their characters ride the range as hag-ridden as was ever Hamlet.[15]

Regardless of the merits of the foregoing selection, the contributions of the authors mentioned, excluding Wister and Adams, have been lumped with the rest of the "westerns," good, bad, and indifferent, that have made the genre. The same dismissal has been applied to the last name of my personal list, and in no case is the margin of error greater than in thus evaluating the writings of Eugene Manlove Rhodes.

Insofar as the public and the critics generally were concerned in his lifetime, Rhodes wrote "westerns." There was one exception to this critical dismissal and a most notable one, Bernard DeVoto, who had known the cowpuncher world as a youth and then had let his cultivated mind play upon that world, upon all the facets of the land he loved, with the genius of gusto given to but few. His regard for Rhodes, as man and man of letters, abided with him for many, many years. Since DeVoto possessed another rare quality—the ca-

---

[15]Ernest Haycox has been credited with introducing the Hamlet strain into the sun-god ancestry. In Mayne Reid's frontier-Gothic romances, you can find the Hamlet strain as pronounced as in anything by Haycox, Schafer, Short, *et al.;* specifically, *The Scalp Hunters*, where Reid made a wondrous switch of James Kirker's name and character.

pacity for rounded maturity—his published appraisals of Rhodes gain added weight. In 1938, he termed Rhodes' stories: "...the only embodiment on the level of art of one segment of American experience. They are the only body of fiction devoted to the cattle kingdom which is both true to it and written by an artist in prose."[16] In 1954, he said again: "Back in 1938 I pointed out that only Gene Rhodes had succeeded in making first-rate fiction out of the cattle business. The statement still stands but the argument would be tighter if Mr. Walter Van Tilburg Clark had not meanwhile published an excellent novel called *The Ox-bow Incident.* ... But Mr. Clark's subject is the mob spirit that leads to a lynching. So his scene might be almost anywhere and though he uses a few stage properties from horse opera, he uses none of its sentiments or traditions." In this same piece, he says of the "western": "...it was turned into the path that has led to its present solemnity by its one novelist, Rhodes, and by the fabulists Harold Bell Wright and Zane Grey."[17]

In 1955, in one of the last pieces turned out before his death, DeVoto devoted himself to a discussion of Owen Wister, his literary origins and the resultant birth of the "western." Speaking herein of *The Virginian,* he summed up his case for Gene Rhodes: "The cowboy story has seldom produced anything as good; apart from Gene Rhodes, it has not even tried to do anything different."[18]

It is comforting to have such a buttress as Bernard DeVoto for purely personal opinions, comforting because it is Rhodes as a precursor of, and practitioner concurrent with, the virgins-villains-varmints school who requires detailed examination.

In the women in his stories, and the best of them have no women whatsoever, Rhodes is at his worst, and that is worse than any other man of stature in the "western" field. If his women are young women, they are passionately and infrangibly virginal, and his heroes move like marionettes in their presence. It is extremely hard to find even the suspicion of a *bad* woman in all his writings; he had known them,

[16]"The Novelist of the Cattle Kingdom," in *The Hired Man on Horseback* (Boston, 1938).

[17]"Phaëthon on Gunsmoke Trail," *Harper's* (December, 1955).

[18]"Birth of an Art," *Harper's* (December, 1955). The first two chapters of DeVoto's unfinished book would have discussed the "western" probably beyond further need. This piece has benefited from an exchange of opinions with Mr. DeVoto on the subject before his death.

seguro que si!, but they had no place in his fiction. Occasionally, an older woman appears fleetingly in his stories after years of frontier abrasion have made her road-weary. Only when this happens is Rhodes' feminine cast at all credible.

In portraying his villains, Rhodes veered wildly from the formula. *Imprimis*, he never cast his villains by the color of their skin. If he has the Hispanic New Mexican in a villainous role, it is because his prototype was that in life. Rhodes' Anglo villains are both *heavy* and *sneaky*, as heretofore defined, but they are that because they were that in life, and whatever category they fit makes but a part of Rhodes' villainous whole—the sons of Mary. His true villains are always those who did not work with their hands—bankers, merchants, lawyers, *politicos*—and who profited, grew swollen and fat, on the lives of those who did work with their hands for daily bread and conquered the frontier while doing it. It would have been easier by far to two-dimensionalize these characters, but Rhodes went to infinite pains in his story construction to show how these villains of his were parasites at the breasts of the country that had nurtured him. He did this because it was true to his experience, true to his country and his people. In doing it, he limned in fiction the salient truth about the west-that-was—a truth unrecognized, overlooked, and neglected for many years by the serious scholars—the truth that the West was the captive, exploited province of the financial, political, and industrial East.

It is only when Rhodes has his villain a proper Easterner that said villain becomes incredible. This is not due to the characterization or motivation of that villain but to the affected mannerisms given him and to his speech.

Indeed, it is the speech he gives to his characters from Western life—a speech far removed from the idiom of the "western"—that has led many critics, and not a few true Rhodesians, to feel that Gene Rhodes' fictional cowboys all talked like Gene Rhodes. There is some truth to this feeling. Rhodes recognized his tendency when he used pages 65-67 of *Bransford in Arcadia* to explain the availability of classical literature to his cow persons through the medium of Bull Durham coupons that were negotiable for volumes in Munro's Library of Popular Novels. Rhodes was a reader, an omnivorous reader, all of his life, devouring everything that came his way even unto *The Congressional Record*. The brave-talking heroes of Sir

Walter Scott's fiction almost ruined him. He revered Shakespeare
and Conrad, and he felt that Stevenson and Kipling had used the
English language more skillfully than any others. So his cowboys'
speech is pricked with allusions and larded with classical quotations.
Yet, he had real-life examples in Bill Barbee, the Texan who revelled
in *Richard III*, in Aloys Priesser, the Bavarian chemist of Engle, in
Henry Touissant, the *Jornada* pioneer whose library contained the
world's classics. There were others, but these three will do to point
this premise: if T. S. Eliot in his plays has made his country, or
country-bred, English families oversubtle in their appreciation of
English literature, so much and no more can be charged against
Gene Rhodes and his riders of the stars. He gave an idealized depiction, in fine prose, of men who had the language within themselves but who lacked the idiom of their readers to say it themselves,
in life, in such wise.

When it comes to the varmints in his stories, Rhodes again
veered wildly from the formula under discussion. You have only to
compare the horses in his yarns—Wisenose, Brown Jug, Buck, Cry
Baby, and Abou Ben Adam—with the horseflesh in other "westerns"
to prove the point. The flora and fauna of his chosen country are
integral parts of his fiction, as they were of the very lives of the
characters he took from life. His people are what they are, do what
they do, because of their country, its needs, demands, and con-
ditionings.

It is the vasty land itself, shimmering in the heat or shrouded in
infrequent mists, eroded, dusty, sun-drenched, as implacable and
as compelling as the sea, that makes Rhodes' canvas for his portraits
of the West-That-Was. Only Walter Van Tilburg Clark can equal
the evocative richness of Rhodes' landscapes and both men share
the inability to enrich certain of their human types.

It is these major differences, both of accomplishment and shortcoming, from the formula "western," past and present, that give
Rhodes his place. There is a reason for these differences, for this
place; reason quite apart from the mechanics of prose construction.

No other writer of "westerns," Andy Adams included, encom-
passed so much living in the trans-Mississippi West they all purported, still purport, to record as did Rhodes. He had had twelve
years of prairie and sky in Nebraska and Kansas—wind, grass,
drought, blizzards, cyclones, grasshoppers, and green buds swelling

in the creek bottoms when spring came—before he came to New Mexico with his father in 1881, "the year that Billy the Kid was killed."

Thereafter, for twenty-five years, he was horse-wrangler, bronc rider, cowboy, miner, wagon freighter, school teacher, road-builder, dishwasher, homesteader, carpenter, water-mason, blacksmith, and rancher who went broke in the losing battle against drought, cow-country interest, and from an uneconomic passion for raising horses in a land where the feral bands were a nuisance.[19]

It is not necessary to live as did Rhodes to write stories about the West, or even "western" stories, as a number of currently prominent practitioners will be happy to tell anyone who cares to write them on the matter. It is the fact that Rhodes *did* live it, that the totality of the free range experience was summated in his personal life, that makes his writings come from the "inside-out," from a deep wellspring of personal experience that was the abiding strength of his life. There is yet another factor in Rhodes' writings that is lacking from those, like this, written wherever the typewriter is handy.

Rhodes wrote his stories, almost all of them that are worth while, far removed from the country and the life he loved; the country and the life he left because his personal code demanded it. His knowledge was sharpened by the expatriate's longing, deepened by distance, enhanced by the frustrations of his exile. His land and his people came out on paper as the remembered mellow haze of a coal-oil lamp seen shining through the cabin window when the man and his world were young. Yet upon what he wrote, you may, as an archaeologist, depend. The people and the land of six New Mexico counties, Socorro, Sierra, Doña Ana, Lincoln, Otero, and Grant, are preserved for all time in the clear amber of his joyous, dancing, illuminated prose.

If the "western" had not burgeoned as it did, only to wither literarily as the inevitable result of incest, Rhodes might have gained in his lifetime the stature which some now feel is his. Certainly, at the time he started his real career, the competition was tough. Stevenson, Kipling, Conrad, London, Stephen Crane, Rex Beach,

[19]It is interesting to note that Rhodes, like Frederic Remington, Charles M. Russell, and Ross Santee, was a horseman and not a cowman. No "cowman right" ever has touched the magic that these four have made. Others may wish to add Will James to this select circle.

Stewart Edward White, all were working the outdoor-action-adventure field on a higher level, of pay and merit, than the dime novel or the emergent forerunners of the pulps. Admittedly, these writers did not specialize in the so-called "western" for which Wister, Hough, Adams, Lewis, and Phillips had made the first rough castings. But, and this is the point to be remembered, everything they did write competed in the editorial market places with Rhodes' fiction. He hit his stride, with his own style and tone and pace, against such competition, and he maintained his place until both his productivity and his critical acclaim were inundated by the tidal wave of "westerns" that crested in the twenties behind Zane Grey's first breaking on the pleasant literary beach staked off by the cognoscenti as their own.

In the rise of "regional" writing in those same twenties, following the blazes of Turner and the steps of Paxson, Rhodes did not seem to qualify, even though New Mexico so claims him today. Certainly, his people, places, and incidents are regional to a degree of being provincial, often happily parochial, while being at the same time universal—meaning anywhere west of the one hundredth meridian and north of a given point. But they were accepted, typed, and dismissed as "westerns." A suitable example comes from the *New York Times Book Review,* November 19, 1933, where *The Trusty Knaves* got mentioned under the section-heading, "Western Loot," while Kenneth Roberts' *Rabble in Arms* got the full treatment under a banner head, "An Epic Tale of the American Revolution." Not to disparage Kenneth Roberts, but to make a point, it can be said that *Rabble* contained no more valid history, no more authentic Americana, no more good writing and reading, than did *Knaves.* It did, however, possess one singular advantage. It was laid in a setting that had no built-in connotations to the critical mind.

There is another factor in Rhodes' critical dismissal. His work in the twenties and thirties ran exactly counter to the mainstream of literary acclaim. Implicit in everything Rhodes wrote are the best traditions, values, customs, and morals—the basic philosophy—of the American physical frontier. This sorted poorly with F. Scott Fitzgerald, Mencken, Nathan, Sherwood Anderson, *et al.,* and, most certainly, had little in common with *The Plastic Age, Little Caesar, Black Oxen, Three Soldiers, A Farewell to Arms,* or Judge Ben Lindsey's theories about companionating. For final and conclusive critical damnation, he wrote for the *Saturday Evening Post.*

Rhodes, himself, contributed to his own neglect. He was dismissed by the literati because he allegedly wrote "westerns," but, while his stories gave great satisfaction to *Satevepost* readers, the great reader market for "westerns" never cottoned to them as books. Rhodes was a poet-cowboy, not a cowboy-poet nor even a cowboy-writer, in his love of words and their uses. Only a writer for radio can appreciate exactly how Rhodes, remembering the tales he had heard in his youth, wrote to fire his readers' minds through their ears and not their eyes. He was a conscious and deliberate prose stylist, an anomaly in his genre, and his plots were incredibly intricate. The humor in his yarns subtly combined the humor of words with a scene sense of the comic situation he had learned from Henry Wallace Phillips. The "western" fan picking up a Rhodes story was apt to react like a pup with his first porcupine and to learn the lesson of abstention with but one experience.[20]

Rhodes' other and greatest contribution to his own neglect was his productivity. He was a slow worker by nature and a spasmodic one, writing not alone for his market but, also, taking inordinate pains that every word would stand up in the minds of those in New Mexico who had known Gene Rhodes as well as Rhodes had known them and their joint country. In adding up the corpus of his life's work, he, himself, could arrive at but 1,200,000 words which is a mere bagatelle alongside the output of Grey, Mulford, Raine, Seltzer, Drago, Tuttle, Cunningham, or a score of others, past and present. Lack of output, ordinarily, is an acceptable yardstick for critical acclaim, but it was not so with Rhodes. More important, practically speaking, is the fact that five-year gaps between books are worse than two-year gaps between major periodical appearances when it comes to keeping an author in his public's mind. And, certainly, such gaps give a book publisher no reason to waste time, money, and effort in promoting the sale of such infrequencies.

Despite Rhodes' lack of productivity, it is interesting to note that he did achieve a very high degree of utilization of what he did write. More interesting is the fact that his work continues to find a niche in the current market place — anthologies, reprints, television, and films — and this despite Frank Dobie's latest feeling that "His fiction becomes increasingly dated."[21]

[20]The sales of his books document this premise. His magazine popularity did not carry over into hard-cover sales.

[21]*Guide to Life and Literature of the Southwest* (rev. ed., Dallas, 1952).

What Don Pancho says, in part, is absolutely true. Rhodes' style, technique, and tone, all are hopelessly archaic in most of his stories. His very early stories are an emetic and, as has been noted, so are his characterizations of women and of Eastern society, people, and manners. But--

The best of his yarns about his own country and his own people retain the nourishing, essential juices of true literature. Coming upon them today, when the expanse of the "western-story" is a vast reach of sheer craftsmanship speckled with great cloud-patches of slipshod writing and escapist plots, Rhodes' stories have the startling impact of an antelope's rump seen shining across long, arid, sun-drenched leagues where no living thing was thought to be.[22]

There is only one obstacle in the way of those who would seek to read Rhodes today, to hone these opinions against the stone of personal experience. Barring one paperback reprint, *Sunset Land*, Eugene Manlove Rhodes is out of print.[23] His published books have been pursued for years by what DeVoto terms "a coterie as select and discriminating as any that ever boosted a tenth-rate English poet into a first-rate reputation." If his books, or his stories in frayed copies of old magazines, can be found today they will ring like a shod hoof on *malpais* in the mind and heart of any purchaser who knows the West-That-Was. They will make, also, a severe dent in the purse.[24] It is this scarcity and price that give solid substance to the partisan literary summation of Gene Rhodes that first was made of DeMaupassant: "He was almost irreproachable in a genre which was not."

---

[22]No attempts has been made here, or hereafter, to select the best of Rhodes' output. As has been said, "One man's fish is another's *poisson.*"

[23]Dell Publications scheduled another one for 1956 to contain more material from *The Best Novels... of Eugene Manlove Rhodes*. There is, however, many a slip between schedule and paperback.

[Fortunately, this statement is no longer true. Hutchinson's tireless efforts have succeeded in restoring most of Rhodes's work to print.—Ed.]

[24]Henry Holt & Co. issued *Good Men and True* at $1.00 net; a good copy of the first edition has been quoted recently at $27.50.

Andy Adams, Cowboy Chronicler

by J. Frank Dobie

Five or six years ago I hunted all over San Antonio for some books by Andy Adams, and I found just one. That was one more than the Austin bookstores then had. A year ago the proprietor of the largest book-shop in Houston assured me that Andy Adams was out of print. Bookstores of Oklahoma, Kansas, and Boston have proved as indifferent. Happily, however, the apathy of some of the book dealers in Texas, particularly in Austin and Dallas, has been overcome. Now, thanks to Mr. W. P. Webb of the University of Texas, the present writer, and perhaps one or two other individuals who have insisted on the extraordinary merit of Andy Adams as a writer and as a historian of the old-time cow people, thousands of his books are being sold over the Southwest and his delayed fame is gaining over the entire country. Katharine Fullerton Gerould and Carl Van Doren have during the past year alluded to him. But the neglect is significant.

The histories of American literature have been singularly silent on him. A contributor to the *Cambridge History of American Literature* mentions him only to show that he has not read him. Boynton and Haney in their recent surveys of the field are silent; that considerate snapper-up of trifles, Fred Lewis Pattee, is silent. Several late authorities, however, mention in one way or another Harold Bell Wright and Zane Grey. Mr. Pattee quotes approvingly somebody's saying that Owen Wister's *The Virginian* is "our last glimpse of the pioneer plainsman and cowboy types, then passing and now gone." By "then" is, I suppose, meant the time at which *The Virginian* appeared; that was 1902. *The Log of a Cowboy* by Andy Adams, his first and perhaps best work, came out in 1903. Following it appeared *A Texas Matchmaker* (1904), *The Outlet*

"Andy Adams, Cowboy Chronicler" by J. Frank Dobie. Originally printed in the *Southwest Review*, 11 (January 1926), 92-101. Reprint permission from J. Frank Dobie, *Prefaces*, Copyright © 1975 by the Capital National Bank, Austin, Texas, Executor of the Estate of Bertha Dobie, granted by the Bank.

(1905), *Cattle Brands* (1906), *Reed Anthony, Cowman* (1907), and *Wells Brothers*—a book for "boys"—(1911).

The first four books are the best perhaps, and I should rank them first, second, third, and fourth just as they appeared. Other readers disagree. *The Log of a Cowboy* is the best book that has ever been written of cowboy life, and it is the best book that ever can be written of cowboy life. With its complement, *The Outlet*, it gives a complete picture of trail cattle and trail drivers. Why has it been so overlooked by critics and historians?

In the first place, twenty years ago literary magazines and literary gentlemen were not concerning themselves with the cowboy. Occasionally an article on that subject got into polite print, but honest matter like Charlie Siringo's *A Texas Cowboy* was bound in paper and sold by butcher-boys—a far cry from this day when the Yale University Press publishes James H. Cook's *Fifty Years on the Old Frontier* and then—with a Ph. D. preface—reprints Captain James B. Gillett's *Six Years with the Texas Rangers*. It is true that Owen Wister was at once accepted, but he went west as an Easterner and wrote of the cattle people not as one to the manner born but as a literary connoisseur. Even before him Frederic Remington with *Pony Tracks* and *Crooked Trails* had been accepted into a well deserved position that he has never lost, but Remington was an artist to whom literature was secondary and to whom the cowboy was tertiary in comparison with Indians and army men. Remington also came into the West looking for local color.

Andy Adams did not come into the cow country looking for "copy." Like Sam Bass, he "was born in Indiana," and again like Sam Bass, "he first came out to Texas a cowboy for to be." He drove the trail as one of the hands. He followed it very much as Conrad and Masefield followed the sea, not as a writer but as a man of the element. The miracle is that when he did write he found such respectable publishers as the Houghton Mifflin Company. He now lives in Colorado Springs, Colorado, aged sixty-six [note that this was written in 1926].

Of course, critics not only arouse interest but they follow it, and Mr. Adams, in a letter, attributes neglect of his books to the fact that he "could never make water run up-hill or use a fifth wheel," namely, a girl. But there is another reason more paradoxical. Generally the development of a particular field by one writer creates a demand for the works of other writers in the same milieu. Unfortunately, however, the demand for cowboy material was first aroused by the "Alkali Bill" type of writers; once aroused, that demand has never been satiated, and an avalanche of shoddy has literally buried meritorious writing. Could Andy Adams have led the van, he might have become as well known in his own field as Parkman became known in his. Only just now are responsible readers coming to wonder what the truth about the cowboy is. It is true that twenty years ago *The Log of a Cowboy* was having something of a run and that the newspapers were recording the usual indiscriminating banalities that they record concerning any Western book, but the present attempt at a serious review is just twenty-three years late.

The great virtue of Andy Adams is fidelity, and *The Log of a Cowboy* is a masterpiece for the same reason that *Two Years Before the Mast, Moby Dick,* and *Life on the Mississippi* are masterpieces. All three of these chronicle-records are of the water, and it is "symbolic of something," as Hawthorne would say, that the themes of three of the most faithful expository narratives of America should be offshore.

Now the one part of America that has approached the sea in its length and breadth and dramatic solitude and its elemental power to overwhelm puny man has been the great plains. The one phase of American life that has approached the life of a ship's crew alone on the great deep battling the elements has been that of a cow outfit alone on the great trail that stretched across open ranges from Brownsville at the toe of the nation to northwestern Montana and on into Canada. All of Andy Adams' books treat of trail life, except one, *A Texas Matchmaker,* and it treats of ranch life in Southwest Texas during the trail driving days. I have no hesitancy in saying that Mr. Adams has as truthfully and fully expressed the life of a trail outfit as Dana expressed the life of a crew that sailed around the Horn; that he is as warm in his sympathy for cowmen and horses and cattle as Mark Twain is in his feeling for pilots and the Mississippi River; and that he has treated of cattle as intimately and definitely, though not so scientifically or dramatically, as Melville treated of whales. Certainly, I have no idea of ranking Andy Adams as the equal of Mark Twain; I do not believe that he can be ranged alongside Herman Melville; but I should put him on an easy level with Richard Henry Dana, Jr. The immense importance of his subject to the western half of the United States makes him in a way more important historically than either Melville or Dana.

Andy Adams has a racy sympathy for the land and for the cattle and horses and men of the land. He savors them deep, but he savors them quietly. Sometimes there are storms and stampedes, but generally the herds just "mosey along." Cattle bog in the quicksands and there is desperate work to pull them out, but oftener they graze in the sunshine and chew their cuds by still waters while the owner rides among them from sheer love of seeing their contentment and thriftiness. One old Texas steer took so much pleasure in hearing the Confederate boys sing "Rock of Ages" that they could not bear to slaughter him. One trail outfit made a great pet of a calf, and for hundreds of miles it followed the chuck-wagon, much to the exasperation of its mother. On another trip there was a certain muley steer that the horned cattle hooked, and at night the boys used to let him wander out of the herd to lie down in a private bed. One spring Reed Anthony, the great cowman, could not find it in his heart to order a round-up because "chousing" the cattle would disturb the little calves "playing in groups" and "lying like fawns in the tall grass." "The Story of a Poker Steer" in *Cattle Brands* is a classic; its delineation of the life of a "line-backed calf" is as quiet and easy as Kipling's portrayal of the life of a seal in one of his best-known stories. Tom Quirk, boarding a train in Montana, thousands of miles away from his Texas home, was sad indeed to part from his saddle horse forever.

No matter whether the theme is a pet calf or a terrible "die-up" in "the Territory," there is absolutely no strain in Andy Adams. This quality of reserve distinguishes him from all other Western writers that I know of. One can but contrast him with the Zane Grey school so ubiquitously exploited by nearly every American institution ranging from a two-bit drugstore to Harper and Brothers. In Zane Grey's *U. P. Trail,* for instance, which has often been hailed as a piece of real history, the men "were grim; they were indomitable;" and the heroine "clutched Neal with fingers of steel, in a grip that he could not have loosened without breaking her bones."

Not long ago a friend was telling me of an incident so expressive that I must repeat it. This friend was camping in a canyon out in Arizona, where he was excavating some Indian ruins. One night he was awakened by unearthly yelling and shooting and the clatter of horses' hoofs. Rushing out of his tent, he met a cowboy whom he knew. "What, what is the matter?" he asked. "Oh," replied the cowboy, "there's a feller coming back yonder who hired us to give him some local color, as he calls it. His name's Zane Grey, and we're doing our damnedest to give him all the hell he calls for."

Now, in Andy Adams *always* "there is ample time," as he makes "a true Texan" say. To quote the words of Gilbert Chesterton on Sir Walter Scott's heroes, "the men linger long at their meals." Indeed, I think that the best things in the books of Mr. Adams are the tales that the men tell around the chuck-wagon and the jokes and the chaff that they indulge in there.

An easy intimacy with the life shows on every page. The man writes of the only life he knows, in the only language he knows. "Now, Miller, the foreman, hadn't any use for a man that wasn't dead tough under any condition. I've known him to camp his outfit on alkali water, so the men would get out in the morning, and every rascal beg leave to ride outside circle on the morning round-up." "Cattle will not graze freely in a heavy dew or too early in the morning." When Don Lovell's outfit received a herd of cattle on the Rio Grande, the Texas boss tallied the hundreds with a tally string and the Mexican *caporal* tallied them by dropping pebbles from one hand to the other. When June Deweese, *segundo,* showed off his boss's horses to a buyer below San Antonio, he had them grazing on a hillside and drove the buyer along on the lower slope so that they would appear larger.

The language that the Andy Adams cowboys use is as natural and honest as the exposition; it is often picturesque, too, as all language of the soil is. I quote sentences almost at random from various of the books. "I'll build a fire in your face that you can read the San Francisco 'Examiner' by at midnight." "We had the outfits and the horses, and our men were plainsmen and were at home as long as they could see the north star." "The old lady was bogged to the saddle skirts in her story." "Blankets? Never use them; sleep on your belly and cover with your back, and get up with the birds in the morning." "Every good cowman takes his saddle wherever he goes, though he may not have clothes enough to dust a fiddle."

A year or so ago in a senseless attack on the historical accuracy of Emerson Hough's *North of 36,* Stuart Henry said that the Texans who reached Abilene in 1867 did not celebrate the Fourth of July. The charge, along with others, was repudiated by some good Texas Americans. Now, as a matter of fact, it is very likely that the Texans of 1867 did not celebrate the Fourth of July in Abilene or anywhere else. I know a few—and they are out of the old rock, too—who still pay more attention to April 21 than to July 4. During the three decades following the Civil War more than ten millions of cattle were trailed north from Texas; they were trailed across every river and into every range of the West, and wherever they were trailed the point-men were Texans. Generally those Texans were either Confederate soldiers or the sons of Confederate soldiers. Andy Adams has been very careful to catch the temper of those Texans fresh from the ranks of the Confederate Army. He has not allowed, like other writers, a mush patriotism to abnegate the justified pride of a section, though in his books the halest of partnerships are formed between "rebels" and Yankees. In 1882, at Frenchman's Ford on the Yellowstone, "The Rebel," a memorable hand in *The Log of a Cowboy,* exulted over a "patriotic beauty" with a toast that went thus: "Jeff Davis and the Southern Confederacy."

When I began reading Andy Adams a number of years ago, the humor of his books did not impress me. Lately I have found it to be one of their highest virtues. Folk yarns salt page after page, and many a good-natured drawl sets me laughing. The humor is as unconscious as the green of grass, but I do not know of anything in Mark Twain funnier than the long story of the "chuckline rider" who blew into a cow camp in "The Strip" about Christmas time and proceeded to earn his board by cooking "bear sign" (the name for doughnuts). The cowboys often play like colts: one of them gets down off his horse and butts his head into a muddy bank, imitative of the cattle; some of them dress up one of their number like a wild Indian and take him to the hotel for dinner. This is horseplay, to be sure, but as it is told it generates health in a healthy reader like a good feed of roast beef and plum pudding.

There are, of course, many shortcomings in Mr. Adams. His books have no plots, but lack of plot sometimes allows of an easier fidelity to facts. He lacks great dramatic power, unless the quiet truth be dramatic. However, there is plenty of action on occasion. "The men of that day," says the author of *Reed Anthony, Cowman,* which like all the other novels but one is written in the autobiographic style, "were willing to back their opinions, even on trivial matters, with their lives. 'I'm the quickest man on the trigger that ever came over the trail,' said a cowpuncher to me one night in a saloon in Abilene. 'You're a blankety blank liar,' said a quiet little man, a perfect stranger to both of us, not even casting a glance our way. I wrested a six-shooter from the hands of my acquaintance, and hustled him out of the house, getting roundly cursed for my interference, though no doubt I saved human life."

The greatest shortcoming, perhaps, is too much love of prosperity.

Andy Adams loves cowmen and cattle and horses so that he can hardly suffer any of them to undergo ruin. The trail has hardships, but it is delightful. The path of the owner and his cowboys is sometimes rocky, but it generally leads down into pleasant pastures. As they travel it, they never go into heroics about their "grim sacrifices," etc.; they take great gusto in the traveling. When I read *Reed Anthony, Cowman,* or *Wells Brothers,* I think of old Daniel Defoe's love for goods of the earth, and I would no more think of holding their prosperity against the actuality of Reed Anthony, Don Lovell, and other prosperous cattle people of Andy Adams' creation than I would think of impeaching the life-likeness of Mulberry Sellers on account of his optimism.

There are no women in Andy Adams, excepting those in the melancholy *Matchmaker.* Well, there were no women in the action that he treats of. Why should he lug them in? Nor has Andy Adams any thesis to advance. He has no absorbing philosophy of life that mingles with the dark elements of earth as in Joseph Conrad. "To those who love them, cattle and horses are good company." Perhaps that is his philosophy.

It is easy to let one's enthusiasm run away with one's judgment. I have waited a long time to write these words on Andy Adams. Perhaps sympathy for his subject has biased me. Perhaps the memory of how a dear uncle of mine used to "run" with him at the end of the trail in Caldwell, Kansas, has affected me. I try to rule those elements out. It is my firm conviction that one hundred, three hundred years from now people will read Andy Adams to see what the life of those men who went up the trail from Texas was like, just as now we read the diary of Pepys to see what life in London was like following the Restoration, or as we read the *Spectator* papers to see what it was like in the Augustan Age. Those readers of other centuries will miss in Andy Adams the fine art of Addison, though they will find something of the same serenity; they will miss the complex character and debonair judgments of Pepys; but they will find the honesty and fidelity of a man who rode his horses straight without giving them the sore-back and then who traced his trail so plainly that even a tenderfoot may follow it without getting lost.

Owen Wister's Cowboy Heroes

by David Mogen

This paper is an examination of the origins of a major American myth-hero: the cowboy as represented by Owen Wister's Virginian —that last pioneer nobleman, roaming a frontier beyond the dominion of a mother culture in the East, representing both its rebellious runaway sons and its most poignant dream of manhood and freedom. The Western as we know it began as a dream of Wyoming in the imagination of a Puritan East, and I have attempted to trace the development of that mythical world in Owen Wister's Western novels, from its origins as a pastoral playground in *Lin McLean,* to its emergence in *The Virginian* as a setting in which an adolescent male fantasy of proving one's manhood can be satisfactorily played out.

If Mark Twain's idyll of boyhood defines the emotional context of *Lin McLean, The Virginian* might be described as that idyll haunted by the restless insecurity of Theodore Roosevelt, providing in the graceful self-possession of its hero an image corresponding to his dream of talking softly and carrying a big stick. The Death of the West, the elegiac theme of these novels, might be described in the first case as the reluctant abandonment of the aspiration to combine independence with boyish spontaneity; in the second, as the process by which Wister's soft-spoken hero must end up blustering about manhood and responsibility after his guns have been abandoned.

1. The West of Lin McLean: Arcadia With Brothels

Much of the atmosphere of *Lin McLean,* Owen Wister's first Western novel, is established in the opening lines. Its West is an immense Arcadia, already vanished as the novel begins, a vast easygoing world of free range and roaming herds, and the hero is a

"Owen Wister's Cowboy Heroes" by David Mogen. From *Southwestern American Literature,* 5 (1977), 47-61. Reprinted by permission of the author and *Southwestern American Literature.*

young man gazing out upon the land in the dawn light. Owen
Wister's first impressions of the West, recorded in his journal during his trip to Wyoming in 1885, reflect this same feeling of exuberance mingled with awe at entering a region remote both in space
and time from everything he had known, a world somehow con-
nected with a primal past, the dawn after Creation. One of his first
journal entries strangely combines the desolate stillness of a landscape on the moon with the green newness of the world in the days
after Genesis; men with their herds of cattle appear here as an almost incongruous intrusion on an alien yet alluring and still untrammeled world.[1]

If the West of *Lin McLean* is not so inhumanly remote and alien
as it appears, it is because Wister has imaginatively seen it through
the eyes of a young man who feels comfortable only in its vast spaces,
who returns from a trip to his origins in an East he has found
cramped, stifling and alien to his spirit and "took heart to see out of
the window the signs of approaching desolation, and, when on the
fourth day civilization was utterly emptied out of the world, he saw
a bunch of cattle and...his spurred and booted kindred. And his
manner took on that alertness a horse shows on turning into the
home road."[2] The cowboys are discovered to be utterly at home in
their immense, empty world, and the narrator of *Lin McLean* has
come to feel something of their easy and natural relationship to it.
He has learned to travel comfortably there without truly being a
part of the world, as Lin is; he has learned to appreciate Lin's life,
to experience it vicariously. Yet essentially he remains only a spectator, a necessary intermediary between the world of history from
which he comes and this strange new world of primal innocence
quickly fading into its inevitable future.

The American frontier has often been protrayed as a virgin world
suspended out of time and history, awaiting the inevitable intrusion

[1] Fanny Kemble Wister, ed., *Owen Wister Out West* (Chicago, 1958), p. 31. See also
the description of Medicine Bow in *The Virginian*, Riverside Editions (Boston,
1968), p. 14. "Houses, empty bottles, and garbage, they were forever of the same
shapeless pattern...They seemed to have been strewn there by the wind...Yet
serene above their foulness swam a pure and quiet light, such as the East never sees;
they might be bathing in the air of creation's first morning.
...many houses in it wore a false front to seem as if they were two stories high.
There they stood, rearing their masquerade amid a fringe of old tin cans, while at
their very doors began a world of crystal light, a land without end, a space across
which Noah and Adam might come straight from Genesis."
[2] Owen Wister, *Lin McLean* (N. Y. 1962), pp. 37, 38.

of civilization. It is a metaphor as old as the nation, which by Owen Wister's time had seen much service both as cliche and propaganda. What is new in Wister's Wyoming is not so much Arcadia as the cowboy; the noble savages and shepherds of a mythical Golden Age appear in the figures of Lin McLean and his "spurred and booted kindred," not as remote figures from a distant mythology or alien race, but simply as decent American boys who strayed into the Garden at an early age, who roam through their vast playground restricted only by the limits of their own resourcefulness. Like the river in *Huckleberry Finn,* the West of *Lin McLean* is an idyllic setting in which a lost world of boyhood is recovered. Essentially it represents a free and spontaneous life in a world unsupervised by well-meaning mothers, a world uncomplicated as yet by the necessity of trying to reconcile sexuality, pre-adolescent romanticism, and the responsibilities of marriage. It is, most of all, a world of true camaraderie, where friendly banter and practical joking reflect both a testing of character and wit and a genuine appreciation of the distinguishing qualities of one's comrades. Like Huck and Jim, the narrator and his cowboy friends have a taste for "philosophizing;" the idyllic atmosphere is the setting for long, rambling meditations beneath the stars.

The central preoccupation of *Lin McLean* is a state of being called "manhood," and the ambiguous implications of the term reflect the ambiguities of Owen Wister's attitude toward his West. Manhood on the one hand signifies simply a certain preeminence within the society of one's cowboy peers, describing the condition of being accepted as wholly a part of the world of the West, of having endured its ceremonial testing of character and mastered its conventions. Yet if the term "manhood" describes the state of having established a recognized position within the world of Arcadia, it can also invoke standards of maturity that threaten to subvert that world altogether. As long as manhood signifies only a condition of proved prowess within the world of the West, it embodies the deepest values of cowboy society, the boy's society of peers; Lin's emergence to the status of man in cowboy camp does not signify the abandonment of youthful pleasures and spontaneity, only a more self-assured and sophisticated indulgence of them. Yet the narrator, the visitor from an older world, employs the same terms to define the difference between his "maturity" and Lin's, and the tone of amused condescension threatens to reduce Lin's stature to that of a picturesque clown.

It is Lin's uninhibited indulgence in satire at the expense of his friend Tommy which precipitates the reflections. "Successes! One ice cream soda success. And she...why even that girl quit him, once she got the chance to appreciate how insignificant he was compared with the size of his words. No, sir, Not one of 'em retains interest in Tommy" (p. 44). The narrator responds to these diatribes on Tommy's limitations with patronizing speculations as to whether "manhood" will ever find its way into the "boy soul" of his friend. Lin's prowess within the cowboy world is defined as "manhood of the body," but the narrator seeks a more elusive and profound quality of the soul, one which is easily ignored in Lin's irresponsible world, which the narrator's more discerning sensibility is acutely conscious of. "I...took an intimate, superior pride in feeling how much more mature I was than he, after all" (p. 45). The narrator is Owen Wister's rather ironically conceived *persona* of himself, of course, and his condescension here is subtly tinged with the envy of the prematurely "mature" for the frivolous indulgences of youth. His patronizing air masks a longing to indulge the foolishness of his own "boy soul," after all; he joins Lin happily in preparing a massive banquet of Tommy's carefully hidden eggs, and in reflecting upon that meal reveals much about the source of his love for the West and his fascination with his friend's life. His feelings of nostalgia are shaded with thinly disguised bitterness at the fact that only in the West, and only for a brief while there, did he enjoy a precariously carefree youth.

It is of the essence of the book's irony that consuming Tommy's eggs with Lin in a spirit of mischievous camaraderie represents to this carefully nurtured sensibility from the East the salvaging moments of his life. "...it is the only time I have ever known which I would live over again, those years when people said, 'You are old enough to know better' and one didn't care!" (p. 46). "Manhood" here appears as a condition of vigilant supervision of one's behavior, in which relaxation of control carries with it the threat of shame for disgracing one's self. To the narrator, the chief instrument of conscience is not morality so much as the fear of appearing foolish, but in any case the manhood it insists upon cannot ultimately be denied. He has introduced a good Puritan conscience into his vanishing world of unshamed youth, and it has the capacity of transforming manhood from a condition of enhanced freedom to one of glum adherence to the demands of decorum. The narrator's bravado over his eggs in line camp is doomed finally to wither before the nagging scorn of his better judgment, just as the West itself must eventually be transformed by the advancing forces of civilization.

It is this sense of fatality, this essentially elegiac feeling for a world doomed by the very innocence of its self-indulgence to succumb to a more severe and sophisticated order of things, that lies at the emotional center of *Lin McLean*. Arcadia must grow up, in the end, and Lin's barbarous lack of self-consciousness give way to finer feelings. The threat posed by Arcadia is of being trapped there, of eating the lotus of good times only to discover that dignity and self-respect are irrevocably lost. One cannot gambol in those pastures too long, for lurking behind the carefree present of Arcadia is a future in which one may appear as worthless, lacking in character and most of all, perhaps, a bit ludicrously contemptible, when all the good-hearted energies of youth no longer suffice to establish one's manhood.

The underlying theme of *Lin McLean* is the conquest of the West, and the agent of conquest is not, finally, the rifle, the wire fence, or the railroad, but a good woman from the East. The narrator's conscience is impotent, after all, to affect anything but himself; the significance of his Eastern background is simply that his intimate acquaintance with the operations of a Puritan sensibility and romantic sentiment provide him with a special consciousness, an awareness of the processes by which the reckless bravado of his cowboy world will be humbled. There is a submerged pathos underlying the brash manner of the West which the narrator is shrewdly perceptive of. " 'How little you understand the real wants of this country,' " he chides Lin, before revealing the nature of that most "important event" that will transform it. " 'It's a girl... A new girl coming to this starved country' " (p. 48). It is this deeply felt need, this "starved" sensibility, which makes the free and irresponsible style of cowboy life vulnerable, for the hunger referred to is not simply that of sexual frustration, but a more elusive hunger of the soul, which nothing in the West provides for.

Lin McLean is a deeply prudish novel, and sexuality is never presented directly in it; indeed, the essentially pastoral atmosphere of the book would be violated if it were. Yet an important aspect of its theme is the abandonment of a world of easygoing, illicit sexuality for the more intense and demanding sentiments of romantic love. The accessibility of prostitutes in Lin's world is referred to more than once, and there are more respectable varieties of available women as well, for those with charm enough to win their favors. Both Lin and the Virginian are granted their successes at seduction, a sign of prowess within the cowboy world which the narrator observes with admiration, and refers to in more intimate moments of conversation with shy rakishness and elaborate tact. Sexuality of this uncomplicated kind is—like drinking, or gambling, or the art of friendly insult, or quitting one's job for no particular reason— one of the indulgences of a carefree and footloose life.

But, as the narrator perceives, there is a hidden, aching need below the happy-go-lucky surface of cowboy life to which the pleasures of red light districts and wild sprees in town after drawing one's time are irrelevant. Beneath the brash, confident manner of the cowboy is a lonely boy looking for a home he's never had; exposure of this "inner man," this sentimental underside of the hearty bravado of Arcadia, reveals a realm of cloying sentiment and latent guilt wholly incompatible with the style of life in cowboy society. When the bishop's sympathetic understanding of these men is compared to the harsh insensitivity of the Puritan minister in *The Virginian,* the language throbs with pathos, as though the mere presence of such a potent father-image transforms the jaunty self-assurance of the cowboy style to a tremulous appeal for guidance and acceptance, "...when they fell he [the Bishop] spoke to them of forgiveness and brought them encouragement. But Dr. MacBride never thought once of the lives of these waifs."[3] There is an "inner West" like Lin's "inner man," a province in which sentiment rules, and it is a vast world without mothers or fathers, filled with homeless waifs keeping a stiff upper lip. The pathos of the cowboy's inner life is the source of those finer feelings which preserve him in the end from contempt. He is both reverential of the finer things lacking in his rude world and regretful of his past vices when confronted with someone deserving of his veneration and respect. By stressing the cowboy's capacity to appreciate finer things when they are present, Wister preserves his cowboy's dignity as well as his freedom to indulge whole-heartedly in pursuits which, in Wister's own world, would be both morally suspect and uncomfortably lower class.

Much of the irony of *Lin McLean* is a result of the incompatibility of the outer West, the happy-go-lucky world of Arcadia, and the inner West, the pathetic interior world of sentiment. Thus, there is no accounting in terms of the exterior realities of cowboy life

---

[3]Owen Wister, *The Virginian,* Riverside Editions (Boston, 1968), p. 149.

for Lin's error of judgment in entering into his first marriage. The "new girl" the narrator referred to proves to be Katie Peck, whom both Lin and Tommy begin courting with determination, and the problem is that she is not "new" at all. She is one of the girls of the Old West, emphatically not a proper vehicle for the romantic sentiment of courtship and marriage. The Virginian attempts to explain Lin's behavior as a simple manifestation of his love of winning— "Lin is determined Tommy shall not beat him. That's all it amounts to." (p. 72)—but this, while providing a motive acceptable to Lin's peers, hardly explains the lapse of judgment that led Lin to enter wholeheartedly into a losing game. Lin has managed to combine the worst of both worlds, and the only explanation for his incongruous error in assigning Katie Peck the part of a romantic lead is that the urgency of the inner man for once overwhelmed the cowboy's shrewdly pragmatic grasp of reality.

Katie Peck, in many ways the most fascinating character in the novel, is everything a lady shouldn't be. She is voluptuously mature, older than Lin by five years, by previous profession, the narrator discovers, a "biscuit shooter" in Nebraska. She seems to have consorted with a good portion of the men of the frontier during her career there, and she is thoroughly, unabashedly, vulgar, from her overripe sexuality to her cynical appetite for money and her abrasive self-sufficiency. The narrator loathes her, and Lin's reappearance in the streets of Cheyenne, trailing in the wake of his bride, confirms his worst apprehensions. It is an abysmal parody of the marriage contract, with its promise of somehow soothing the weary spirit of the cowboy's inner self. The cowboy is tamed, but the lost boy still has not found a home, and glumly accompanies his frilled, boisterous termagant who is no more receptive of his inner self than were any of his cowboy friends, and lacks their tactful reserve.

Katie Peck capitalizes on Lin's absurd misconception of her nature only until her interest flags and Lin's money runs out. She is as footloose and irresponsible as the cowboys she lives among, dedicated to good times and lighting out for new country when the spirit moves her, and is no more concerned finally to "tame" Lin, except as a passing entertainment, than to provide solace to his sensitive inner self. Rather, she embodies the seamy underside of Wister's Arcadia. Her presence in the novel evokes a sordid mirror image of the pastoral scenes of cow camp, the Wild West of the towns, where the unbridled freedom of cowboy life loses its aura of innocent and natural spontaneity to appear as chaotic debauchery.

Lin's courtship and "marriage" to Katie Peck are essentially material for farce, but they have a serious, pathetic side, and in the aftermath of their separation the atmosphere of pastoral languor shifts to allow for the more heart-rending emotions of sentimental melodrama, culminating in the most maudlin of sentimental conventions, a strangely Dickensian Christmas scene in which Lin roams the streets of Denver, having abandoned his comrades to their saloons, and finally lures a group of suspicious but eager street waifs out to Christmas dinner and the opera. One of them proves to be the runaway son of Katie Peck and her first husband, and, after carefully winning the boy's trust and affection, then nursing him through a nearly fatal fever, Lin adopts him as his own and takes him back to cow camp. The "inner man" is in the open for all to see. All that is lacking is the "new girl" to provide a home at last for Lin and his lost boy.

Her name is Jessamine Buckner: she's strong and sweet, profoundly moral, and has the capacity to render grown men foolish with a glance. The potency of her goodness is immediately felt, even by the narrator, who has experienced such things before but is disconcerted to stumble upon such a paragon of healthy decency so far away from home. "...[her] straight look seemed like the greeting of some pleasant young cowboy. In surprise I forgot to be civil, and stepped foolishly by her to see about supper and lodging" (p. 164). Jessamine's penetrating gaze succeeds where the forces of law and order have been repeatedly humiliated. In Separ, the small prairie railroad town where she has disembarked, a tradition has been established among the cowboys of terrorizing the local railroad agents and shooting up company property. It is all done in a spirit of madcap good humor, but one sheriff has been returned tied to the cow catcher, and another accidentally shot to death. In the process it has become a matter of principle to the local cowboys that they not lose face to the railroad. The one force which they have not reckoned with is the one which, at Lin's instigation, the company employs. The taming of the West in *Lin McLean* is represented by a cowboy's foolish grin, as all the anarchic violence of the Wild West shrivels into shuffling, embarrassed politeness before the mocking wholesomeness in Jessamine's eyes.[4]

[4]See *Lin McLean*, pp. 223-24, where the cowhands descend in a howling mob to terrorize the new railroad agent "...Honey Wiggin tromped in foremost, hat lowering over eyes and pistol prominent. He stopped rooted, staring...his hand went feeling up for his hat and came down with it by degrees...in a milky voice he said, 'Why excuse me, ma'am' Good morning.'

If the West is tamed by Jessamine, it is buried with the soiled frills and finery of Katie Peck. Jessamine's determination that she and Lin cannot marry while the other woman lives, despite the fact that Lin and Katie were never truly married, is an exercise in fastidiousness that bewilders everyone. The entire episode makes no sense, even to the most stringent morality, but it does possess a certain psychological suggestiveness: the new order refuses to establish itself until the last vestiges of the old are buried and out of sight, as though by the very militance of her goodness Jessamine were demanding the last full measure of triumph over the Old West she displaces. Lin can only enter into his new life by first laying to rest the shameless spirit of his past. But the death and burial of Katie Peck is, curiously, the passage in which *Lin McLean* achieves its greatest lyrical intensity. The death itself is an extravagant melodrama, which retains a haunting power and appropriateness despite all the maudlin histrionics with which Wister presents it. Katie's last fling is the elegiac climax to the novel. Before she dies, poisoned by an overdose of the laudanum to which she is addicted, "a big pink mass of ribbons, fluttering and wrenching itself" (p. 279) in the midst of the revelry in the saloon, the flamboyant and vulgar exuberance with which she destroys herself seems to have invoked all the energies of a dying West in one last orgiastic celebration of its past.

Drybone on Katie's last night is the Old West in the most dissolute and riotous celebration of its freedom. It is appropriate, perhaps, that the West invoked in this final elegiac passage is not the gentle, pastoral West of cow-camp but the West most abhorrent to the spirit of Jessamine Buckner, with all the drunken clamor and defiant bravado of its saloons. There is a dreamlike quality about this closing episode, as though Drybone were already a ghost town, and the shouting and revelry in its streets some mysterious recreation of a dead past invoked by Katie's presence, which must fade away after her death, back into the memories of which Drybone itself is an emblem. The "shouting and high music" echo in the graveyard, "Drybone's chief historian," where "Beneath its slanting headboards and wind-shifted sand lay many more people than lived in Drybone" (p. 264). At Katie's grave the milling mob of cowboys, mostly hungover and woozy, but eager to pay tribute, appears to Lin as an hallucinatory parody of his youth. "'It feels—it feels like I was looking at ten dozen Lin McLeans'" (p. 298). The debris of the past,

---

'Good morning, gentlemen,' said Jessamine Buckner."

"broken bottles and old boots" (p. 298), litters the spaces between the buildings, and when the crowd leaves, "their faces full of health, and sun, and the strong drink" (p. 297), there is a curious sensation that the playing cards in the grass have long since inherited the town. "Soon their voices and themselves had emptied away into the splendid vastness and silence, and they were gone. ... In Drybone's deserted quadrangle the sun shone down. ... and the wind shook the aces and kings in the grass" (p. 300).

Lin McLean ends with a marriage which is, ostensibly, the consummation of its hero's dreams, but it is a resolution which, though inevitable, seems curiously insipid in the aftermath of Katie Peck's burial. It is possible to discover the explanation for the vagueness and resigned sentimentality felt here in the character of Jessamine Buckner. Wister was aware that his virtuous heroines somehow remained wooden, despite his efforts to bring them to life. Yet perhaps the problem with this final marriage is not so much a result of the bride's personality as of the fact that the "inner man" of Wister's cowboys is simply too infantile and pathetic, so that to preserve their character at all it is somehow necessary to keep them from that home they so urgently long for. One might imagine Wister's West as populated by Huckleberry Finns who lit out from Miss Watson for new territory, and perhaps marriage still signifies at the end of his novels, not so much entrance into a new strength and maturity as a return to being "civilized." At the end of Owen Wister's Western novels it almost seems there is nothing for his heroines to do once they've married their cowboys, except tuck them into bed.

2. *Playing by the Rules: The Heroic West of* The Virginian

The Virginian created our mythical West, the heroic West, with its gunfighters, its grim code of honor, its ritualized violence. It is the West as hushed setting for the showdown, the hero as softspoken, graceful perfectionist of the kill, that have become the institution of the Western. Owen Wister's discovery in *The Virginian* was the Western hero as the embodiment of cool, who proceeds from apparently genial banter to the inevitable bloody showdown with hardly a change of expression. Wister's other cowboy hero, Lin McLean, has many of the Virginian's qualities, but he lacks this particular sinister yet engaging opaqueness. "I began to know the quiet of this man was volcanic" (p. 15) the narrator observes shortly after stepping off the train, and it is just this suggestion of hidden and volatile depths, of a sense of a self aloof and fiercely proud behind the easygoing cowboy manner, that suggests nobility in disguise.

Lin lacks the Virginian's drawl, that suggestion of Southern gentility somewhere in the background. Something of the legend of the chivalric South has been imparted to Wyoming in *The Virginian*,[5] like the Sir Walter Scott South satirized by Twain, it is a society governed by an heroic code of gentlemanliness and manhood, resorting to the ritual violence of the duel or feud as the final arbiter in questions of honor. The Virginian's drawl is a sign of his prowess within this heroic system; it signifies his aristocratic instinct, his fine sense of the proprieties and demands imposed by the code. The charismatic power with which Wister has endowed his hero is part of a more fundamental change in his depiction of the West: from the West as a world of recovered boyhood and good fellowship, to the West as sifter of men, where the deepest values are embodied, not in play itself, but in winning. It is the lethal power gracefully communicated in the Virginian's gentle manner, rather than Lin's easygoing, boyish charm, which fascinates Wister here, and the difference of emphasis is felt in the worlds they inhabit.

The pastoral West of *Lin McLean* is essentially a vision of uninhibited, youthful camaraderie, a world in which no man aspires to be better than another. This youthful world of natural equality lurks somewhere in the background of *The Virginian*, but essentially the character of its West has been transformed. The Virginian's world is not so much an Edenic playground as a romanticized Darwinian arena of struggle[6] where the noblest and strongest rise naturally to eminence, and the Virginian himself is not simply an especially engaging and attractive resident there, as Lin is: rather, "he was one of thousands drifting and living thus, but (as you shall learn) one in a thousand" (*The Virginian*, p. 37). The "inner man" of the Virginian is not simply a good boy; he is a natural nobleman, emanating a magnetic force which the narrator observes with almost embarrassingly enthralled admiration.

The ability to dominate one's peers would be irrelevant to the cow

---

[5]See David B. Davis, "Ten-Gallon Hero," *AQ*. 6 (Summer 1954), pp. 111-25. [See p. 15 in this volume.]

[6]For an interesting discussion of social Darwinism in *The Virginian*, see M. C. Boatright's article, "The American Myth Rides the Range: Owen Wister's Man on Horseback," *SWR*, 36 (Summer 1951), pp. 157-163.

camp of *Lin McLean,* but the drama of *The Virginian* derives precisely from depicting its hero's qualities of leadership, his emergence as indisputably a member of the "quality" rather than the "equality."[7] The vision of democratic boyhood has become an intricate adolescent scramble for status, where men constantly take the measure of each other through elaborate symbolic confrontations.[8] Card games provide the novel's deepest metaphors for life, "the game," as the Virginian refers to it while discussing Browning with his fiancee, which he proceeds to define as "Life, ma'am. Whatever he [Browning's hero] was a-doin' in the world of men" (p. 213). The world of men operates as a kind of poker game in which character can be judged, ultimately, by calculating one's winnings, as another of the Virginian's literary reflections suggests; Falstaff might win at whist, but in poker, where the real stakes are, mere brains are no match for Prince Henry's nobility (pp. 97-98).

Two almost incompatible themes embodied in the Virginian's career are brought together in the poker metaphor: poker on the one hand is a symbolic equivalent of the heroic code, a system in which honor is won and tested through ritualized combat; on the other hand, it is a game played for money, and though success in the game is to be construed here as a sign of inner qualities, the game in this aspect is essentially a business venture. If the Virginian on the one hand is a disinherited prince of romance whose noble birth is made manifest by the style with which he plays "the game," he is, on the other, an Horatio Alger figure pulling his way by his bootstraps out of his lower class status. The West of *The Virginian* combines a world of romance in which the cowboy appears as the last free spirit with an essentially Puritan world of social and economic struggle where industry and virtue are rewarded. In the attempt to identify the romance hero's pursuit of honor with a worker's desire for promotion, Wister introduces values of a Puritan society which threaten, as they do less drastically in *Lin McLean,* to subvert his hero's romantic identity altogether.

[7]See *The Virginian,* p. 93: also, see Neal Lambert, "Owen Wister's Virginian: The Genesis of a Cultural Hero," *WAL.* 6 (Summer 1971), pp. 99-109, for an interesting discussion of Wister's abandonment of his "vernacular" hero (Lin McLean) for the more dignified figure of the Virginian, his gentleman cowboy.

[8]The showdown at the end of the novel which has become a staple scene of the Western is in some ways a vulgarization of the novel's more subtle confrontation between the Virginian and Trampas. This is not the gunfight, but the battle of tall tales and verbal repartee on the train ride, in which the winner establishes his position as leader of the crew.

Once the Virginian is advanced to a position as foreman and shows himself moved and honored to be placed above his fellows, the entire romance world of the cowboy is called into question. Indeed, Wister's glorification of cowboy life on occasion took on the tone of a businessman's dream of a hearty, contented, cheap labor force — "They are of the manly, simple, humorous, American type which I hold to be the best and bravest we possess and our hope in the future. They work hard, they play hard, and they don't go on strikes" (*Owen Wister Out West,* p. 246) — so that his Old West embodies an early Republican nostalgia for simpler times, when manhood manifested itself as unquestioning devotion to hard work. Within this context the Virginian's promotion from labor to management is a proper and inevitable recognition of qualities that set him apart from his comrades. But once cowboy life is seen as something to rise out of, the bunkhouse as only a cheap, inferior home, the emotional context which defined the cowboy as a romantic figure is dissipated, his anarchic splendor and freedom transformed to mere healthy dutifulness.

A disinherited prince inherits his kingdom by right of birth once his identity is revealed, but a capitalist hero cannot have his until he has saved money to buy it, and it is difficult to maintain a laborer dreaming of higher status and a comfortable home of his own as a prince of romance. "It [his new position] meant everything to him: recognition, higher station, better fortune, a separate house of his own, and — perhaps — one step nearer to the woman he wanted" (p. 144). Thus, the cowboy, whose lineage Wister traced rhapsodically to the knights of medieval romance in his essay in *Harper's,*[9] appears here as simply a poor fellow who has not yet attained what all ambitious Americans seek. The Virginian's courtship of Molly Wood and his career as a rising entrepreneur both place him in the ignoble position of an inferior seeking admission where his cowboy background implies only shiftlessness and lower class status. The man whose inner self knows no equal is referred to condescendingly by the boss he reveres as "pretty nearly as shrewd as I am. And that's rather dangerous in a subordinate" (p. 57), and the most unkind remark from Bennington is not the concern for his bloodthirsty past, but the observation that Molly "has taken a sort of upper class servant" (p. 225). Perhaps most difficult to reconcile

---

[9]"...upon land has the horse been his [the Saxon's] foster brother, his ally, his playfellow, from the tournament of Camelot to the roundup of Abilene..." From "The Evolution of the Cowpuncher," quoted in *Owen Wister Out West,* p. 257.

with his dignity are his own sentimental pieties to the system of "making it" that has granted him a promotion.

"After a while...I noticed a right strange fact. The money I made easy that I wasn't worth, it went like it came. I strained myself none gettin' or spending it. But the money I made hard, that I *was* worth, why I begun to feel right proper about that. And now, I have got savings stowed away. If once you could feel how good that feels..." (p. 168).

The sententious preachiness of this speech reflects the degeneration of the arrogant, cool poise of Wister's hero into cornball earnestness, a process that can be discerned in the very style of his speech, as a loss of imaginative vitality. The Virginian's newly rhetorical folksiness reflects his emergence as a spokesman for a kind of official morality of manhood, closely tied to social Darwinian theory and Republican politics. His new style of speech is the end product of a process of assimilation, whereby the supple, playful cadences of his youth are transformed to a style of earnest exhortation characteristic of an older Puritan society.

The narrator's original fascination with the society of Wyoming was due in large part to his awe at the bewildering ingenuity of its conversation, the delight at extensions of language into absurd realms of innuendo and double meaning, disguised always as simple exchange of observation, which leaves him perplexed and dazzled at the bizarre originality of the cowboys' laconic speech. The narrator's observation that "this wild country spoke a different language than mine" (p. 21) contributes to an aura of romantic exclusiveness about cowboy life, inverting the traditional theme of the novel of manners so that he, the aristocrat, is required to master the subtleties of a society whose standards of conduct and speech are more elusive and demanding than those of his own; "that speech of the fourth dimension" from which the cowboys drop into "direct talk" (p. 21) is expressive of the spirit of an Old West united by common experience and sensibility, which often manifests itself as cool disdain for the straight world of dudes.

The narrator is aware that his very presence is sometimes utilized as the cowboy's "telephone" (p. 21) for communication in some unfamiliar dimension of meaning, and, on the train ride which most severely tests the Virginian's prowess within the society of the West, the narrator is mystified both at the hostility he encounters and the manner in which it is expressed; he is aware that he has acquired a protector, though the nuances of the battle escape him. The irony is that the Virginian's mastery of this oblique art of communication, evocative in the opening chapters of a playful camaraderie that recalls the world of *Lin McLean,* is employed ultimately to manipulate his former comrades in the interests of his boss. And, finally, with the abandonment of that slyly exuberant cowboy poetry for the rhetoric of Sunday school, he embodies a heavy-handed moralism his more irreverent youth would have regarded with quiet contempt.

The Virginian walks stolidly off with the chips in the end, destined for a successful life as husband and businessman, "merely a tall man with a usual straw hat, and Scotch homespun suit of rather better cut than most in Bennington" (p. 302). But by then the game is over, and the book's happy ending brings with it a realization that his true genius lay, not in piling up winnings, but in playing the game with a daredevil recklessness that had no concern for a future or for proprieties imported from the East. "'I don't guess,'" says Lin McLean, after the announcement of the Virginian's engagement, "'that you and I will do much shufflin' of other folks' children anymore'" (p. 224), and the elegiac impact of the observation derives from the memories it evokes of a more rebellious past, and a younger hero with a flair for caricature of the forces of nicety and moralism advancing upon the carefree spontaneity of his world: the Virginian and Lin McLean, sending unwitting parents home from the dance with the wrong babies, in the Old West's last flamboyant gesture of defiance toward the encroaching world of mothers and gardens; or the Virginian, keeping the dogmatic evangelist preacher awake all night with increasingly lurid confessions of his sins of the flesh, until the fierce old man rides off in furious realization of the indignity he has been subjected to.

The Virginian, like Lin McLean, must lay his past to rest before entering into his new life, but the heroic world of *The Virginian* is made of sterner stuff than the pastoral world of *Lin McLean,* and the Virginian is required not only to witness the death of his past, but to participate in its destruction. The lynching of Steve, the Virginian's companion in days preceding the narrator's entrance into the West, is a nightmare equivalent to the elegiac night on the town in *Lin McLean,* evoking a lost world of companionship and innocence in the anguish of the Virginian's renunciation of an alternate self surviving out of his past. "You have a friend, and his ways are your ways. You travel together, you spree together confidentially, and you suit each other down to the ground…And the years go on, until you are a foreman of Judge Henry's ranch and he —is dangling back in the cottonwoods" (p. 242). At this death scene the heroic code of the Old West ironically reasserts itself. The Virginian and Steve, who since parting company have played by different rules in their concern to win, play out this final act by the old rules, where only honor is at stake: Steve goes calmly to the rope discussing his coming death as though he had "lost a game of cards" (p. 240), and the Virginian remains cool to the last, playing hangman to this version of himself which played a losing game without betraying an emotion.

It is only in the ghostly aftermath of the hanging, when the Virginian's heroic identity disintegrates in hopeless grief and remorse, that the emotion held in check by the demands of the heroic code is fully revealed; the inner nobleman gives way to a lonely frightened child, as though the very severity of the heroic system had transformed the boyish inner self of Lin McLean into a terrorized, helpless infant. "…blamed if I can coax the little cuss to go to sleep again! I keep a-telling him daylight will sure come, but he keeps a crying and holding on to me" (p. 254).

The Virginian's honeymoon on the island, prissily Victorian as it is, with his division of the island into His and Hers sides for bathing, is curiously appropriate. For it is on this island, poised between the heroic world of the game he has played all his life, and his future as "an important man, with a strong grip on many enterprises" (p. 304), that this lost child of the Virginian's self is recovered and accepted for the first time. Observing a small animal frolicking in the lake, he interprets it as an embodiment of some buried part of himself, unconcerned both with responsibility and heroism, asking "What's the gain in being a man?" (p. 298), and he dreams of finally relaxing, to "become the ground, become the water, become the trees, mix with the whole thing" (p. 299). For a while the hero is only a "dreamy boy" (p. 299) with nothing to prove or defend against; he is Huck floating down the river, and the serenity works a kind of enchantment, suffusing his features with a youthfulness his bride has never seen, and "filling his face with innocence" (p. 299). He will resume the burden of manhood when he leaves, but for this interlude at least there is a feeling of resolution in the peculiarly American allegory played out in Owen Wister's West, as the abandoned youth of the West languishes at last in the bosom of the East, before entering into his fruitless middle age.

The Archetypal Ethic
of *The Ox-Bow Incident*

by Max Westbrook

One of the most sensible of all critical principles warns the reader that he must not choose indiscriminately what questions he will ask of a work of art. To ask a significant question is to impose the conditions of possible meanings. Philosophers and literary theorists—Susanne Langer, for example, in *Philosophy in a New Key*—have written learned and convincing studies of the principle and its applications. The legal mind is alert to this principle in the court room, realizing that what is admitted as evidence depends as much on questions asked as on answers given. The practical critics of Walter Van Tilburg Clark's *The Ox-Bow Incident*, however, have allowed circumstances to mislead them into asking the wrong questions; and the evidence thereby granted relevance has confused our reading of the novel.

In 1940, when it was first published, *The Ox-Bow Incident* was immediately recognized as an exception, as a cowboy story of literary merit; and it is still conceded to be, on critical grounds, the best or at least one of the best cowboy novels ever written. Some such judgment has prompted reviewers and critics to ask why this cowboy story is superior to other cowboy stories. But the question suggests that the excellence of *The Ox-Bow Incident* consists in Clark's having handled skillfully what is normally not handled skillfully in works of sub-literary merit. The approach might have worked had critics compared the novel with the fiction of Western writers like Willa Cather, John Steinbeck, Frederick Manfred, Vardis Fisher. The comparison, however, is between *The Ox-Bow Incident* and the formula cowboy story, which is about as profitable as trying

"The Archetypal Ethic of *The Ox-Bow Incident*" by Max Westbrook. From *Western American Literature*, 1 (Summer 1966), 105-18. Reprinted by permission of the author and *Western American Literature*.

to find the meaning and excellence of *Moby Dick* by limiting yourself to a discussion of ways in which it does not fall into the cliches
and ineptitudes of the formula sea story. Clark's critics have tried
to analyze the novel by negation—the narrative is not loose, the
cavalry (in this case the sheriff) does not gallop unrealistically to
the rescue—and the result is an impoverished criticism amounting
to little more than praise for a tight and suspenseful narrative.[1]
Placing a work of art in its proper genre is essential to criticism,
but the discovery of that proper genre must itself be an act of
criticism.

Certainly Clark chose the setting with reason. *The Ox-Bow Incident* is Western in a significant way, and its craftsmanship is
excellent. The novel, however, cannot be called a cowboy story
except in some perversely abstract sense, except in that sense in
which *The Scarlet Letter* is a true-confessions story or *Hamlet* a
detective-mystery. Nor can the injustice of lynch-law be called the
subject of the novel, for surely the subject of a work of art must be
something which is investigated. Hemingway's *A Farewell to Arms,*
for example, includes an investigation of the subject of loyalty.
Frederic Henry is a conscientious volunteer who deserts, and neither
his devotion to duty nor his desertion is overtly condemned. The
problem is subjected to aesthetic study. But in *The Ox-Bow Incident*
there is no evidence that lynching, under any circumstances, is just

[1]See, for example, Ben Ray Redman, "Magnificent Incident," *Saturday Review
of Literature* (October 26, 1940), XXIII, p. 6. Redman is representative in that his
review is very favorable, with only minor reservations, and yet contains no significant analysis. For the most part, he praises the tension in the novel, the suspense, Clark's abilities in craftsmanship. Typical of the general criticism on Clark
is Chester E. Eisinger's essay in his *Fiction of the Forties* (Chicago, 1963), The
University of Chicago Press. Eisinger writes that Clark has no interest in "society"
or in "ideology" (p. 310) and then describes *The Ox-Bow Incident* as a philosophical
novel, as a "deliberate commingling of social and moral issues" (p. 311). Eisinger's
basic strategy is also typical: Clark is a transcendentalist, his novels do not constitute an accurate development of transcendentalism. Instead of concluding that it
is therefore mistaken to call Clark a transcendentalist, Eisinger stubbornly concludes that Clark is therefore incoherent. Vernon Young does the same thing in his
"Gods Without Heroes: The Tentative Myth of Van Tilburg Clark," *Arizona Quarterly* (Summer, 1951), VII, pp. 110-119. Two critics I do not agree with, but whose
positions I respect and whose articles I recommend, are John Portz. "Idea and
Symbol in Walter Van Tilburg Clark," *Accent* (Spring, 1957), XVII, pp. 112-128;
and Herbert Wilner, "Walter Van Tilburg Clark," *The Western Review* (Winter,
1956), XX, pp. 103-122. Easily the best article on Clark, in my judgment, is John
R. Milton's "The Western Attitude: Walter Van Tilburg Clark," *Critique* (Winter,
1959), II, pp. 57-73.

or even expedient. Most men consider lynching wrong, both legally and morally, and the novel does not question that judgment. It questions something else.

If the reader is not distracted by comparisons with the formula cowboy story—or by the belief that the book is an allegorical warning against Nazi tyranny, an approach which, in 1940, appealed to reviewers and even to Clark himself—he will find, I think, that the story itself suggests a quite different and much more rewarding set of questions.

Why does the novel begin and end with Art Croft and Gil Carter despite the fact that neither plays a major role in those events which are central to the novel? What is the relevance of the long gambling scene which opens the novel? What is the relevance of the discussion of Art and Gil's emotional problems built up on winter range? What sense are we to make of Davies, who seems the most admirably moral character in the novel and is yet allowed to disintegrate into pathetic helplessness? Why is Gerald Tetley—the novel's second most articulate spokesman for morality—made to be so weak that he is disgusting to Art Croft the narrator? Why does Clark spend so much time—in an economical novel—getting the lynchers started, and why is the lynching not stopped? If Davies' academic explanation is wrong, what is the answer? If Davies is right, what is the relevance of his finely-drawn distinctions to the hard-headed realism which characterizes the tone of the novel?

The passages which give rise to these and to comparable questions share a common emphasis. Clark repeatedly focuses our attention on pent-up emotions and internal meanings, on the difficulty of giving external shape to the internal, and on the danger of fragmented projections of the inner self. In the opening paragraph, the land, not yet unpent from winter, is working its way out into Spring. It is the same with Art Croft and Gil Carter, for "winter range stores up a lot of things in a man, and spring roundup hadn't worked them all out."[2] Once in the saloon, working off their "edge" with drinks and kidding, Art and Gil discover that the ranchers around Bridger's Wells are also pent-up, also on "edge," for someone has been stealing cattle. Gil joins a poker game and begins to win heavily, but "with his gripe on he [does not take] his winning

[2]Walter Van Tilburg Clark, *The Ox-Bow Incident* (New York, 1942), The Press of the Readers Club, p. 4. Since this edition seems the most readily available, I have used it for the convenience of my readers. Subsequent references to this edition are cited parenthetically in the text.

right," (21) and Art begins to worry about Farnley, who "wasn't letting off steam in any way." (22) The scene becomes structurally relevant when Farnley does "let off steam" by becoming the symbolic leader of the lynch mob. The pattern continues with Major Tetley, the actual leader, and with Davies and Gerald Tetley, who are the voices of conscience, and with numerous minor characters: inner feelings must be projected into practical action, but there must be an integrity if that projection is to be healthy, and there is the constant danger—in small matters as well as in the lynching— that what is inside man will be given a distorted projection, and the result will be a horror, at best a helplessness. This value-system, I think, underlies language and event throughout the novel, but it is given its most straightforward expression in a comparatively minor passage. Art Croft, almost parenthetically, offers a brief description of Kinkaid, the cowboy whose supposed death the lynchers want to avenge:

> He was only an ordinary rider, with no flair to give him a reputation, but still there was something about him which made men cotton to him; nothing he did or said, but a gentle, permanent reality that was in him like his bones or his heart, that made him seem like an everlasting part of things. (36)

Kinkaid's character does not consist in deeds or words, that is, in either the pragmatic or the rational, but in some quality of "bones" and "heart" which expresses a sense of "permanent reality" and expresses it with balance and unity, as "an everlasting part of things." These values, I hope to show, are comparable to those which C. G. Jung describes as archetypal. They are the property of the unconscious mind, and the rational mind—like that of Davies— finds itself incapable in their domain. The rational mind can comment and analyze, even with some validity, but it cannot project its ideas into action. Man can only feel himself into accord with archetypal reality, and then aesthetically and ethically successful action may occur, but the rational mind cannot will a sense of "permanent reality" into the concrete events of human activity.

The American Dream, however, in direct opposition to Jungian principles, has emphasized individuality, which is both the price and privilege of democracy. As it releases man from cultural and political tyranny, individualism also begins to imprison man within the confines of his own temporal powers of creation. Too often, the emphasis on free will leads to an emphasis on ego and degenerates into greed and into an exaggerated evaluation of the male ego. Clark—again like Jung—holds that the male ego tends to separate man from the permanent, to distort projection. The intellect, also severed from the permanent, is associated with a degrading version of the feminine. Thus the lynch mob in *The Ox-Bow Incident* misappropriates for itself a monopoly on virtuous masculinity, and thus the protestations of Davies and Gerald Tetley are repeatedly associated—both in language and action—with a degrading femininity. But unlike Jung, Clark puts the archetypal to work in problems of American democracy, and thus he assigns to man's unconscious an ethical responsibility which is normally associated with the rational mind. Whether playing poker or joining a lynch mob, man is morally responsible for projecting his responsibility onto the human stage of action; and this projection, though it is properly subject to the judgments of the rational mind, cannot be generated by the rational mind. If man balks before the burden, if archetypal energies are betrayed by the fears or by the ambitions of the self-conscious intellect, terror is let loose.

Twenty-eight men, ostensibly led by Major Tetley, pursue, capture, and lynch three men believed to be guilty of cattle rustling and murder. During the pursuit, Gerald Tetley protests to Art Croft that he thinks their mission despicable. Gerald is a character type, the weak and sensitive son of a stern father and a doting mother. His father bullies him, demanding that he develop the pride of aggressive manhood. His mother, now dead, had always interceded, protecting her son from a stern father and a cruel world. Having to face the Major by himself, Gerald is helpless, and he is doomed. Yet what he says represents one extreme of a polarity essential to the structure of *The Ox-Bow Incident.*

Denouncing the "cheap male virtues" of physical courage, (136) Gerald argues that all men fear the pack, the mass of society which bullies its members, forcing each person to become brutish rather than risk exposing to mass contempt his own inner tenderness and weakness. Each man has dreams, but, says Gerald, "nothing could make us tell them, show our weakness, have the pack at our throats," (137) and yet these dreams are true. No man, Gerald continues, wants to hear the truth: no man wants to hear the confessor: "We're afraid that sitting there hearing him and looking at him we'll let the pack know that our souls have done that too, gone barefoot and gaping with horror, scrambling in the snow of the clearing in the black woods, with the pack in the shadows behind them." (138) Gerald is uncomfortably right, and his rightness can be seen in emotional details which constitute the real cause that led to the effect of lynching three innocent men. Even Art Croft, after hearing Gerald's confession and after admitting to himself the truth of that confession, goads Gerald with the threat of "cheap male virtues": "'I'm not wrong about your being here, am I?'" (140) It is wrong for Art to question Gerald's loyalty to honest citizenship, to make him protest that he is not on the side of the rustlers, and Art knows it is wrong, and feels "mean" to ask the question, but he does ask it. Clark's irony here is missed unless we remember that neither Art (who later admits to Davies that he felt all along the lynching was wrong) nor Gil (who keeps remembering, though he is reluctant to confess it, an earlier hanging he had seen and been horrified by) wants to join the lynch mob. Both are participating in murder because they fear an inner reality. Both give in to society's divisive value system which associates virtue with a willingness to join the he-man lynch mob. Repeatedly, Art and Gil show themselves ready to fight with fists or with guns in order to show their allegiance to a cause in which they do not believe.

Jung describes the same fear, placing it in the realm of the unconscious and thus in the domain of the archetypal. People, he explains, are "afraid of becoming conscious of themselves." That fear, furthermore, is different from that reserve prompted by the good manners of one's society. "Beyond all natural shyness, shame and tact," Jung writes, "there is a secret fear of the unknown 'perils of the soul.' Of course one is reluctant to admit such a ridiculous fear." Jung's explanation of the danger of "secret fear" is strikingly relevant to *The Ox-Bow Incident:*

> There is indeed reason enough why man should be afraid of those non-personal forces dwelling in the unconscious mind. We are blissfully unconscious of those forces because they never, or almost never, appear in our personal dealings and under ordinary circumstances. But if, on the other hand, people crowd together and form a mob, then the dynamics of the collective man are set free—beasts or demons which lie dormant in every person till he is part of a mob. Man in the crowd is unconsciously lowered to an inferior moral and intellectual level, to that level which is always there, below the threshold of consciousness, ready to break forth as soon as it is stimulated through the formation of a crowd.[3]

[3]C. G. Jung, *Psychology and Religion* (New Haven, 1963), pp. 14, 15, 16. Of particular relevance, also, is "Positive Aspects of the Mother-Complex," part four of Jung's *Psychological Aspects of the Mother Archetype.* The second paragraph of part four would do quite well as a brief statement of Clark's world view.

Man's unconscious, then, for Clark as for Jung, is both his hope for contact with archetypal reality and, when pent-up, when joined with mob-energy instead of with the energy of nature, the source of horror. As mentioned earlier, however, Clark believes man must learn to think through unconscious archetypes for the purpose of making ethical distinctions. We see this most obviously in Art Croft's reflections on Gerald's outburst:

> I realized that queerly, weak and bad-tempered as it was, there had been something in the kid's raving which had made the canyon seem to swell out and become immaterial until you could think the whole world, the universe, into the half-darkness around you: millions of souls swarming like fierce, tiny, pale stars, shining hard, winking about cores of minute, mean feelings, thoughts and deeds. To me his idea appeared just the opposite of Davies'. To the kid what everybody thought was low and wicked, and their hanging together was a mere disguise of their evil. To Davies, what everybody thought became, just because everybody thought it, just and fine, and to act up to what they thought was to elevate oneself. And yet both of them gave you that feeling of thinking outside yourself, in a big place; the kid gave me that feeling even more, if anything, though he was disgusting. You could feel what he meant; you could only think what Davies meant. (139)

Here are the central argument and the typical image of Clark's allegiance to the West. Though his sin, in a general way, is the same as Major Tetley's, Art Croft is an appropriate narrator for a novel of that allegiance in that he is moving toward the acceptance of ethical responsibilities in a world of archetypal realities. He wants to think outside himself, to a reality more objective than the personal projections of the romanticized individualist. The objectively real, furthermore, must be felt, a requirement which suggests mysticism, or knowledge of the real apprehended by a means beyond human analysis. Gerald, however, in stressing the imaginative at the expense of the practical, disgusts Art, who does not like to see a man pour "out his insides without shame"; and Art admits also a deep admiration for Davies, whose intellectual and very unmystical approach also gives "that feeling of thinking outside yourself." Art Croft has thus accepted a Western version of the American paradox. The universal principles of justice, as formulated and intellectualized by Davies, are real. They represent a part of our history, and the American of integrity cannot take D. H. Lawrence's advice (given throughout his *Studies in Classic Ameri-*

can Literature) and ignore an ethical duty because it is not honored with the ontological status that is the exclusive property of the unconscious. Clark's hero is obligated to grant the rights of the internal self, the ethical duties owed to others, and unlike his Eastern counterpart, to accept also the primary reality of the archetypes of the unconscious. He intellectualizes nervously (all of Clark's heroes are painfully rational, none are mindless), he is concerned with the practical world (law in *The Ox-Bow Incident*, adjustment problems from boyhood to manhood in urban America in *The City of Trembling Leaves*, the settling of the West in *The Track of the Cat*), and he realizes or comes to realize that the unconscious mind must be in tune with primordial reality. The goal for Clark, and here again he is of the West, is unity.

Neither the mystical nor the intellectual, it should be emphasized, leads to unity. Throughout Clark's works, characters who seem mystical or unusually sensitive are either disgusting, like Gerald, or ineffectual, like Arthur in *The Track of the Cat*. The intellectual, like Davies, is sympathetic but ineffectual, and the intellect—when associated with the coolness of a Major Tetley—tends toward cruelty and self-destruction. Unity, which Clark associates with balance, cannot be achieved by a narrow personality.

The Reverend Osgood, for example, is right intellectually, and, according to Art, sincere; but he is a failure as a man and as a minister. The fact that his advice to the lynchers is legal, ethical, and sensible is irrelevant. His words do not spring from generative unconscious, and thus they come stillborn into the world of action, and make men turn away, ashamed. Osgood, of course, is not a whole man. He represents man's cowardly severance of parts from a whole he is neither humble enough nor brave enough to sense. This severance, quite understandably, is for Clark an ugly operation. The foot torn from the body, however pitiable, is grotesque. The sense of the whole must be felt with such courage and conviction that it results in a projection which has an honest face, which is dramatically effective.

Osgood's failure, therefore, is described in aesthetic terms. Since his position obligates him to stop the lynching, the Reverend tries, but he goes about it "busily, as if he didn't want to, but was making himself." (41) His intellectual concept of an official duty, that is, cannot give birth to genuine emotion or to genuine action. His efforts are fragmented. He starts, and then stops, unable to get going, unable to speak with force or persuasion, incapable even of persuading himself. (The lynch mob has excessive energy, but it is distorted mob-energy, repugnant to man's ethical sense, and thus the mob too starts and stalls, has difficulty getting under way.) He waves his hands, nervously, thrusts them in his pockets again, and looks, at one point, "as if he were going to cry." (40) Art notices that his "bald head was pale in the sun," that the "wind fluttered his coat and the legs of his trousers," that he "looked helpless and timid." (41) He "was trying to do what he thought was right, but he had no heart in his effort," (41) and he makes Art feel "ashamed," "disgusted." (41) His voice "was too high from being forced," and, Art concludes, "He talked with no more conviction than he walked." (41)

Osgood, as a man, is embarrassing, which is not to say that brave men have a full head of hair or that men with high voices are cowards. Clark has chosen to describe Osgood's pathetic and ineffectual efforts in aesthetic terms because he is concerned with the necessity of the archetypal source. Osgood flutters his hands as a nervous reaction to his own incompetence. He speaks in a voice "too high from being forced" because his source is his own sterile will instead of the energizing archetypes of the unconscious. He has given himself over to officialdom's grotesque separation of man from the totality to which he belongs. He has alienated himself from that essential unity of thought and things—and truncated man is a disgusting sight to behold.

This alienation, I think, explains why Clark began the novel with a brief study in restoration. Though close friends, Art and Gil have succumbed to the tension of winter range, and they have argued and fought. They must now ease out of their divisive feelings, but the restoration can take place only if there is a sense of balance, a sense of the whole. They do not "dare talk much," and they are eager "to feel easy together again." (4) The clipped and ironic conversation, the mask of jokes to cover a bitterness which must not be allowed to grow, and the ritual of restraint represent a sense of the whole of which Osgood is unaware.

Art and Gil's entrance into Bridger's Wells, with its suggestions of rites of passage, is immediately contrasted with Monty Smith, whose degraded insensitivity makes him one of the most despicable villains in Clark's archetypal world. He is a "soft-bellied, dirty fellow," who wears a "half-shaved beard with strawberry patches showing through, sore and itchy." (5) Though opposite Davies and Gerald, though worse even than Osgood, he too is an embarrassment. He is a sponge, the town bum, and he cheapens manliness by pretending to be a genuine cowboy able to buy a round in turn. Gil is too much a man of feelings to be an ideal Clark hero, but he does feel with a roughhouse kind of honesty, and the certainty that Monty Smith will try to sponge a drink makes him "sore." He reins his horse sharply, and Art says, "Take it easy." (6) Gil does not reply, nor does he tell Art what he feels. Art has enough insight (he is apparently a writer) to know what his partner feels, and both know that what is important cannot be shaped into words.

Inside Canby's saloon, Art and Gil begin to drink. Behind the bar is a large and ludicrous oil painting entitled *Woman with Parrot*, but called by Canby himself "The Bitching Hour." The painting shows a large woman, half draped, lounging, holding a parrot. Behind the woman appears a man who seems to be sneaking up on her, or perhaps he is being lured by the woman to his destruction. Gil complains that the man "is awful slow getting there" and thinks the woman "could do better." (8) Canby defends the man, who is always "in reach and never able to make it." He thinks the woman has a "mean nature." (8)

The painting, it seems to me, makes an ironic comment on major action. The tension in the painting is frozen, caught for all time and, as a result, melodramatic, unrealistic. The tensions of the real world, by contrast, must be resolved in action. Almost every character in the novel, at one time or another, feels himself unmanned or at least that his manhood is doubted. Because of the high value placed on the male ego (Sparks is about the only one who escapes its tyranny), tension is built up, pent-up emotions demand satisfaction, gross or otherwise. Tyler and Osgood swell around pathetically trying to assert their authority. A feeble old man and an irate woman tongue-lash the reluctant lynchers. Smith, as a fraud, finds his manhood constantly in jeopardy, specifically when he must bum a drink from Art and then leaves, "hitching his belt in the doorway to get his conceit back;" (11) and it is this need which makes him eager to participate in the lynching. Even Gil is unsettled for having lost his girl, an unmanly thing to do, and Major Tetley, of course, is determined to prove both his own manly leadership and the courage of his son. In general, the ability of Bridger's Wells ranchers to protect their own cattle is in question. As a result of these small and large distortions, the lynching occurs.

This, I think, is the relevance of the opening scene, one instance in which resolution takes place with a sense of the whole, and the means to a better understanding of the entire novel. During the banter about the painting, Art reflects that Gil and Canby "said something like this every time we came in. It was a ritual." (8) And the word *ritual,* of course, suggests that unconscious realities are being shaped into the world of actuality. It is with ceremonial implications, then, that Art takes his cue from Canby, whose "face stayed as set as an old deacon's," (10) and begins describing the fight he had with Gil. Ironic and friendly insults are then swapped by Art and Gil. Gil justifies having knocked Art across a red-hot stove by saying a man has to have exercise. Art, he complains, is not much of a fighter, "but there wasn't anything else handy." (10) Art counters by kidding his partner's inept singing. They are "talking off their edge," and Canby puts "in a word now and then to keep [them] going." (11) The tension built up during winter range cannot be ignored nor can it be allowed its natural expression. It must be shaped.

The ethical, therefore, stands in a curious relation to the aesthetic. There are qualities and shades of qualities. Clark's vision, I think, reveals reason and feeling as neither good nor bad. What is desired is unity, a sense of the whole, with reason and feeling in their proper place, that is, with feeling (or the unconscious) as man's contact with reality and reason as man's conscious recording device for what the unconscious has taught. Davies, after all, pleads for feeling more than for reason. He is not the cold intellectual without heart. His failure is in his effort to make the rational do the work of the unconscious and in his resultant inability to give his beliefs the shape of dramatic conviction, which is not to imply that Clark has stooped to formulas.

Certainly Major Tetley is a master performer, and his ability to control the lynching party is an actor's ability. He speaks to a man without looking at him, keeping his own face full camera, and thus keeps "inferiors" in their place. He knows when to pause, how to ignore an opponent, when to turn rebellion by a soft reply. He is cunning, which is an archetypal characteristic of pent-up and distorted energies. As the master of male ego, he is the natural leader. Gil Carter, for example, offended by Farnley's accusations at the card table, rouses his manliness and knocks Farnley flat. Offended by Major Tetley, he again asserts his manhood, fully prepared for a gunfight, only to be turned into helplessness by Major Tetley's quiet sophistry. Gil is left in the frustrated position of feeling right but looking wrong, which happens, in different ways, to Osgood, Davies, and Gerald, and which happens also, in the climax of the novel, to the three victims of the lynching.

The lynching is simply a culmination, a gross increase of numerous minor injustices which occur throughout the novel and which are enacted according to the same ground rules that permit murder. The long poker game is a direct preparation for what takes place at the Ox-Bow. Gil begins to win, but he does not win in the right way. He neither apologizes nor gloats. Rather, he rakes in the pot as if he expected it. And Farnley, the heaviest and most disgruntled loser, also refuses to play the game right when he calls for double draw, even though he is not dealing, even though double draw is not "real poker." The judgments made after their fight are made by the same code, except this time Gil does it right. Canby knocks Gil out with a bottle, and then starts to take his gun. Art shakes him off. He knows his buddy, and his buddy will take it in the right way, and that he does, coming out of it slow, but joking. There is a right way to play poker and a wrong way, a right way to fight and a wrong way. One of the final comments in the novel is Gil's statement that he will not fight the sophisticated dude who took his girl. "I don't know how to start a decent fight with that kind of a guy," (287) he says, and readers will be reminded of Art's hope, just before the lynching, that Martin would "make the decent end he now had his will set on." (240) The Mex, who has held center stage and earned the admiration of everyone by removing a bullet from his own leg, spits in contempt when old Hardwick buckles, saying ironically, "This is fine company for a man to die with." (243) But in the end the Mex goes to pieces and screams, talking "panicky in Spanish," (246) and Art comments: "In the pinch Martin was taking it the best of the three." (246) How to die, how to fight, how to play poker, how to stop a lynching: all are studies in the same world view.

After it has become known that the three hanged men are innocent, Davies flagellates himself, embarrassing Art with a destructive confession. Davies does make some valid points—his denunciation of the sins of omission for example—but his confession is repugnant, for it comes from a part-man. Art, though enough of a moral coward to confine his opposition to "safe" actions like the fetching of Judge Tyler, though he puts aside his conscience and does not vote to delay the hanging, is a more complete being than Davies. His insight into people characterizes the novel, and he has at least some contact with the unity of all things, but he is also remarkably acute in reading the motives of Davies' rational will. He does miss Davies from time to time, but his understanding of the rational mind is a mark of Clark's American revision of Jungian archetypes. That revision is a fairly complex one. It is certainly bold. By what guilt or fate, then, have twenty-eight men come to the horror of lynching three innocent men? Clark's answer—or the closest thing to it for an author who feels that questions are more legitimate than answers—is his dramatization of the horrors of divisive lives. It is contained in the portraits of Judge Tyler and the Reverend Osgood and the obscene ethic of their narrow little roles as half-men, in the bumbling but honest frustrations and hi-jinks of Gil Carter, in the sympathetic obsession of Davies' doomed but honorable intellectualism, in the embarrassing but insightful confession of the girl-man Gerald Tetley, and even in the melodramatic tyranny of Major Tetley, the master play-actor of male ego.

The reality which lies behind the archetypal ethic of *The Ox-Bow Incident* is a reality one apprehends best by belonging as an "everlasting part of things." Man does not achieve his real self in idea or office or emotion, but as an individual part of a larger whole. Man's only hope is to act from a sense of the integrity of that larger eternity, and his most shocking failure is to murder innocent men on behalf of his own dedication to a severed piece of man called the male ego. When that failure occurs, his victim will be most probably a man like Martin, an innocent, naive in the affairs of the manly world, the natural prey of mob-beast that grows from man's neglected unconscious.

The subject of *The Ox-Bow Incident*, I have tried to suggest, is not a plea for legal procedure. The subject is man's mutilation of himself, man's sometimes trivial, sometimes large failures to get beyond the narrow images of his own ego. The tragedy of *The Ox-Bow Incident* is that most of us, including the man of sensitivity and the man of reason, are alienated from the saving grace of archetypal reality. Our lives, then, though not without possibility, are often stories of a cruel and irrevocable mistake.

The Novelist and His Background[1]

by Vardis Fisher

When it was suggested that I should take as my topic this evening "The Novelist and his Background," I felt dismay, even though it may be supposed that serious writers know something about the subject. Mention of "serious" writers invariably brings to my mind the story of that tedious congressman who, after wearying his colleagues with a long-winded speech, turned to Henry Clay and said, "You, sir, speak for the present generation but I speak for posterity." Clay, you will remember, said to him, "You seem resolved to speak until the arrival of your audience." All serious writers like to believe, with the congressman, that they speak for posterity; but as we approach old age we understand more and more clearly that we do well indeed if we speak for ourselves.

I felt dismay at the thought of talking to this group because I am not in any special sense of the word a folklorist. Still, any writer, I suppose, is a folklorist, or any artist of any kind. My dictionary says that folklore is the customs and beliefs of a people or a study of them. In that sense folklore is as broad as human life itself, and a novelist's materials are surely a part of it. In a narrower sense, folklore is myth. Myth, any myth, it has been said, is an effort to explain a custom or belief whose origins have been forgotten, or, more likely, were never known. Myth, it may be, is the more spacious formula in which the lore is contained; and myth, I understand after so many years of writing, is the chief thing in a novelist's background.

I do not know how well this matter is understood by people generally. Many years ago when I was a college teacher I was called on the carpet by an angry president, who was tired of hearing complaints about me from parents, the alumni, and the board of regents.

"The Novelist and His Background." From Vardis Fisher, *Thomas Wolfe as I Knew Him, and Other Essays* (Denver: Allan Swallow, 1963), pp. 79-89. Reprinted by permission of Mrs. Vardis Fisher.

[1]A talk given to the Western Folklore Conference and to the Writers' Workshop at Denver, July 17, 1953.

Pacing back and forth while wondering whether to fire me or reform me, he suddenly turned and asked, "Fisher, what in the devil do economics, sociology, psychology, and all these things have to do with courses in writing?" If a university president can be so limited in his view, we hardly dare suppose that there is much comprehension of the way folklore and myth and their wealth of symbols fill and overflow our lives.

In his book on Thomas Wolfe, Mr. Herbert Muller says that Wolfe tried to create the American myth. That statement startled me. Recently, when looking over the first issue of the *Denver Faulkner Studies*, I was again startled, when I found this author called an epic mythmaker. How, asked the critic, is one to understand Faulkner the mythmaker? It seems to me that here we have confused thinking. No man creates a myth. All myth is a product of the folkmind. It may be true that Wolfe was trying to represent what he conceived to be the American myth; and it may be that Faulkner is trying to search out the substance and color of ancient myth in the American South. But an effort to perceive in what ways myth shapes and determines life today is quite different from creating the myth itself.

Freud, toward whom in some quarters it is now the fashion to be indulgent, thought that myth "corresponds to the displaced residues of wish fantasies of entire nations." Otto Rank conceives of myth as an intermediate between collective dreams and collective poems. As the dream draws off the subconscious repressed emotion, so does the myth, creating for itself a "collective symptom for taking up all repressed emotion." Which, in both Freud and Rank, is another way of saying that if our reach does not exceed our grasp, what's a heaven for? It is another way of saying that emotion will create for human yearning those goals which mind cannot establish as fact. For according to Stucken, all myths are creation myths.

For Mr. Muller, myth is "not a way of disguising or evading the shocking facts of life but a way of ordering and accepting them." In accepting the shocking facts they are, of course, disguised. Muller goes so far as to suggest that all literature, philosophy, religion, yes, and even science, is mythology. It would be a great comfort at the moment to know that the atom bomb is a myth. Thomas Mann thinks that the mythical is "the pious formula into which life flows when it reproduces its traits out of the unconscious." I see no reason to call the formula pious, unless Mann intended to imply that the creative act is untouched by irony or doubt.

All these definitions we need not press too far. It may be that we do not quite know what myth is, for the reason that we have not been able satisfactorily to explore the unconscious mind. The mystic, who depends so much more on that mind than most of us, or who in any case makes fuller use of it, is still a riddle. Freud admitted that research in the concepts of folk psychology—that is, myths, sagas, and fairy stories—had not by any means been concluded; and though research has revealed a good deal since his death, we still walk in the dark with dim lanterns.

We can, of course, observe myth-making all around us. We can, that is, observe the creation of legend, which myth absorbs. In 1922 Professor James Weber Linn said to a group of us at the University of Chicago, "I felt like a lion in a den of Daniels." He claimed the witticism as his own, though it was old before he was born. In the *Reader's Digest* for March, 1950, Herbert Corey solemnly attributes the witticism to Willmot Lewis and gravely informs us that since Lewis first said it in 1931, it had enlivened the orations of hundreds of speakers. In such manner people build up their heroes. In some such manner, we may assume, myth is born. The stature of demi-gods all around us rises in legend, the embellishments of which will coalesce eventually to make the myth, which will become a part of biographies yet to be written.

As I see it, the chief task of the novelist is sufficiently to liberate himself from his background to be able to see it in fairly clear perspective. That he was unable to do this up to the time of his death was the tragedy of Thomas Wolfe. He was so enmeshed, so suffo-cated, so much the captive of all the forces that had made him, that he actually could place himself, as in *Look Homeward, Angel,* as a diapered babe, still unable to walk or talk, in the position of a sardonic and matured adult. In varying degrees we are all guilty; and we are guilty because the lore and myths of our world enfold and imprison us, embellishing what we take to be meanings, and enhancing our pitifully small egos. We have in some manner to break free, without on the one hand losing touch with the stuff that made us, without on the other mistaking our self-protective illusions for truths. The threat of a deeper and deeper schizophrenia broods over the struggle.

A novelist's background, it seems to me, is to be found less in the physical accidents of his life—in parents, neighbors, and geography—than in the past which produced the child. Many years ago a novelist published a story called *What Makes Sammy Run.* Sammy was a Hollywood heel, and in an effort to understand what had made him a heel, his creator went back to Sammy's childhood. But Schulberg never found out what made Sammy run, any more than in a later effort he found out what made Fitzgerald run. I had just read this novel when I said to my friend, Prof. Don MacRae, that it would be interesting to do the same job for some college professor— not that I intended to imply that all, or even most, college professors are heels. MacRae almost at once set himself to the task. The result was his Houghton Mifflin Fellowship novel, *Dwight Craig*. But I don't feel that MacRae was able to tell us what made Dwight Craig run. Some of you may be aware that I once rather exhaustively explored a man's childhood, with the hope of explaining how he came to be what he was. I also was unsuccessful, and the sense of my failure grew with me down the years.

Those who try to find the man in the child are unsuccessful because the man is not there. The man is in all the centuries of our past. One of Faulkner's critics says that in a Faulkner story everything has been said that it is necessary to say about the part of today that yesterday is. How wonderful if that were true! For if that were true we could now say what makes Sammy run. It would mean that we could talk quite precisely about the novelist and his background. In the midway of this our mortal life, wrote Dante, I found myself in a dark wood, astray. It would mean that we had come out of that dark wood. No man knows, says a line of poetry, through what wild centuries roves back the rose. It would mean that we would know the rose all the way back. In plain truth, we do not. Not even Faulkner, who so long and faithfully has explored these matters, knows that. Understanding what is necessary to say about the part of today that yesterday is is exactly the novelist's task. It is a task that still defeats us.

More than twenty years ago I realized that I had not been able to explain the man in terms of the child. I became aware that the author of *The Red and the Black,* great modern that he was, and so unflinching in his devotion to truth, had not explained Julien. I fell into such a fit of depression—in psychological jargon, into such a sense of frustration and failure—that I must have been in the condition of the man who, despairing of his sanity, went to see a psychiatrist. What he needed, the psychiatrist told him, was to get out and away from himself. The great comedian Grimaldi was in town; why didn't he go hear him and laugh and forget his troubles? And the poor miserable wretch replied, "Great God, *I* am Grimaldi!"

After some months of despair, devoid, I'm afraid, of the saving grace of irony, I came to the conclusion that to be able to explain what makes Sammy and all the rest of us run we must go to the past — which means, simply, that we must explore and try to understand the folk mind, and all the myths and symbols it has produced. For an exploration of that vast field one lifetime would never be enough. It is not only that we haven't the time; it is also that we know too little about the marvelous variety and richness of the symbols which the folk mind has evolved, and which still shape and direct all of us in ways that we never suspect. All the savagery of the past, said the great James George Frazer, lies so close to our surface that it constitutes a standing menace to us and our civilization. Proof of that we seem to have had in abundance in our time.

Perhaps without impropriety I may tell you that in the past twenty-five years I have read about two thousand learned books about the past, in those fields most closely related to the novelist's background. If I had the time and the eyes to read another twenty-five years, I think I should be right where Grimaldi was when he sought help. I have learned a few things about the evolution of myth; I have stood aghast before the thousands of symbols whose meanings are now a matter of record; but chiefly I have merely opened a window on a tremendous vista which I shall have neither the time nor the mind to penetrate.

I may then be pardoned a touch of annoyance when I read that in a Faulkner story everything about the past has been revealed which is today relevant to the present. Mr Faulkner, I am sure, must have been amused if he read that statement. He also has been exploring myth and symbol, and with an ingenuity which none of his contemporaries seems to possess, he has been manifesting the past in the present. Another Faulkner critic has said that one of his stories may be compared to the transition from the pagan to the Christian era. I do not know if Faulkner so intended it, but there was no such transition. Nineteen centuries of Christianity have done no more than to elaborate on and in some instances to refine ancient myths. I raise this point only to suggest that the knowledge of the best of us is still so inadequate that in almost no matter can we be sure that we do not err.

I have stated it as my view that the principal part of a writer's background is the myths that have shaped him. There is a luminous statement in Harold Bayley's two-volume *The Lost Language of*

Symbolism: "Little or no distinction can be drawn between classic myth and popular fairy-tale: myth was obviously once fairy-tale, and what is often supposed to be mere fairy-tale proves in many instances to be unsuspected theology." This field is so vast that we have time to look at only one instance. The principal myth of the Western world is not God or the Mother but what we call the Christ; that is, the myth, found with practically all ancient peoples, of the deliverer, the savior, and with all but Jews, the sacrificial offering on the fructifying tree. The wealth of folklore, drawn from so many sources, that went into the making of this symbol is one of the marvels of human history. The tenacity with which the Western world has clung to this symbol suggests its depth in human yearning.

From a great many I choose this myth-symbol with the hope that it will indicate the scope of our problem, as well as its difficulties. We are all aware of that need in mankind for heroes, which Carlyle expressed so well. Heroes we possibly must always have, of some sort, which means only symbols to which we aspire—or if we do not aspire, being too indolent, symbols that can serve as points of reference, and as moral and spiritual nourishment. When hero-worship, so strong in the Greeks, was combined with the sacrificial scapegoat, which also was commonplace in the lore of the ancient world, mankind got its symbol of the savior—and in the process brought women to that degraded level the record of which is one of the most repulsive chapters in human history. We must understand the myth and its sources before we can understand the modern Western woman, or even, one is tempted to add, the sensational appeal of Mickey Spillane.

Today, Professor Richard W. Boynton has said in a recent book, we are beyond mythology, or should be. Possibly we should be but we certainly are not. It is not clear that we should be, for the reason that myth has always been the vehicle for what in any generation passes for truth. In regard to the Christ symbol, see what form it is taking today! We all know that the Christian churches are fighting for their lives. We all know that there is a force abroad in the world that passes loosely under the name of Communism. We all know that this force has had an extraordinary appeal to a great number of intellectuals; and though I have steadily resisted it, and for seventeen years have been publicly speaking out against it, I was forced to face some unpleasant realities before I turned away from that dark wood. That so many have been, and are still being, disillusioned in this new force, which some have called a religion, is of no interest to us this evening, save as we must wonder what direction the myth will now take.

The thing called Communism—it is not, of course, Communism at all—is, as well as I can make it out, a revival on the one hand of ancient emperor worship, which served the Caesars so well, and on the other an invasion, for its dupes if not for its exploiters, of the great spiritual vacuum being left by the slow withdrawal of Christianity. Boynton thinks the Christian churches should scrap their antiquated dogmas and replace them with a religion of human values. In short, he would abandon the myth. But myth will not be abandoned, and the hunger for heroes will not be put aside.

What we have then, as I see it, is a return to unabashed hero-worship, during this fateful time when an immanent and personal deity is being dethroned. Many people call that godlessness, but it may not be that at all. It can hardly be that as long as the myth is vigorous. That it is vigorous is established by the obvious facts, not only that so many persons tend to deify their political leaders, including the late Mr. Roosevelt, but also that a cradle-to-the-grave security, which the political messiahs promise, is taking the place of the older belief in a life after death. The political messiah is replacing the ecclesiastic, and the "emergency" is replacing hell.

We are today witnesses to this shift in the direction of an ancient myth. All things are yours, Paul told the simple folk who were the early Christians. Under the Christian myth all things were theirs in a life to come, in which inequities would be no more and wrongs would be redressed. As Professor Shotwell has said, "There is no more momentous revolution in the history of thought than this, in which the achievements of thinkers and workers, of artists, philosophers, poets and statesmen, were given up for the revelation of prophets and a gospel of worldly renunciation." That gospel of renunciation, the reward of which is a higher glory in another life, has been the very heart of the Christian myth.

Our conflict today is between that gospel, struggling to survive but inevitably doomed to extinction, and the gospel of the blessed and abundant life here and now. The myth has veered and changed color, but it is the same myth. God, again as remote and lost as that symbol was in the time of Jesus, when the symbol of his Son came down to restore the divine intimacy, now finds his attributes taken from the ecclesiastic and invested in the politician. It is tempting to speculate on the development of the myth in the years ahead; to inquire how long it will survive and what purpose it will serve; and to wonder if disillusionment in the myth's new form will be greater than in its old. All that lies beyond us tonight, but we should note in passing that certain eminent writers, who loathe the form the myth is taking, have fled the scene, and sought a haven in a moribund Church. Mr. T. S. Eliot has said that a rational civilization will never work; to which, I should think, it is enough to retort that we can never know until we try it.

Now all this is surely an important part of a writer's background in a time of stress and change. It may well be that we apprehend only dimly, if at all. Novelists of a later age—if the novel as an art form survives, which is doubtful—will understand far better than we what makes Sammy run. Today, those who strive to understand are able to see, in broad but dim perspective, the outlines of some of the ancient forces which have shaped us. There are many important myths, an exploration of which might well constitute the highest form of intellectual adventure. Sometimes, it is true, we weary in this struggle to look inside the riddle; and though we may not walk out into the sea, as Virginia Woolf did, or jump off a ship into an ocean at midnight, as Hart Crane did, we do feel the need to shut out the past, which presses with such intolerable insistence upon the present.

In such moments we feel as William James felt about his guests. "Are we never," he impatiently asked his wife, "are we never to have an evening alone? Must I see people every night?" His faithful wife replied, "I shall see that nobody bothers you this evening." But at the first sound of the doorbell William was there, behind his wife, looking over her head and exclaiming with delight, "Come in! Do come right in!" And so it is with us, caught between these persistent guests from the past, whose presence wearies us, and the need to press on and re-establish our kinship with all things.

I have mentioned only one myth among many that are a part of the novelist's background, and of the background of all of us. It has been said that all fiction is autobiographical, and that of course is true. Of autobiography, Professor Boynton says that it "may be somewhat cynically described as the art of informing the world in print what you wish you had been, instead of giving it a portrait of what your enemies and hostile critics said you were." Our hostile critics usually manage to have their say. It is true, nevertheless, that not much fiction, past or present, can stand the scrutiny of enlightened minds. To build it strong and true enough to stand that scrutiny becomes more and more the duty imposed upon us. It is the great achievement of Stendhal, whom a critic as eminent as Taine read fifty or a hundred times, that he wrote strong and true for his day; and though the most famous literary critics of his time rejected him, and his contemporaries refused to read him, we are proud today to place him high above his enemies. For his intuitive anticipation of certain psychological truths are now commonplace.

I might have talked to you of more immediate matters in a novelist's background—of the clues which he must try to find—the clues to his nature and problems. But those clues, it seems to me, all lead back to more remote times, whether they be clues to his emotional hermaphroditism, or to his schizophrenia, or to the multidude of symbols in his dreams. They are clues that go back to Job's question, and to Pilate's, both of which remain unanswered. They are clues that go back to the ages, out of which came the stuff that makes today's child. We have gained so much in knowledge while losing so much out of memory. I am fond of Jean Paul's profound observation that language is a dictionary of faded metaphors. How true that is, any standard work on symbolism will reveal. Which of us, asked Edward Carpenter, has ever seen a tree? Not one of us has. For ancient peoples a tree was a house of God, a phallic symbol, a miracle standing in the earth-womb, an act of divine creation, a living breathing thing with speech, powers, and spirit. If we cannot see a tree, we have strayed a long way from the wisdom of the ancients. We must suspect that a great deal remains to be refound and a great deal to unlearn, before we can see Shelley plain. "All I have written and published," said Goethe, "are but fragments of a confession." We have only fragments still.

But as we explore, as we become more familiar with the knowledge which thousands of obscure scholars have put before us; as we understand with Joubert that a man of imagination without learning has wings but no feet; as we make knowledge serve our intuitive insights, and our insights feed more on knowledge and less on caprice—we shall add more and more to the great confession which is the history of the human race. We shall lose our self-protective illusions; we shall have to abandon one comforting myth after another; but we need never lose the deep truth which Emerson saw:

> 'Tis not in the high stars alone,
> Nor in the redbreast's mellow tone,
> But in the mud and scum of things,
> There always, always something sings!

Fact or Fiction: The Blend of History and Legend

by Vardis Fisher and Opal Laurel Holmes

When we said to a California librarian that Hubert Howe Bancroft often spun legends instead of writing history she replied sharply that she did not agree. Stefansson in his book *The Standardization of Error* says that errors widely and generally accepted are more convenient for most people than truth, because, as the late Professor Wendell Johnson, distinguished semanticist, put it, error "agreed upon and firmly fixed in legend and in law, is something one can count upon from day to day, even from century to century." As so many people still count upon Bancroft. It is simply a fact of life that most persons prefer the mythmakers and legend makers to the scholars; indeed, most of them have never heard of scholars and would think them very dull if they tried to read them. Professor Kent Ladd Steckmesser in his excellent *The Hero in History and Legend* says the serious historians lost the Western field by default, meaning that when they ignored "such presumably adolescent subjects as cowboys and Indians" they left a vacuum that the glamorizers have filled. Prof. David H. Stratton reviewing Helen Addison Howard's *Northwest Trail Blazers* in the Spring, 1965 issue of "Montana: The Magazine of Western History" points to the

reluctance to give up old myths and legends. It is still possible to read in popular histories of the Northwest that Sacajawea was responsible for the success of the Lewis and Clark expedition, Marcus Whitman saved Oregon for the United States, and Chief Joseph was a "Red Napoleon." On the other hand, scholarly works of history are often

"Fact or Fiction: The Blend of History and Legend." From Vardis Fisher and Opal Laurel Holmes (Mrs. Vardis Fisher), *Gold Rushes and Mining Camps of the Early American West* (Caldwell, Idaho: The Caxton Printers, Ltd., 1968), pp. 1-12. Reprinted with the permission of Mrs. Fisher and The Caxton Printers. References within this selection to other parts of the book that are not included have been left unchanged in the interests of clarity.

too stodgy for the general reader and get no further than the college
library shelf and the reading list for advanced history courses.

It seems to us that Steckmesser and Stratton haven't put their case
very well. It's not so much that scholarship is stodgy, that is, thick,
heavy, stuffed, and lumpish, or that historians lost the Western
field when they failed to write tales for adolescents about Indians
and cowboys, scouts and marshals; it is that most of those who read
books about the past, or the present for that matter, don't want to
know what the facts are, if knowing about them will disturb their
standardized errors. With no love of knowledge for its own sake they
have no wish to discover whether their beliefs are false. If you tell
them that Wild Bill was not the great civilizer of the West, and as a
pistoleer was only an average shot, that Wyatt Earp was largely an
imposter and braggart, and that Kit Carson, a small man, was not a
Hercules with muscles of steel plate and a perfect command of
English, they will want to run you out of town.

If a person wishing to know the history of the American West
were to read a few hundred books and articles about it, chosen at
random, he would come out of it with his head well crammed but
there might be few historical facts in it. Even some professors and
professional historians have a most unscholarly credulity, not to
mention encyclopedias, for the *Britannica* as late as 1961 was telling its readers about the "McCanles gang." Too typical of Hall's
four-volume history of Colorado is his account of Billy the Kid, in
which, says Ramon Adams, there is not a single fact. Professor Grace
Hebard's childlike approach to the demi-gods is revealed in her
breathless words about Wild Bill: "No desperado that disputed his
authority lived to repent it. He was the terror of evil-doers. Members of the McCandlass [sic] gang once leagued together to put him
out of the way when he was a station guard on the mail route, and at
one time a roomful attacked Wild Bill alone. When the smoke had
cleared away it was found that ten men had been killed, and Wild
Bill had received three bullets, several buckshot, and numerous
knife cuts." There is not a single historical fact in that. When a
professor for whom the history of the West was a major interest can
go off into the wild blue of legend without knowing it we need not
be surprised to find ex-President Eisenhower telling the people that
he was "raised in a little town of which many of you may never have
heard. But out in the west it is a famous place. It is called Abilene,

Kansas. We had as our Marshal, a man named Wild Bill Hickok."[1] If Eisenhower grew up in ignorance of Hickok's true nature and his deeds we must wonder how completely the legend makers have taken over our public school system.

In no other field in which we have read widely have we been so frustrated as in this field of our Western history. So, now, the reader is warned. He is to suppose that there are many errors in this book, for the simple reason that in many areas we don't know, and no person yet knows, what is fiction and what is fact. In an effort to dodge the errors we have based a great deal of this book on primary rather than on secondary sources. Let us admit at once that some things probably can never be determined, such as the number of men Hickok killed (though this can be of little interest to anyone except those who make heroes of killers), or whether Murieta actually lived, or Calamity Jane was a psychopathic liar. It will take a lot of research to settle the innumerable discrepancies in the thousands of books already before us. It would, for instance, be a sizable task to determine which of two competent writers is correct, or if neither is, in their conflicting statements about Stratton and Cripple Creek. Except in the physical sciences when we enter books about the West we are in the realm of legend, and if we are not to get lost in it we must be alert on every page. Some authors have tried to justify their indifference to the historical facts by quoting J. Frank Dobie: "If this story isn't true to facts, it is true to life"; or Mark Twain: "This tale may never have happened, but it could have happened." Some writers include in their bibliographies books that are worthless as history — such as, to give absurd instances, a life of John Wesley Hardin by John Wesley Hardin or of Polk Wells by Polk Wells. It is never-never land when writers accept as fact the lives of criminals written by the criminals themselves. In this book we have tried to be guided by such statements as Dimsdale's: after giving a calendar of crimes that led to the vigilance committees in Montana he said his task had not been pleasant but "the historian must either tell the truth for the instruction of mankind, or sink to the level of a mercenary pander, who writes, not to inform the people, but to enrich himself." His words may sound harsh to this self-indulgent age in which the accumulation of money is generally assumed to be the chief reason for living.

[1]Steckmesser, 158.

In this introductory essay we shall try to suggest how valueless, as history, most of the writing about the West is, not by citing instances over the whole broad field of it, though this one could easily do, but by looking at a few persons who have had hundreds of books written about them. The reader who wants a longer look at this matter can find it in *Burs Under the Saddle,* by Ramon F. Adams, in which six hundred double-column pages expose a few thousand errors in four hundred and twenty-four books. Though historian Bloom finds Mr. Adams sometimes chewing on trivia with considerable relish he admits that he writes "with great authority." The reader who wishes merely to sample this huge exposure of errors could turn to page 113 to see what happens to only one of the many books on Calamity Jane. Another excellent book in exposing the vast areas of nonsense has already been cited here, Steckmesser's *The Hero in History and Legend:* this is a fascinating study of what the mythmakers have done with Kit Carson, Billy the Kid, Wild Bill, and General Custer.

There are books, literally hundreds of them, that present some of the badmen of the West as Robin Hoods. Of Jesse James, for instance, who became a national idol, James Horan asks the question, What was he like? and says: "The answer is simply that he was a cold-blooded killer and a thief. There is no credible evidence that he ever gave one cent to a widow, or to anyone else in need, or took up arms for the helpless or the downtrodden." His teacher had been Charles Quantrill, the "'bloodiest man in American history.' A slim, handsome man, former teacher and a superintendent of a small Bible school, he was Jesse James' teacher in the art of murder, horse stealing, arson, and butchery." George D. Hendricks in his *The Bad Men of the West* undertook to delineate their traits and characteristics but like most people with a thesis he pulled leather and rode hard. He classified Black Bart...as a poet, on no evidence except a few scraps of doggerel, and approved the opinion of an unnamed person that this road bandit was "a great reader of classics and Bible." Wyatt Earp he presented as a man over six feet tall with a "powerful frame," yet who weighed only 155 pounds. If his book is to be judged by what he says about Murieta, the legendary Mexican Robin Hood, it is worthless; and this is sad, for in his Introduction he says he is a Doctor of Philosophy. Mr. Adams gives ten columns to exposing the errors by this doctor of philosophy who majored in history, and says of his book that it "has been kept in print for over twenty years and seems to have been a popular seller, which makes it all the more regrettable that it is loaded with errors." Typical of his indifference to facts is his statement that "a mob hanged Jack McCall for shooting Wild Bill Hickok." We are aware of the need of heroes in most persons—today they are called images—of the Kit Carsons, Wild Bills, and John F. Kennedys and on the other side the Klondike Kates and Baby Does and Elizabeth Taylors; but it is going pretty far when Kit Carson, who was a small man, is compared to Hercules and other giants of myth, with enormous shoulders, a "voice like a roused lion," and the habit of creeping through thickets with his heavy rifle barrel held by his teeth; when a man who could barely read faced a bully and said, "Shunan, before you stands the humblest specimen of an American in this band of trappers, among whom there are, to my certain knowledge, men who could easily chastise you; but being peaceably disposed, they keep aloof from you. At any rate, I assume the responsibility of ordering you to cease your threats, or I will be under the necessity of killing you." Such preposterous bombast was seized on by biographers and anthologists and repeated word for word. No wonder that when Colonel Inman showed Kit the cover of a journal that had him protecting a trembling woman while dead Indians littered the acres all around him, he said, after studying the picture, "That thar might be true but I hain't got no reckerlection of it."

Another national hero of Homeric proportions was described by one who knew him as a "short, slender, beardless young man. The marked peculiarity of his face was a pointed chin and a short upper lip which exposed the large front teeth and gave a chronic grin to his expression." Joseph Henry Jackson called it sob-sistering—the outpouring of tears and prayers and hysteria and the almost frenetic idealizing of various brutal killers in the old West. What touched off the worship of the homely little brute known as Billy the Kid? for the Bonney legend, says Steckmesser, "has penetrated every level of American culture" and Billy the Kid country "draws thousands of hero-worshipers each year and is the subject of articles in national travel magazines... Buildings have been restored, markers erected, and an annual Billy the Kid pageant is staged in August." What explains it?—repressed fears and hostilities, hatred of authority, chronic anxieties?—for there he is, enthroned in "one of the great All-American legends"—a youngster who was "a tough little thug, a coward, a thief, and a cold-blooded murderer." That is one view and it is far closer to what he was than the view that he was a brave and gallant crusader for right and justice.

The people who knew him are certainly better judges of what he was than those who have nothing better to do than to create folk heroes for the uneducated. On his death, "The general reaction of the press was one of relief." One newspaper said that those unfamiliar with William Bonney's criminal record "cannot comprehend the gladness that pervades the whole of New Mexico and especially this county. He was the worst of criminals." Another said that despite the glamorizing of him "by sensation writers, the fact is he was a low down vulgar cut-throat, with probably not one redeeming quality." And so for a while after his death he was "an out-and-out villain, a cold-hearted wretch who giggles while his victims writhe in their death agonies." For a quarter of a century that's all he was, but then the sob sisters got busy and the satanic Billy became the saintly Billy, and the officer he shot down without giving him any chance at all became "a snarling, foulmouthed bully," though at the time of his death every newspaper that wrote about the killing was horrified and shocked by the cowardice and brutality of it. Walter Noble Burns, a specialist in stardust for those spurning the earth, endowed Billy with all the virtues stored up in the saints' legends. Hollywood's producers pitched in to help, other writers eager for profit and acclaim took up the cry, and lo and behold, Johnny Mack Brown, All-American football player, becomes Billy the Kid for millions. The historians with their stodgy pages and devotion to truth can't make any headway against that—against a little squirrel-toothed runt who has become a giant who avenges insult to his mother and then is persecuted and hounded by all the human monsters of the Southwest, but manages to kill a few hundred of them and ride off into the sunset with the little girl who stuck to him through thick and thin. Today, in August, down in New Mexico you can see thousands of the graduates of our public school system going solemnly to the shrine where rest the bones of one of the most vicious and merciless killers in American history. In an earlier time, in California, the good and virtuous ladies took "fresh flowers, delicate viands, fine wines" to the brutal murderer Tiburcio Vasquez when he was in jail, and, in Nevada, to the equally brutal strangler of Julia Bulette.

"Today's student," says Jackson, "will wonder what the good ladies of San Jose saw in the little man (he stood barely five feet seven in his boots), with his retreating forehead, his sullen look, and the thick mane of coarse black hair." Jackson obviously had little knowledge of the stuff heroes are made of: Kit Carson is said by some to have been only five feet six, and the Kid was shorter than that, but so was Napoleon, who fills countless volumes. It's not only the good ladies who idolize the repulsive creatures: when the judge sentenced Vasquez he said to him that he had "one unbroken record of lawlessness and outrage, a career of pillage and murder," yet one of the idealizers of badmen has blandly written, "Even the judge who sentenced Vasquez stated that he did not believe him guilty." When the facts of history get in the way of those dedicated to the apotheosis of criminals they don't stand much chance. Look again for a moment at the James brothers. Popular opinion from the beginning was on their side and became so strong that it "was impossible for peace officers to enter Clay County. There was no need for Jesse and his gang to hide out now; they had their own 'iron curtain' of sympathizers, frightened sheriffs who were often in their pay, and kinfolk." When a harassed governor posted a reward of ten thousand dollars for Jesse, dead or alive, and for the reward a coward shot him in the back of the head, the kinfolk and sympathizers would have torn Bob Ford limb from limb if they could have laid hands on him. As for Jesse, he was buried in such style that one wag expressed the opinion that on resurrection day he would be mistaken for a banker. The governor who had dared to offer a reward had his political career ruined. That you can understand if you have before you the facts that on an occasion when Frank James was acquitted of the charges against him "the crowd went wild trying to shake his hand"; that invariably when a James or a Younger was jailed long petitions were presented which begged for their parole; and that Jesse's death made front page news over the nation. Among the words on the white shaft above his grave were these: "Murdered by a coward whose name is not worthy to appear here." But our favorite of all the sobsister incidents is told by Dimsdale. When Charles Forbes, a Plummer bandit without a single virtue, was acquitted of a murder he had boasted about, "Judge Smith, bursting into tears, fell on his neck and kissed him, exclaiming, 'My boy! My boy!' Hundreds pressed round him, shaking hands and cheering...." It's a fact of history that a substantial part of the people is always on the side of the more spectacular criminals, and that the idealizing of them takes every possible form, including paintings of them, such as the one of Murieta in this book. As Jackson says, it didn't even pretend to be a likeness of this bandit, if in fact he existed, but was nevertheless accepted "by devout believers as an authentic portrait."

Edward Zane Carroll Judson, who called himself Ned Buntline, was a "frisky fellow of many pursuits,...drunkard, temperance lecturer, beggar, promoter and jailbird," who decided to write what became known as dime novels. Between 1869 and 1933 seventeen hundred such novels were written about Buffalo Bill alone, and thousands more about other idols. Among the common people there seems to be a "voracious, wolfish hunger" for heroes. This Bill, a killer of helpless beasts, a show-off and braggart, was blown up into a figure of almost cosmic proportions. Jackson points out that magazines devoted to the West, such as the *Overland Monthly*, the *Argonaut*, and *Sunset Magazine*, "doubtless with the best of intentions, printed almost entirely the inventions of rewrite experts and sensational feature writers," who based their unhistorical moonshine on such sources as the *California Police Gazettè*, which in turn often copied from pamphlets or booklets in which it is hard to find a single fact. As Jackson says in regard to the heroes, "almost nothing that has been written since 1900...contains more than a bare speck or two of truth. ... What it comes down to; then, is that you find the truth...only by going to original sources and then exercising your wits as nearly in the manner of Mr. Sherlock Holmes as you are able. When you have done all that you can, you are still painfully aware that there are holes in your account." Jackson points out the significant fact that some of the sheriffs performed their dangerous tasks with great courage but are seldom mentioned in books about the West, much less transformed into national idols, as so many have been who were merely spectacular outlaws. As an instance there is Thomas J. Smith, marshal in Abilene, who probably had ten times the courage of Wild Bill or Wyatt Earp, yet has aroused the admiration of practically no one. Jackson hoped that some day writers would give such men their due. That is a lot to hope for: they were on the wrong side of the law. Of Tom Pollock, one of the· bravest marshals a hell town ever had, Zamonski and Keller observe that had his "career coincided with the westward push of a railroad or with the great cattle drives or with the better publicized cowtowns, Pollock might have joined that select and legendary few who seem to have blazed all the trails, dug all the gold, punched all the cattle, tamed all the towns, and fought all the Indians all by themselves."

When errors are corrected they still persist, not only year after year but decade after decade. If they are the kind that appeal to the unenlightened and the unthinking they are likely to persist until the last cow comes home. Though we published a novel about the

Lewis and Clark expedition to the ocean, and made it plain in the introduction and in the story that the Indian girl did not act as their guide; and though other writers have pointed out the same obvious fact, she is still acclaimed in programs over the air, and will be in countless books yet to be written, as the bird-woman who led the men all the way from Mandan to the ocean—this ignorant child who could hardly have been more than thirteen or fourteen and whose notions of geography would have made the worst of the old maps of the West look divinely inspired. Though we gave most of two years to the research for and the writing of a book on the death of Meriwether Lewis, and pretty well exploded the myth that he was an alcoholic and a lunatic who killed himself, as late as March 12, 1965, *Time's* book editors told their readers that Lewis "died in alcoholic ruin." Such perversions of fact in the interest of sensationalism and best sellers could be cited by the thousands.

In the libraries of nonsense that make of small men the giants of legend nothing is more unrealistic than the accounts of their shooting. For our autopsy in this matter we choose Wild Bill, the most deadly shooter since William Tell shot the apple off the head of his son, and "monumental figure in the tall-tale mythology of the West." Though Frank North, Hickok's friend and fellow scout, has said that he never saw Hickok handle a gun with his left hand, James Butler nevertheless shoots with unerring accuracy and simultaneously with both hands in both directions. In exposing the fictions in this legend Ramon Adams cites a hundred and seventy-nine page references, and could, of course, have cited ten thousand more. It seems very unlikely that as a shot this man was in the same company with Phoebe Anne Oakley Mozee, known as Annie Oakley, the girl who got her gun, yet he is gravely presented in book after book as the great civilizer of the West who did his magnificent job with two forty-fours. The hypnotized writer in the *Encyclopedia Americana* tells the world that Hickok "never killed but in self-defense or line of duty"; and even Stewart Holbrook took leave of his senses when faced with this legend and set it down as imperishable fact that Wild Bill was a "quiet and courteous" gentleman who "seldom swore, drank even less, and was a little quicker with Mr. Colt's Patent Revolving Firearm than any of the many ugly customers he found it necessary to shoot in the process of civilizing the frontier."[2]

[2]*Esquire*, May, 1950.

He was in fact a tinhorn gambler, an ardent patron of the soiled doves, a chronic drinker, and a coward in more gunfights than one; but as Steckmesser says, you have only to make him a dead shot and fill him full of social purpose and you're on your way to the image of the great civilizer. You have only to take the word of J. W. Buel who, in 1880, published a thing he called a biography. He said it: "He was essentially a civilizer.... Wild Bill played his part in the reformation of pioneer society more effectively than any character in the annals of American history." Seventy years later Stewart Holbrook solemnly repeated it, though a more preposterous falsehood it would be hard to find in all the writings about the West.

"It wasn't love at first sight. It was just a case of goggle-eyed, moon-struck hero worship. Colonel George Ward Nichols, an Eastern galoot, couldn't help himself." He looked into the eyes of James Butler Hickok, "eyes as gentle as a woman's," so gentle indeed that "you would not believe that you were looking into eyes that have pointed the way to death for hundreds of men." Whether Mr. Horan is right in thinking that the Colonel was goggle-eyed we do not know but there can be no doubt that he set the legend on its sturdy legs and gave it a push toward the twentieth century. Richard O'Connor thinks that Nichols had a case of "girlish enthusiasm" when he told the world about Hickok in *Harper's Monthly* in February, 1867, but O'Connor himself, whose book on Wild Bill Adams thinks one of the best, is not entirely free of the girlish attitude when he writes such words as these: "nearly blind, Wild Bill outdrew and shot gambler Phil Coe...a jigger of whiskey jostled out of his hand, and four men hit the sawdust." There is no evidence that Hickok was nearly blind at any time, and the four men dead in the sawdust are only a brilliant facet of the legend; but it must be admitted that by the time Mr. O'Connor tackled the job a few years ago it took a mighty man to wrestle with this legend. Ramon Adams has shot it full of holes, and Professor Steckmesser has given it a very bad time, but it must have at least a hundred years of life left in it. This we sense when we find O'Connor apparently accepting the oft-told feat of "having a tomato can thrown into the air and riddling it with twelve bullets before it fell back to the ground." With two six-shooters fired by both hands. He doesn't make clear whether he believed the story that Hickok could drive "a cork through the neck of a whiskey bottle at about twenty paces." Men who accept such nonsense have surely never fired a gun, or even discovered the nature of tin and glass. His eyes full of stardust O'Connor does gravely tell us that Hickok was "often a walking arsenal. In addition to a pair of .44s strapped to his thighs he would carry a brace of .41 Derringers in his side pockets, a Bowie knife in his belt, a shotgun or repeating rifle crooked in his arm." If there had been a seven-inch breech-loading howitzer around no doubt he would have also carried that. What we need to be told is why a man who could put twelve bullets in a small falling can in two or three seconds needed all those weapons to protect himself.

How Nichols ever got to be a colonel is also a mystery, for he must have been a timid man forever on the run if he had need of such a ferocious hero. It was he who put in circulation the outlandish story that Hickok killed McCanles and five other desperadoes with six bullets, and (as Horan puts it) "cut four more to death in hand-to-hand combat, and walked away from the carnage in fair health except for eleven buckshot holes and thirteen stab wounds." There were only three unarmed men, and Hickok, hiding behind a curtain, shot them. Nichols told his readers that he asked the great civilizer, Have you ever been afraid? and that James, who by that time had become Wild Bill, said yes, he allowed as how he had been. It was in the Wilson Creek fight. "I had fired more than fifty cartridges and, I think, fetched my man every time." That makes him as big a liar as Wyatt Earp. No less a person than Henry Morton Stanley confided to the *New York Herald* that Hickok had told him, "I suppose I have killed considerably over a hundred." O. W. Coursey, whom Horan calls "one of the more open-mouthed biographers," brought his quivering emotions under control while he told of this civilizing episode: "Wild Bill, facing the desperate character who entered the front door, had shot him with a revolver in his left hand, while with his right hand he had thrown the gun over his left shoulder and shot the man coming in from the rear. History does not record a more daredevil act, a more astute piece of gun work." Astute means sagacious; under sagacious the dictionary cites this instance: "He was observant and thoughtful." Sagacious shooting is pretty fancy shooting, in any land or clime, but Adams spoils it by saying "there is not one shred of evidence" to support this over-the-shoulder sagacity.

Other instances of astute shooting are, as Adams summarizes them, "cutting a chicken's throat with a derringer shot without breaking its neck, shooting a hole through a silver dime from fifty paces, tossing a wooden block in a stream, flipping it into the air with a bullet striking underneath it, and then riddling the block before it could fall back into the water." Riegel's *America Moves West*, written for the schools, includes the chicken neck, dime, and telegraph pole stories, and introduces an apple. He tells the children that Hickok could cut the stem of an apple with the gun in his left hand, and hit the falling apple with the gun in his right hand. Checking school texts against the known facts about Western history might show that many of the books ought to be given to libraries in those countries where our libraries are most likely to be burned. In Appendix C of our book on the death of Meriwether Lewis we cite a few errors, most of them by nationally known professors. We quote from that Appendix:

> Professor Albert Bushnell Hart in his *School History of the United States:* "The party of forty-five men, for which Congress appropriated only $2500...guided by the 'Bird Woman'." There we have three errors in seventeen words. Professors Bourne and Benton tell students that "only one Indian had been killed," an error found also in Hall, Smither, and Ousley, *The Student's History of Our Country*, though Lewis wrote as plain as day in his journal that two Indians were killed. Professor Fite says that "forty-five members were included in the party" which reached the Three Forks the "next spring." Both statements are false. Casner and Gabriel say the party wintered in "the lodges of the Mandan Indians" and were "guided by a French trapper and his young wife." Both statements are false. Sometimes the errors are simply fantastic. Boyle, Shires, Price and Carman in *Quest of a Hemisphere* say that "many times" the Indian girl "saved the white men when their lives were threatened by hostile Indians." In not a single known instance did she save their lives. Thwaites, Kendall, and Paxson in their *History of the United States* (for the schools) say that "After many thrilling experiences with fierce currents, inclement weather, grizzly bears, they spent a long, bitterly cold, and almost starving winter not far from the present Bismarck, North Dakota." Thwaites at least should have known that the fierce currents and the grizzlies came after the party left its winter headquarters. Professor Frederic L. Paxson (the same Paxson) in his students' edition of his *History of the American Frontier* says that when Lewis wanted to converse with Indians "he was forced to rely upon his mulatto body servant, who by chance spoke French." Lewis had no servant of any kind. Paxson goes on to commit another whopper when he says that on "May 14, 1804, he led his band of thirty-two across the Mississippi and up the Missouri." It remained for S. P. Lee, with Louise Manly, in their *School History of the United States* to misspell both names

(Merriwether, Clarke) and to say: "Up the Missouri and its great branches and through the wild mountain ranges of the northwest they pushed their way to the Pacific slope. Here they found the two rivers which today bear their names. Down these they went, until the two rolled together into the Columbia." Students who use this text and have a map of the Northwest before them must conclude that it was Lewis and Clark who rolled together into the Columbia.

If famous professors can't do any better than that shall we expect accuracy from the biographers of James Butler Hickok and Wyatt Earp? No wonder Wild Bill sickened on it after Buffalo Bill lured him into his circus. The exterminator of the "McCandlass gang" had to murmur these tender romantic words: "Fear not, fair maid; by heavens you are safe at last with Wild Bill, who is ever ready to risk his life and die if need be in defense of weak and helpless womanhood." Though the applause may have been deafening that was about the last thing on earth that the lover of the crib girls was ready to die for. When he could no longer gag it down he left the show.

The deadly shooting by the deadeye Dicks doesn't seem very deadly after you have read some descriptions of it by trustworthy witnesses. Dimsdale saw a duel between Ives and Carrhart, two of Montana's deadliest pistol toters: "Carrhart stood still till Ives turned, watching him closely. The instant Ives saw him he swore an oath, and raising his pistol, let drive, but missed him. ... Carrhart's first shot was a misfire, and a second shot from Ives struck the ground. Carrhart's second shot flashed right in Ives' face but did no damage. ... Carrhart jumped into the house, and reaching his hand out, fired at his opponent." The two then blazed away at one another until the Ives gun was empty and Carrhart had one shot left. Eleven shots fired and neither man was touched. Then: "As Ives walked off to make his escape Carrhart shot him in the back." It is Dimsdale who also tells about the duel between two gamblers named Banefield and Sap. When one of them called the other a cheat the two men drew their guns and fired at close range, and though neither was hit, a dog named Toodles, lying under the table, was shot three times and killed.

If objection is made by the admirers of Western gunmen that we are citing only second raters, let's move on to the very top, noting, on the way, Otero's statement that when he was in Las Vegas, New Mexico, in 1880, Wyatt Earp stopped there to settle an old score with a man named White. In a saloon at close quarters they fired many shots at one another and the only result was a bullet scratch across White's spine. But let's see Earp in action, as he himself told it. After his brother Morgan was shot through a window, at night, probably by a coward named Frank Stilwell, and Stilwell was ambushed and slain, probably by Earp and his friends, a warrant was got out for Earp, and while dodging it, he and his dead-shot buddies headed for Iron Springs, unaware that an outlaw known as Curley Bill and his cattle rustling gang were there. This Bill, according to some death-less prose, was the greatest outlaw in the Southwest in those years and about as deadly with a gun as anyone you ever heard of. The only story of what happened at the Springs—if in fact anything at all happened—was told by Wyatt Earp.

After a ride of thirty-five miles he and his men were weary and off guard, and so were within gunshot of Curley's gang before they sensed danger. Thinking they had been ambushed all but Earp fled, who at that moment was walking and leading his horse, a shotgun in his hand. Only a few yards ahead of him was Curley Bill, and he had a shotgun.

> I can see Curley Bill's left eye squinted shut, and his right eye sight-ing over that shotgun at me to this day, and I remember thinking, as I felt my coat jerk with his fire, "He missed me; I can't miss him, but I'll give him both barrels to make sure." I saw the Wells, Fargo plate on the gun Curley Bill was using and I saw the ivory butts of Jim Hume's pet six-guns in Hume's fancy holsters at Curley Bill's waist as clearly as could be. I recognized Pony Deal, and as seven others broke for the bottomwoods, I named each one as he ran. ...

That amusing nonsense has been solemnly accepted as fact by nearly all the writers on Earp and Tombstone whom we have read. Anyone who has used guns knows that if Earp was close enough to see that Bill's left eye was shut, and the plate on the gun, and in turn to identify eight men as they ran, he was close enough for Bill to hit him with a shotgun. Earp says he emptied both barrels in Bill's chest and practically blew him to pieces. But what was Bill doing while Earp observed the shut eye, the stolen guns, the holsters, and the eight men running away? The fact is that in his old age Earp talked to a bewitched Stuart Lake and really filled him full, and that most of the writers on Earp have accepted Lake as gospel. Adams takes forty-three columns and fourteen thousand words to demolish the thing that Lake called a biography. Frank Waters, one of the best of the writers about the West, spent a lot of time digging out the facts. He says:

> The truth about Wyatt Earp lies, not in his fictional exploits on a legendary frontier, but in his lifelong exhibitionism and his strange relationships with Doc Holliday and his three wives. It will not add to his posthumous fame and the almost psychopathic interest in him manifested by the general public. But it will be a healthy sign if we can now face up to how this pathetic figure—an itinerant saloon-keeper, cardsharp, gunman, bigamist, church deacon, policeman, bunco artist, and supreme confidence man—has conned us into believing him America's most famous exponent of frontier law and justice.

And along comes Ed Bartholomew with two volumes, so that now, as Joseph W. Snell of the Kansas State Historical Society puts it, "the image of Earp's fantastic career lies broken and trampled. He was not, it turns out, the man he said he was." Bartholomew shows us, says Snell, "that Earp was once arrested for horse stealing in the Indian country, nearly killed himself by foolishly loading the sixth chamber of his pistol, protected his prostitute sister-in-law with his Wichita policeman's badge, and in many cases was nowhere near the action he claimed to have been involved in." Nevertheless, persons back East were prepared to believe everything. After the gunfight at the O.K. Corral, proudly placed by some writers at the head of the list of all the most ferocious and frightening gun battles of the old West, it was reported in Eastern papers that Earp was found with nineteen bullets in his body, yet was still breathing. The editor of the Tucson *Star* took up his quill:

> Pshaw, that is not half nor a twentieth part. The Marshal had fifty-seven bullets extracted and it is believed there is about a peck yet in his body. Only a short time ago a cowboy had a Henry rifle rammed down his throat and then broken off; he spit the gun barrel out with the loss of only a tooth. It is stated as a fact that more than four-fifths of the inhabitants of the district carry one or more bullets in their body. One instance is of record where birth was given to an infant who came forth armed with two bowie knives. ... Every house has port-holes from which the cowboys are shot down. It is a great place for suicides; if a fellow wants to die with his boots on, he just steps out on the street and yells "you're another," and immediately he is pumped through from all sides. Sports play at cards with a knife in the left hand and a six-shooter in the right. It is no uncommon occurrence to see twenty men dumped out of a card room in the morning, and pitched

down some mining shaft where the ore has petered out. This is but a faint picture of the situation. Our New York exchanges had better try and get the facts.

One fairly aches with sympathy for the poor Tucson editor, for it was impossible to make the matter look ridiculous by trying to exaggerate it, since no exaggeration could be more fantastic than what was accepted as fact.

In a book before us a full professor is saying that Wild Bill "could probably draw faster and shoot more rapidly and more accurately than any other man then living. He killed many men, most likely twenty-seven, although nobody cared to ask him." Such innocence in full professors is pretty painful; many persons asked Hickok how many persons he had killed and he was tickled silly every time. The same professor goes on to say: "He was always within the law and justified.. quiet mannered, absolutely fearless, and always in control of himself." The Great Civilizer, that is, who single-handed opened the West to the wagon trains and the pioneers.

Cowboy and Gaucho Fiction

by S. Griswold Morley

The cowpuncher is not an exclusive product of the United States of America. Wherever cattle thrive on a large scale there must be men to manage them. Here, what with long grass country, short grass country, Rocky Mountain plateau, part of the deserts, and a slice of the Pacific Coast, there are some 800,000 square miles over which beef critters, as well as buffalo and antelope, have roamed.

Turn now to the south of us, to the Hispanic countries of the Western Hemisphere. Large scale cattle raising is conditioned necessarily by the geography of the land. Extensive plains must exist, and a suitable climate. Going from north to south, the following nations possess a cattle industry of importance: Mexico, Colombia, Venezuela, southern Brazil, Uruguay and the Argentine. Each has its type of cowboy. In Mexico he is called a *vaquero;* in Colombia and Venezuela, a *llanero* (plainsman); and in the regions along the River Plate, a *gaucho.* The name *gaucho* first appears in the late eighteenth century, and its origin is unknown.

Not by mere chance is our cowboy known in the Southwest as a "buckaroo," corruption of the Spanish *vaquero.* His art and his technique are strictly Spanish, by way of Mexico. The horsemen and the cattlemen existed in Mexico and Spanish California before they did in the United States, and from them we learned the tricks of riding and throwing the lasso. If proof is wanted, consider the Spanish origin of the terms of the trade. Lasso, lariat, quirt, rodeo, caviya, mustang, cinch, hackamore, bronco, stampede, are all of Spanish derivation. Some of our cowboy's customs are the offspring, though he did not suspect it, of old Spanish sports: for example, the "lancing game," where the rider, going at full speed, tries to thrust a lance through a pendant ring. This was a Moorish pastime, described in full detail by Perez de Hita in the late sixteenth century. The Ar-

"Cowboy and Gaucho Fiction" by S. Griswold Morley. From *New Mexico Quarterly Review*, 16 (Autumn 1946), 253-67. By the courtesy of Virginia Morley Brooks.

gentine gaucho, so far away from Texas, but drawing on the same tradition, had his *juego de la sortija,* or ring game.

Here is a more curious instance of identical origin. Readers of two celebrated gaucho novels, *Soledad,* by Acevedo Diaz, and *Raquela,* by Benito Lynch, have been struck by an episode which they thought lurid and exaggerated: to put out a prairie fire, men kill a mare and drag its body along the line of flame. Lynch has even been accused of borrowing the idea from his predecessor. No borrowing is here, only the description of an actual technique. It was standard practice among our cowboys, who slaughtered a steer, fastened two lariats to fore and hind legs, and, as they called it, "straddled" the fire. Whether this too came from Spain, or merely originated in both countries from the exigencies of plains life, I do not know.

In essential details, the cowpuncher technique of Texas, Venezuela, and the Plate is alike. If you read a description of a rodeo or a bronchobusting in Will James or Philip Rollins, and another in a Uruguayan novel of Reyles or a Venezuelan novel of Rómulo Gallegos, you will think it is the same scene. True, some personal accoutrements are different. The gaucho used a *facón,* a hilted knife half a yard long, for his private fights, while the cowboy flourished his six-shooter—that is nothing more than superior Yankee mechanical genius. The *gaucho* had another singular weapon, unknown in the North, the *bolas* or *boleadoras:* two or three stone balls sheathed in leather and united by strands of rawhide. These terrible implements were thrown to trip ostriches, horses, and cattle, and they found a place in war as well as in ranching. Since the bolas leave the hand entirely, they have a longer range and require less preparation for hurling, than the lasso; hence they are quicker. It is a reproach to the white man's powers of invention that he did not think of the bolas. The Spaniards of the South took them from the Indians of that region. Our Indians had not devised them, and so our cowboys lacked that weapon.

The cowpuncher, in whatever land he lived and plied his profession, was a proper epic figure. Always on horseback, living day and night with his beasts, he became an extension of the horse, or the horse of him. Gait and physique showed his occupation: one cowboy was known as "wedding-ring Bill," from the rear view of his legs. The literature of both North and South is full of admiration for expert and daring horse taming, feats of balance and muscle reading, skill in roping and herding cattle. But cowboy and gaucho were more than mere horsemen. Alike they developed a special code of honor, a pride in skills, a spirit of discipline, and obedience to unwritten laws of the trail. They risked their lives again and again. They performed their work in every weather; they went for days without sleep, if necessary, like a sailor or soldier. A broken arm or leg was all in the day's work if the cattle were delivered on time. Courage was taken for granted. Both plumed themselves upon generous hospitality to every stranger, and their code was firm to ask no questions of him.

In these respects the two were alike. In others they differed. The cowboy must have been among us from the moment the Great West was explored, but not until the Indians were cleared out of the plains could cattle raising become an industry. When, in 1846, the British officer George F. Ruxton crossed the plains from Santa Fe to Fort Leavenworth, and Francis Parkman explored the start of the Oregon trail, they found immense herds of buffalo. These had to be removed. The second half of the nineteenth century and the beginning of the twentieth were the cowboy's best days. Also, he was, in the last analysis, a hired hand on horseback, despite Gene Rhodes's brilliant protest against the term. He was a law preserver not a lawbreaker, and worked for a wage.

The gaucho antedates our cowboy by a hundred years or more, and his background is as dissimilar as possible. He began as a smuggler, a *contrabandista;* he stole before he guarded, unlike the cowboy, who guarded before he stole. The gaucho carried on an active trade in hides, dodging the Spanish tariff. He formed the backbone of armies, and his lawless upbringing made him apt for civil war. If he did not wish to fight in the ranks, he was impressed by force. If he deserted from the army, he became a *gaucho malo,* or bandit. He had, therefore, a backdrop of violence and tragedy, whereas the cowboy of this country, though pursuing a very dangerous profession, was in the main a law-abiding citizen like any other workingman. The gaucho began as an outlaw and was tamed by time into a farmhand; the cowboy began as a cattle hand and by exception strayed into banditry.

Moreover, the gaucho, as a good Latin, was a devotee of music. Our northern cowboy sang songs, as everyone knows, and part of his trade was to soothe the cattle with his tunes at night, when he rode herd; but he did not travel with a guitar slung across his saddle; he did not, like the gaucho, esteem skill in improvising verse as second only to skill in dueling. The Spanish song contest (*payada*) took place in saloon or patio, and a description of one is likely to come into any novel.

The gaucho, then, in comparison with the cowboy, was a many-sided being. He was an expert horseman and cattleherder, and that is where the two meet. But he was also soldier, bandit, musician, picaro and gambler, politician at the orders of his local boss, and a cattle owner or cowman (for the word *gaucho* covers all these). For my present purpose I must leave out of account all the phases of his life that do not coincide with those of our cowpunchers, and I must consider him strictly as a cattle hand.

Gaucho and cowboy are alike picturesque figures; more, they are heroic figures. And if, to form an epic legend, perspective must be had, and the mist of remoteness must curl about the characters and blur the realistic sharpness of the faces, that too is present. The palmy days of the cowboy are past. He still exists, but his domain has shrunk. The farmer, the nester and his barbed wire have taken over much of it. The Chisholm trail and the Goodnight-Loving trail are only memories. The great cattle drives from Texas to Montana belong to the past. Agnes Morley Cleaveland's *No Life for a Lady* graphically depicts the change; so do the accounts of Douglas Branch and Philip Rollins. And in the Argentine, the real gaucho has passed from the scene. When Sarmiento broke the power of the tyrant Rosas in 1852, he rang the knell for the old wild, free life, and struck down the gaucho. He is now only a heroic legend and, as such, fit material for folklorists and novel writers. Cowboy and gaucho both deserve an adequate literature. What have they had?

Our cowboy has been lucky from the start in the writers who described him as he was. From Charlie Siringo and Andy Adams down to Will James and Douglas Branch and Philip Rollins and Agnes Morley Cleaveland, there are portrayals of Western ranch life written with knowledge, color, and enthusiasm. It takes no more than the plain truth about a cowboy to hold the reader. The facts about him are better than the fiction. The farther the narrative strays from pure observation, the weaker it becomes. Even old Andy Adams (*A Texas Matchmaker,* 1904), rambling along without literary pretension, has a surer vision of life than Owen Wister.

Fortunate in his historians, the cowboy has been unlucky in his novelists. No thoroughgoing account of cowboy fiction exists. Douglas Branch's *The Cowboy in Literature* (1922) has many gaps, and the general histories of our literature concede only passing allusions to the "western" novel—very properly, if one considers its slight artistic value. It appears that Owen Wister was the first to write a cowboy novel with a plot. Wister was a competent writer, but *The Virginian* (1902) set a vicious pattern. Every novelist since his day has followed it. The hero, I need hardly say, is a cowboy of surpassing skill; he is stronger than anyone else, more graceful than anyone else, he throws a lasso better and with less effort than anyone else; he can shoot quicker and straighter, ride harder and faster than anyone else; the toughest bronco has no terrors for him. If he is ever injured it is because someone takes unfair advantage of him. He is always mentioned on the first page of the novel. If he has any bad traits we do not hear about them, or they are he-man sins.

There is also a villain without the least redeeming feature; he is homely, brutal, underhanded. In *The Virginian* he isn't even a good horseman or a good poker player, and you only wonder why the hero didn't finish him off in the second chapter instead of the next to the last. Then, there is the girl. In the early novels she used to be an innocent schoolmarm just arrived from the East; she had to be taught not only how to ride a horse but also the facts of life. However, the latest fashion of "westerns" (the current trade term) casts aside the innocence. I quote advice to writers of pulp westerns as given in the *Writer's Digest* of August, 1942:

> Keep away from that innocent virgin stuff. Lay off that pure-as-the-driven-snow. In selecting a heroine for this Vaquero of mine [he is describing how he himself composed a western] I selected someone to match his temperament: a little black-haired, black-eyed French girl, who was a mystery in town.

She doesn't have to be a black-eyed French mystery. Sometimes she is the wealthy daughter of a cattleman; in that case she is an expert horsewoman and condescends to the cowboy. As an example of this type let me quote from Emerson Hough, *North of '36* (1923), page 2, as the heroine appears in the room where a crowd of cowboys are eating breakfast:

> Obviously now, she was tall, slender, supple, rounded to a full inheritance of womanly charm unhardened by years of life in the saddle and under the sun. More, she was an actual beauty. Anywhere

else she would have been a sensation. Here, she spoiled each unfinished breakfast.

In any case, cowboy meets girl, and with the very happiest of
consequences.

In short, "westerns" are not cowboy novels, but two-gun novels;
and the lay figures who function in them might just as well be placed
in the gangster jungles of Chicago as on the plains of Texas and
Montana. They are the successors of the "detective story" and "wild
west romance" of the 1890's. One may even carry their lineage much
farther back, and compare them to the medieval romances of chivalry.
In both, the characters are puppets, and the strings that pull them
are the same. The sentiments of Amadis toward Oriana differ scarcely at all from the Virginian's adoration of his Molly. When Geraint
the son of Erbin slew three giants with his potent sword, he com-
ported himself no more nobly than gallant Charlie See, who in the
poolroom of a saloon, with his mighty arm hardened on the baseball
field, put six gun-toting cowboys to flight with billiard balls. The
ancient author and Eugene Manlove Rhodes conceived the drama in
like terms; only the setting differs.

The number of westerns now flowing from North American type-
writers is enormous, though less than that of the mysteries. Besides
hundreds of full-length novels, a dozen pulp magazines, paying half
a cent a word, are devoted exclusively to western stuff. In a list of
the most popular authors the average cultured reader would recog-
nize only a few. You have heard of Peter B. Kyne, Zane Grey, Rex
Beach, and Dane Coolidge, but only addicts and librarians react to
the names of B. M. Bower, C. E. Mulford, M. Brand, E. Cunningham, D. Dresser, and J. Gregory. There are scores more, and most
of them never went near a cowcamp. In 1940 Hurst Julian, who described himself as a cowboy temporarily in hospital recuperating
from the natural accidents of his calling, wrote an article in the
Saturday Review of Literature complaining of the technical inac-
curacy of westerns. He claimed to have read some three thousand
such books and stories, and nearly all misused the terminology of
the range. The only names he excepted were Will James, Eugene
Manlove Rhodes, and Ernest Haycox. Mr. Julian could have added
a few to his list of good angels, I think, for Dane Coolidge, Emerson
Hough, and Owen Wister himself (did not Teddy Roosevelt read
and criticize his manuscript?) knew range life well. Ignorance of
the subject matter was not their taint, but the adolescent tradition of
the western.

Eugene Manlove Rhodes deserves a special word. A cowboy himself, he was more proud of being able to ride anything with hair than he was of composing successful novels and poems, yet no man worked harder over his style. He it was who advised a novice writer to read his own stuff aloud three times, once to himself, once to a sympathetic auditor, and a third to one hostile or indifferent. By this means, he said, all faults would come to light. The result of such severe self-criticism is one of the most solid and distinguished styles written by any North American novelist. I would call Rhodes a first-rate writer of third-rate novels, for their sentences, humor, accuracy, and color are as admirable as their characters are distorted and impossible. His heroes are flawless and his heroines flabby, in the good Wister tradition. It is an advantage that there are not many heroines. At least two of his novels have no female characters at all.

Some fairly famous names are found among the writers of westerns. O. Henry, in *Heart o' the West* (1904), turned out playfully sentimental sketches with ranch background. Harold Bell Wright took a whirl at the game, and James Boyd, author of *Drums,* recently with little luck combined the picaresque and cowboy patterns in *Bitter Creek* (1939); one can only say that he spoiled both.

No North American novelist of the first rank has yet tried his hand on the cowboy. The reason may be that he does not bulk large enough in our civilization. His sway extended over thousands of square miles, yet he was only a hireling. The owners were the ones who molded history. He was not worth the ammunition of the big guns.

So, as the real cowboy fades from view, his passing chronicled and lamented by a few informed spirits, his debased and spurious ghost sinks lower and lower, till it reaches the subliterary plane. As Fred Lewis Pattee remarked, "The cowboy theme has been chased in every direction until it has found final refuge in the vast swamp of the movies." The last decade has seen some indications that clearer understanding and truer art may yet await ranch life. Real talent has here and there turned toward the great plains and the desert. But John Evans' stunning *tour de force, Andrew's Harvest* (1933), is the love story of a nester, not a cowboy. Walter Van Tilburg Clark's *The Ox-bow Incident* (1940) is a psychological study of lynch-spirit in Nevada; there are cowboys in it, but so far as their emotions go, they could have been factory hands in Pittsburgh or white-collar workers in San José. Perhaps such writers, or others of equal gifts, will some day discover the heart of the cowboy. Gene Rhodes and

Will James saw the heroic stuff in him well enough, but they could not handle it. The cowboy, like the railroad man, is a hero who has not found his Homer.

When we turn to South American prose fiction about the gaucho, we step into another world. It is an adult world, not an adolescent. It is a world in which tragedy is the natural accompaniment of life. Out of his violent origins, continual civil war and pervasive injustice, the gaucho trails with him an aura of melancholy and frustration that contrasts as abruptly as possible with our naïve northern notion that all will come out right in the end. The gaucho has many enemies, and no defense save his own *facón*. The police were against him. The local judges were party tools, and unless he stood well with the proper faction the *gaucho* could expect no justice. If a petty rebellion was current, and it usually was, he found himself without choice but to fight on one side or the other, according to who was his protector. If made prisoner, if arrested on a false charge, he was forced into the army for the dreaded frontier service. He could not escape without being branded a deserter, and if he deserted he necessarily become a bandit. The gaucho did not object to fighting, to be sure, but he preferred to do it in his own causes. The sanguinary civil wars of the Plate region were largely fought by gauchos, and captained by *gaucho caudillos.* With such an origin and such training, it is not surprising that the cowboy of Hispanic fiction lives in sorrow and ends in violence.

Of the cattle-raising countries south of our border, only two have produced fiction that actually depicts the lariat-thrower in his reality. Mexico has some bandit novels, and Venezuela, with the celebrated *Doña Barbara,* gives the reader a glimpse of *llanero* life, but in none of these is the cowpuncher the center of action. In Uruguay and the Argentine, on the contrary (two nations that are one in geography and origin, and are separated only by a freak of chance), gaucho literature is extensive, vital, and stirring. There are epic poems, chief among them the famous *Martín Fierro;* there are dramas, songs, histories, descriptions of customs, as well as novels. Gaucho character and habits of thought have penetrated the regions of the Plate to the marrow. In 1926 Manuel Gálvez wrote:

> The *gaucho* and the border chieftains have disappeared, yet they still
> live among us. The pampa penetrates Buenos Aires in a thousand
> ways. It gives its Argentinian touch to poetry and painting, to novel
> and drama. Through the medium of the horse and the cult of the horse

it seeps steadily into all the social layers and colors the slightly yankeeized soul of the great city.

Imagine yourself trying to write such words about New York or Chicago, as Gálvez did of Buenos Aires, and you will measure the difference between the status of the cowboy there and here. As a result, the prose fiction of the Plate is, one may say, planted solidly on the old gaucho tradition. In the United States of North America the cowboy is relegated to the rubbish corners of literature; in Uruguay and Argentina, authors of the first rank are proud to interpret him. Javier de Viana, Carlos Réyles, Ricardo Güiraldes, Benito Lynch—there are no more distinguished names. The fiction of these and other writers covers every phase of that Protean being: soldier, bandit, submerged peon, politician, musician, lover, cowboy. Only the novels that touch his life as horse tamer and cowhand are my present concern. For that reason I must exclude from consideration many novels that seem at first glance to belong there. Thus, Benito Lynch's *Romance de un gaucho* tells the love story not of a cowboy, but of a *patroncito,* the son of a cattle owner. Lynch's *Los caranchos de la Floridá,* too, describes a ranch owner. Viana's *Gaucha* is a naturalistic study of abulia in an environment of degraded ranch life. *Soledad,* by the elder Acevedo Díaz, portrays barbaric passions and instincts among gauchos who could as well be Australian bushmen. Very few are the novels that examine the skills and emotions of the man on horseback who has charge of cattle. Those few are of high rank. Barring the early sensational "police dramas" of Eduardo Gutiérrez, a sort of inferior Dumas, père, even the weakest of South American gaucho novels rates as genuine art. In them fiction stands on a level with factual description, and not, as with us, below it. And there are factual accounts of gaucho life both truthful and well written; some of the best are in English by Cunninghame Graham, Black Bill Craig, and that "Argentinian who preferred to write in English," as the Argentine scholar Tiscornia calls him, W. H. Hudson.

I have on several occasions asked well-qualified Latin Americans to select a title that should represent their fiction at its best; so that, if a man from Mars (or the United States of America) were allowed to read only one novel, he might receive the most favorable impression. It is an unfair question, I know, and no one could expect unanimity in the answers. But a surprising number of experts picked *Don Segundo Sombra,* by Ricardo Güiraldes (1926). This happens to be also the supreme gaucho novel, or one of two. Such a choice could not possibly happen in this country. No cowboy romance would fall within the first hundred. And this fact shows as well as anything the contrast between the obscure footing of the cowboy in our economy and the prominence of the gaucho along the river Plate.

Auturo Torres-Rioseco prefaced his critique of *Don Segundo Sombra* with these reflections upon various types of novels and their admirers:

> It is likely that there are as many classes of novels as there are readers. Those who are fond of Dumas père will not enjoy the psychological novel in the order of *Le rouge et le noir;* he whose favorite reading is *Les Miserables* will not have the patience to follow the complicated analyses of Proust....

Bernardo De Voto expressed the same idea and carried it a little farther when he wrote, in his early-Mencken manner:

> There is a discouragingly large amount of literature which breaks in a sharp curve just as the reader swings at it. It will not behave, it will not order itself according to his requirements.

He was trying to say that some books do not conform to accepted rules of the art of writing, and yet they are good. I should hardly cite these two opinions, not original surely, except for one reason: both these distinguished critics were writing about cowboy novels. DeVoto was making a straight-out apology for Gene Rhodes, whom he was prefacing, and Torres was making a veiled apology for *Don Segundo Sombra.* For when a critic begins his discussion of a work by saying that there are all sorts of novels and that what fits one man's taste may not fit another's, that is a manner of intercession for his author. It is as much as to say: "This novel is a bit queer, I know; it's not quite up to standard in some ways, but still it has its points, as I hope to show you." That is what both DeVoto and Torres proceed to do. The faults of *Don Segundo Sombra* are in no way comparable to those of Gene Rhodes, but they are faults.

Who is Don Segundo of the shadowy name? He is a middle-aged wandering cowboy and horse tamer. In his diversified career he has laid up no wealth save that of experience, tact, and knowledge of the pampa world. He never makes a mistake; he always meets an emergency in the right way. He is a figure of mystery. He drifts into the story by accident, and at the end drifts out again. Nothing is known of his family or antecedents. By mere chance he takes up with a lad of fourteen who lives the gaucho life. Segundo's relation to him is sometimes like that of Baloo to Mowgli—mentor and friend. The youth turns out to be a rich heir, Segundo stays with him three years to give him the proper start; then, his task completed, he says farewell and rides away over the hills. The only conflict in this story is between the lad's passion for a free life and the shackle of his sudden wealth.

It is a beautifully written book. The style of Güiraldes is sober, economical, full of overtones and undertones. The date of action is purposely left indefinite. The hero, drawn from a friend of the author, is a literary synthesis of the finest qualities of a gaucho—of a middle-aged gaucho, to be sure. He is a cowhand as Willa Cather might have seen him, had she chosen to try. He is ,without fault. Critics have compared him to Don Quixote and the picaro Lazarillo de Tormes; not rightly, to my mind, for they are human, and Don Segundo is an object of worship.

So I would not consider Güiraldes' classic narrative the great gaucho novel of all time. It is too limited and too much in the nature of an essay. In 1931, five years after it appeared, the following words were penned by Carlos Reyles, the celebrated Uruguayan novelist:

> The master novel is not yet written, that shall convey to the reader a living, definitive sensation of the wild land, of the primitive cattle ranch, of the *gaucho* and his tragic adventures. So far, only certain aspects, certain anecdotes, have been brought out; but the great trinity remains intact, awaiting the iron hand that shall grasp it, compress it, and in a supreme effort squeeze out its succulent juices. How grateful we should be if we possessed a native Don Quijote, a Hamlet or a Cid! Our essence has not yet found its complete expression.

In the following year, 1932, Reyles himself made his contribution to the gaucho novel, *El gaucho Florido*. I do not know whether he believed that it fulfilled the need he had just expressed; I suspect that he did. His novel does embrace all of his three phases of gaucho life, the *campo bagual* or untamed land, the *estancia cimarrona* or ranch in its pristine state, and the tragic career of the gaucho. The subtitle of *El gaucho Florido* is precisely "The Novel of the Primitive Ranch and the Unspoiled *Gaucho.*"

If Reyles failed in his ambitious enterprise it is not because he did not understand the problem, or because he lacked technical knowledge. His novel pictures more sides of a gaucho's life and character than *Don Segundo Sombra,* more than any other novel in Spanish.

We have the usual horse race, the usual feats of horse-taming and bull-wrangling, but also a developed account of ranch life, with its wise owner (a marvelous person more skilled than his men at throwing the bolas and the lasso), its *curandera* or witch-woman, a favorite type, and a throng of accurate minor characters. Florido himself, the expert cowhand, the handsome Don Juan, borders a little on the North America hero, and the villain Manduca is as black as Owen Wister's. The women of the book are drawn with sympathy and skill. The gaucho was neither sexless nor saintly. The innocent schoolmarm had no place in his history; if she existed she stayed with her own kind. The gaucho had a *china* or two to keep him company, and he might marry one or he might not. He was not separated from women for months at a time, like our cowherders, for the simple reason that his plains were smaller and he never remained long far from a ranch. Women occupy a normal position in the gaucho novel. The two loved by Florido are refreshingly natural. They and their friends create an atmosphere of reality more convincing than the man's world of Don Segundo. The special gift of Reyles, his power to transmit the force of passion with unfiltered directness, shines and glows in these pages.

Reyles had within his grasp a truly great novel, but it slipped from him. Deficiencies of temperament entailed the strange lapses of taste that one associates with Iberian literature more than with Hispano-American. Violent scenes of unjustified jealousy and abrupt and unmotivated ending mar the whole, and many details show the same lack of balance. The novels of Reyles have a way of starting out on sure and prancing feet, only to stagger wearily into the finish.

These two are beyond doubt the best of the straight cowpuncher novels of Latin America. Many more are excellent. Zavala Muniz turned a reminiscent and realistic eye upon the lives of his own ancestors in three *Chronicles*, which alternate between savage battles and pungent countryside. The younger Acevedo Díaz, renouncing the sanguinary manner of his father, composes conscientious evocations of gaucho plus Indian—*Ramon Hazaña, Cancha Larga*—with a certain ingenious and niggling psychological verity. Other less ambitious tales are equally successful. The weakest of them is superior to the best of our "westerns."

Our inferiority may be due to a number of reasons. I am unwilling to admit that North America has no novelists equal to those of Argentina and Uruguay. The good ones simply do not consider the cowboy worthy game. I think he is worthy game, and I can adduce two arguments for his being better game than the gaucho for a novelist. First, the tough climate with which he had to contend. The gaucho lived in a sort of earthly paradise, if paradise consists in benign natural surroundings. His hardships resulted from human weakness and hazardous occupation, not from environment. To cite an Argentine author:

> The pampa has a fertile soil, plenty of water, a climate where winter brings nothing lower than 40°, and summer nothing higher than 85°; where snow is unknown, and storms, winds and rains, with rare exceptions, are never violent. This environment is not of a sort to produce such a toughened character as Don Segundo Sombra.

But the North American cowboy fought against Texas northers and the snows of the Rockies. Nature was his bitter enemy. And the magnitude of his undertaking was vastly greater. The gaucho drove his herds from estancia to estancia, following the petty needs of the ranchers. It is only five hundred miles from Buenos Aires to the Andes. Nothing in his efforts was comparable to the tremendous drives from Texas north over the Chisholm trail or the Goodnight-Loving trail. To herd three thousand cattle a distance of twelve hundred miles in five months and deliver them safely was an epic feat. The foreman faced hostile Indians, rustlers, flooded rivers, stampedes, and storms. He counted the beasts at regular intervals. He kept his men contented and in health. He was a manager and a fighter, a captain as well as an expert roper. He deserved better of the writing fraternity than a few thousand two-gun pulps.

In cowboy fiction, the contrast between North America and South America is as sharp as possible. On the one side you find snappy narrative and juvenile psychology; on the other, the studied writing of masters of the novel who have learned their art in the European tradition. Perhaps the carry-over of that same tradition explains the still more marked contrast in the underlying spirit. In these United States, whether one reads a tawdry thriller or an authentic account of the cowpuncher's daily feats, one receives a sense of abounding strength, of optimism for the future. This cowboy never doubts that he is in a splendid profession. He can leave it if he likes, but he doesn't like. He may be a hired hand, but he is the master of his soul. He is not a victim, either of fate or circumstance. He embodies a healthy pioneer energy — the same force that carried the emigrants

to California. He does not spend his hours in voluble self-pity, like
Martin Fierro, bewailing his misfortunes (certainly great), or, like
the lad in *Don Segundo Sombra,* pondering the mysterious ways of
fate. Gaucho novels terminate on a note of stark tragedy, excepting only *Don Segundo Sombra,* which moves on a calm and even
level throughout, and Benito Lynch's absurd parody of melodrama,
Raquela. In *El gaucho Florido,* the heroine is shot on her bridal
night, for no particular motive, by an unknown party, who catches
her and the plot quite unprepared, and the hero takes to a life of banditry. In Viana's *Gaucha,* the villain, a very wicked "western" bad
man, murders the hero and with his gang rapes the heroine and
leaves her to die, naked, bound to a tree. In Lynch's *Romance of a
gaucho,* the hero commits suicide on the pampa, and his body is
devoured by buzzards. In the same author's *Los caranchos,* father
and son kill each other. In Zavala Muniz's *Crónica de una reja,*
the hero, a harmless shopkeeper with no enemies, is unexpectedly
shot in a skirmish by a man he hardly knew. If the "western" runs to
an infallible wedding in the last chapter, the gaucho novel goes as
far in the other direction. As a matter of faithfulness to life, marriage is at least as real, and more frequent than suicide, rape, and
murder.

No one can object to tragedy, with which we must all soon or late
make friends, but it is a source of wonder to me that in new countries,
undeveloped, peopled by vigorous explorers, their descendants are
always victims of something. Tragedy pursues them; they have no
confidence in the future. Even the confidence of Don Segundo, who
knows no fear, is that of a stoic, not of an adventurer. Is this an element of the unhappy inheritance of Spain, a nation that exhausted
its immense energy and aspiration in futile warfare? Is it due to the
turbulence of the early colonial years or to a mixture of races that
never were quite fused?

In seeking an explanation, we must not forget that the gaucho was
a political being, and not merely a social being. Since his sphere
of action was more ample than that of our cowboy, he had to pay the
inherent penalty. Politics rules his existence. The dictator Rosas
was the most powerful of the gaucho chieftains, and when he fell in
1852, he dragged his supporters down with him. The new policy of
education necessarily entailed the persecution of the gaucho, and his
ultimate disappearance. Thrown on the defensive, he and everything
associated with him received the brand of suffering.

These, it appears, are the elements that combine to produce the melancholy tone, now severe, now plaintive, of the gaucho novel. The fact is that the United States cowboy was hardly even a citizen of our social order. Did he vote? Did he care who governed the states that he drove cattle through? Certainly he never joined a union. He was in no way caught in political cogs. The police never touched him unless he shot up a town. The army was outside his ken. Why should he worry? His pioneer spirit could function freely.

In the last analysis, the spiritual difference between the gaucho and the cowboy reflects the society from which they came. The tradition of Spain springs out of lengthy political coils that tangle feet and cramp minds. They lassoed the wild roamer of the llanos. But in the free atmosphere of this young democracy, the cowboy cracked his heels in the air, waved his hat, and let life buck. When it finally threw him, he landed on his feet, with no regrets, qualms, or philosophies.

English Westerns

by James K. Folsom

One of the more remarkable—some might say disappointing—developments of nineteenth century literary history was the startling, and by and large unexpected, influence of James Fenimore Cooper on European literature. A Spanish critic who wrote in 1853 that *El último de los Mohicanos* was "a masterpiece which has become a classic in every language of Europe" probably stated no more than the simple truth. In Germany the immediate and lasting popularity of the *Lederstrumpferzählungen* attests to Cooper's overwhelming importance in that country, as does the presence of numerous imitators, of whom only Karl May is at all widely remembered today. And in France Cooper's work was incorporated at once as a welcome graft to an already venerable primitivistic tradition.[1] Even today the anomaly of French and German Western films attests at once to Cooper's continuing popularity and, more significantly, to a perennial European fascination with the American West.

In England fascination with the American West was also great, though it took a different form from that which developed on the Continent. In Great Britain there was little direct imitation of Cooper, though his works were widely read; but without much question his influence is to be traced to the immense number of later English books about the American frontier.

Two significant differences are immediately apparent between English and Continental treatments of the American West. First of all, on the Continent the American West ossified with the frontier

---

"English Westerns" by James K. Folsom. From *Western American Literature*, 2 (Spring 1967), 3-13. Reprinted by permission of *Western American Literature*.

[1]See Clarence Gohdes, "The Reception of Some Nineteenth-Century American Authors in Europe," in *The American Writer and the European Tradition*, ed. Margaret Denny and W. H. Gilman (Minneapolis, 1950), especially pp. 112-113; and, more generally, Hoxie Neale Fairchild, *The Noble Savage, A Study in Romantic Naturalism* (New York, 1928).

of the early Leatherstocking Tales. Few European writers in the Western tradition follow the American West across the Mississippi, and as a result they ignore what have become the staples of later American Western writing: cowboys, wagon trains, cavalry patrols, and indeed the whole physical and moral geography of the Great Plains are almost totally missing from Continental western fiction. English Westerns, in contrast, are almost ostentatiously up-to-date; they chronicle the events of the California gold rush, of cowboy life on the Great Plains and of trapper life in the Rockies, and even, on occasion, of very particular historical events such as the Mormon migration to the Great Salt Lake.[2] Indeed, three of the most prolific writers of English Westerns knew America more than casually at first hand, and consciously wrote to give the impression that they were conveying incontrovertible, eyewitness information about the Western frontier.[3] The second difference is that English Westerns were confessedly written as juvenile fiction, in contrast to Continental western fiction which, however much it may have been read by juveniles, was like Cooper's fiction ostensibly written for adults. This juvenile bias of English Westerns is probably their most obvious single distinguishing characteristic, and it serves to separate them on the one hand from the usual Continental and on the other from the ordinary American method of writing Westerns. Since it may serve as well to isolate English attitudes toward the American West and indirectly to throw into bolder relief some of our own habitual attitudes toward our Western experience, a more careful analysis of these heretofore ignored works of juvenile fiction may prove of value both to the historian of taste and, hopefully, to the student of more serious literature.

The juvenile bias of English Westerns is perhaps most easily

[2]The plot of Captain Mayne Reid's *The Wild Huntress* (London, 1861), for instance, depends upon the allegation—often made at the time because of the Mormon custom of polygamy—that the Latter-day Saints were engaged more or less openly in the White Slave trade.

[3]R. M. Ballantyne (1852-1894) was a clerk for the Hudson's Bay Company in Canada from the age of sixteen until twenty-two, later recording his Canadian experiences in *Hudson Bay, or, Everyday Life in the Wilds of North America* (London, 1876); G. A. Henty (1832-1902) visited the California gold fields, where the scenes of many of his American stories are laid; and Captain Mayne Reid (1818-1883), who wrote largely about the Southwest, came to America in 1840, obtained a United States Army commission as captain in 1845, and distinguished himself in the Mexican War, in which struggle he was wounded during the assault on Chapultepec.

seen in their omnipresent moralizing. It is probably fair to say that all juvenile fiction—or at least an overwhelming majority of it—is written with some kind of overtly conceived moral purpose. On the simplest level, at least in English Westerns, this moralizing often represents nothing more than training in the basic tenets of Christian morality. R. M. Ballantyne, a clear example, writes from a Scotch Presbyterian background mostly in disparagement of smoking and drinking; and some of his novels, notably *The Red Man's Revenge* (1886), also serve as fairly simple moral homilies showing the necessity for the conversion of the Indians to Christianity. The commonplace story of the conversion of the Indians indicates the next level of didacticism in English Westerns, the notion of the "sugar pill"—that the real purpose of these stories is to impart miscellaneous information of various kinds, using the vehicle of an adventure tale to hold the reader's interest. Ernest R. Suffling, for instance, who in his preface to *The Fur Traders of the West* promises a story "full of adventures of a thrilling nature," concludes his tale by asking his "young readers one favour, and that is, to take an atlas and prosecute an imaginary voyage of their own, by following and noting every place" mentioned in the book. "Having done this," he assures them, "they will have taken a step to advance their knowledge."[4]

Insofar as English Westerns are indeed a kind of education in esoterica one can have nothing but praise for the accuracy of the various authors' observations. Only rarely do the novelists convey factually inaccurate material, and then usually because of the inadequacy of their sources. G. A. Henty is once trapped into a somewhat uneasy report of the dangers of meeting a "hydrophobia cat," a "pretty little beast marked black and white, and about the size of a big weasel." When it bites you, Henty's juvenile hero is told, you face "sartin death; thar ain't no cure for it; the best plan is to put your Colt to your head and finish it at once." The animal is of course a skunk, for which the early explorers of the Great Plains had an exaggerated respect; but Henty could not bring himself to tell his young British readers the apparent whopper—which he probably did not believe himself—that the only animal which his intrepid frontiersmen were "regular feered of" was not the grizzly bear, or the cougar, or even the prairie wolf, but only the harmless,

---

[4]*The Fur Traders of the West, or, Adventures among the Redskins* (London, 1896), pp. viii, 320.

albeit occasionally somewhat personally offensive, skunk of their acquaintance.[5]

Nor is the author solely to blame for the various tall tales which now and again intrude in his stories as sober fact. R. M. Ballantyne, who during his residence in Canada never actually settled farther West than Winnipeg, often used accounts of trappers and other employees of the Hudson's Bay Company as sources for his stories of life on the Great Plains and in the Rocky Mountains. The temptation of pulling the leg of the sober young Englishman who had asked for a story of life on the plains apparently proved, on occasion, too strong to resist. At least once Ballantyne tells as sober fact a story which must have provided considerable quiet amusement to the other listeners. He recounts at great length the Indian method of hunting buffalo by forcing a herd to mill together in a circle while the pursuers gallop around the outside spearing or shooting their prey with arrows. So far so good; the story is eminently true and, more to the point, easily verifiable. The alleged conclusion of the hunt, however, trades the world of fact for that of fantasy. "Sometimes," Ballantyne soberly reports, "a horse got jammed in the centre of the swaying mass, and could neither advance nor retreat. Then the savage rider leaped upon the buffaloes' backs, and springing from one to another, like an acrobat, gained the outer edge of the circle, not failing, however, in his strange flight to pierce with his lance several of the fattest of his stepping stones as he sped along."[6]

On the other hand, the omnipresent instructional purpose of these various Western stories does weaken them esthetically. Not only does it tend to make the novels anecdotal and to give an occasional hard wrench to an already creaky plot in order to allow the author the opportunity of including some factual material which he could not otherwise slip in, but it makes the tales slow-moving, always a grave danger in stories of adventure. Typically the ostensible plots of these stories will continue uninteruupted for a chapter or two when a suitable opportunity will present itself to the author for a lengthy digression explaining how to build a canoe, or to hunt buffalo, or to lure an antelope within rifle range. The comparatively few stories—notably by G. A. Henty—which are not written in this way tend to attain the same educational goal

[5]*Captain Bayley's Heir: A Tale of the Gold Fields of California* (London, 1889), pp. 170-171.

[6]*The Dog Crusoe. A Tale of the Western Prairies* (London, 1861), pp. 94-95.

through questions (by the juvenile hero) and answers (by the frontiersman being questioned). The question to this answer, for instance, is not difficult to conjecture. " 'Oh, these Colts carry a long way,' the cow-boy said carelessly. 'They will carry four hundred yards, though you can't depend upon their shooting a man over a hundred'." Henty, who is the master of this kind of exposition by question and answer is usually more successful, however, even given the artificiality of the technique. The cautionary lesson of *caveat emptor* could scarcely be more masterfully instilled than in this scene from *Redskin and Cow-boy* where his juvenile hero Hugh goes to buy a horse. The implied question, of course, is how one should keep his wits about him when purchasing a horse from strangers.

> "That is something like a horse," the man said. "Five years old, strong, and up to anything, clean-limbed, full of courage, and fast."
>
> "He has got a temper," Hugh said as the horse laid back his ears and made a sudden and vicious snap at the man's hand.
>
> "He is a bit playful," the man said.[7]

The most important didactic dimension of English Westerns, however, is without question to be found in their attempt to instill in their youthful readers a set of attitudes. It must not be forgotten that these stories are conceived as fiction to be read by youthful empire-builders, and are very consciously aimed at training future bearers of the white man's burden in the station to which Providence will call them. They bear comparison with other juvenile fiction such as Kipling's *Jungle Book* and Conan Doyle's *The White Company*, and indeed with more adult adventure fiction like Rider Haggard's *She* and Charles Kingsley's *Westward Ho!*

At times this has its ludicrous side, as when, for example, a certain Mr. Gunson is lecturing the young heroes of *To the West* on the amenities of life in the wilderness. "Nothing like a good tea meal out in the wilds," he says heartily, "to put life into one. Why I've known days when we've been ready to break down, or give up, or go back; then we've formed camp, got a bit of fire on the way, boiled the kettle with a pinch of tea in it,...and been fit to do anything after."[8] Or when Kate, the young heroine of "A Sioux Raid," acknowledges the efforts of the Black Fox and the Owl, two good Indians who have just spirited her way from captivity among

---

[7]*Redskin and Cow-boy, A Tale of the Western Plains* (London, n. d.), pp. 143, 144.
[8]G. Manville Fenn, *To the West* (London, 1891), pp. 199-200.

the Sioux. "How good of you and the Owl," she graciously says to the Black Fox, "to come all this way to rescue me!"[9] However comical this attitude may appear on the occasions when it deteriorates into stiff-upper-lipness, though, it is meant to be taken seriously. The story of *The Fur Traders of the West,* its author says, "shows that courage and energy are traits to be admired," and "also goes far to prove that truth, sincerity, and magnanimity also form integral parts in the composition of the character of the boys of Great Britain." Nor are these boys just humdrum young men. The hero of *In the Heart of the Rockies,* whose family, significantly, had all been seafarers, had, Henty tells us, "in his blood a large share of the restless spirit of enterprise that has been the main factor in making the Anglo-Saxons the dominant race of the world.[10]

Another significant difference which sets the English Western apart from both American and Continental counterparts may also be traced to its juvenile aspects. This lies in the very different way in which conflict is handled in English Westerns. Even a casual delver into English Westerns will notice immediately the far greater importance which is placed on natural peril than in other Western literature. The physical dangers of the Wstern environment—prairie fires, stampeding buffaloes, losing one's way, and even on occasion attack by wolf packs or rabid skunks—are emphasized to what seems to an American reader an excessive degree. Concomitantly, the perils represented by evil human beings become, in English Westerns, relatively muted and, equally important, relatively generalized.

This is not to say that human evil is either unknown or unrecognized in children's fiction, but rather to point out a peculiarity in its presentation. Perhaps this can be made clearer by recalling for a moment William Golding's *Lord of the Flies,* which is among other things a serious parody of R. M. Ballantyne's most famous children's story, *The Coral Island.* At the end of *Lord of the Flies* the English officer who has come to pick up the castaways mentions *The Coral Island* and gives as well a kind of capsule statement of the didactic purpose of it and other such juvenile fiction "I should have thought," he says, "that a pack of British boys...

---

[9]G. A. Henty, "A Sioux Raid. A North-American Story," in *Fifty-two Stories of the Brave and True for Boys,* ed. Alfred H. Miles (London, n. d.), p. 362.

[10]*The Fur Traders of the West,* p. viii; G. A. Henty, *In the Heart of the Rockies, A Story of Adventure in Colorado* (London, 1895), p. 16.

would have been able to put up a better show." Ralph, the juvenile hero of Golding's novel, has no reply. He can only weep, Golding tells us, "for the end of innocence, and the darkness of man's heart."[11]

The point is very simply that, though a great amount of children's fiction may well be about the end of innocence, relatively little concerns itself with "the darkness of man's heart." In other words, evil in juvenile books is generally done by easily recognizable villains—pirates (as in *Treasure Island* and *The Coral Island*) or, in English western fiction, Indians. In English Westerns the villainous Indian is almost everywhere. The plots of a sizable number of these books concern themselves simply with the successful conquest of Indian peril; and even in the pages of those books which are only peripherally concerned with Indian trouble lurks many a dastardly red man ready to loose an occasional random arrow at his juvenile opponents. One stock figure of the American Western, however, is almost totally unknown; the apparently good man whose respectability is nothing but a cover for his evil machinations is notable in English Westerns only by his absence. The counterpart of many an American Western which, like Max Brand's *Destry Rides Again*, tells of the hero's eventual discovery that the villain he seeks is a trusted friend is simply not to be found in English Westerns; a much more usual plot in these stories is an almost exact converse, telling of a young man who has been misunderstood but finally manages to clear himself of the disgrace into which he has been unjustly thrust.[12]

This in turn emphasizes another significant difference between American and English Westerns. English Westerns are primarily concerned with educating young men who presumably will eventually take places of leadership in society; consequently, the stories they tell are in general stories more or less in praise of that society. The American Western, contrariwise, tends to be set up in terms of at least a fictional choice between two sets of values—those of the frontier on the one hand, and of civilized society on the other. The habitual American method of presenting Western material, which follows a tradition begun by Cooper, is by means of two parties with diametrically opposed sets of values. The one party, the "party of the past," stands for conservation of whatever order is being threatened by the other party, the "party of the future."

[11] (New York, 1959), p. 248.
[12] For clear examples see G. Manville Fenn, *To the West,* and G. A. Henty, *Redskin and Cow-boy.*

Except in a general way the values represented by these two parties are not constant, nor does any particular type of Western character —the cowboy or trapper or miner—necessarily always belong to one party. The only constant feature is the polarity itself, in which one party, representative of the past (be they trappers, or cattlemen, or Indians) resist the encroachments of the other (be they settlers, or nesters, or cowboys), representative of the future. Moreover, the fictional stance of the American Western has traditionally been nostalgic and retrospective, identifying for dramatic purposes at least with the old order of the party of the past. T. B. Thorpe's Mike Fink, "the last of the riverboatmen," sets the tone as early as 1842 for later literary frontiersmen.

> "I knew these parts afore a squatter's axe had blazed a tree; 'twasn't then pulling a — sweep to get a living, but pulling the trigger done the business. Those were times, to see; a man might call himself lucky. What's the use of improvements? When did cutting down trees make deer more plenty? Who ever cotched a bar by building a log cabin, or twenty on 'em. Who ever found wild buffalo, or a brave Indian in a city? Where's the fun, the frolicking, the fighting? Gone! Gone![13]

The English Western, in contrast, is not at all suspicious of progress, nor does it develop its story by means of this common American polarity between the party of the past and that of the future. Typically the English Western details the fortunes of a young man who for some reason or other goes West in order to get the Wanderlust out of his system and to make his fortune. The resolution of an English Western affirms the values of society without qualification; nor are there to be found in English Westerns characters like Leatherstocking who are both sympathetic and admirable yet who at the same time profess values which are antithetical to social ones.

A brief glance at the plots of a few of these English Westerns will serve to make the point clearer. R. M. Ballantyne's *Over the Rocky Mountains* (one of a number of Ballantyne's stories, parenthetically, which recounts the fortunes of a juvenile hero significantly named "Wandering Will") tells the adventures of a young man who inherits a property in the Rocky Mountains which he sets off to visit. After numerous adventures he arrives at the property

---

[13]The Disgraced Scalp-Lock, or Incidents on the Western Waters," in *Half Horse Half Alligator: the Growth of the Mike Fink Legend*, ed. Walter Blair and Franklin J. Meine (Chicago, 1956), p. 71.

and, with a number of friends, proceeds to work it for gold. He ultimately returns to England where he marries and settles down, leaving his friends behind in California to mine his gold claim, which has turned out to be immensely profitable. The end of this tale, which concludes the "Wandering Will" series, finds the hero once again ensconced in the bosom of society; his wanderings have enabled him to take on the appurtenances of civilized life by giving him a sufficient fortune to allow his return to England where he can live as a gentleman.

G. A. Henty's "The Golden Cañon" tells a very similar story of two young Englishmen who join a party which sets out from San Diego to pack into the Arizona back country in search of a lost gold mine. Though they have only an enigmatic map to guide them they eventually find the mine and, after a running battle with Indians, manage to carry away the gold which has already been mined by an earlier party. Each boy brings home as his share of the booty a hundred pounds of gold, worth about £5000 sterling. With it they buy shares in a maritime company and eventually become both sea captains and owners of their own ships. "Neither," Henty tells us, "had any inclination ever to embark again upon the operation of gold-mining."[14]

Henty's *Captain Bayley's Heir*, one of the best of these English Westerns, tells a closely allied story. In this book one Frank Norris is wrongfully accused of stealing and flees England in order to make his way in the world. After numerous adventures in America he succeeds in amassing an immense fortune, returns to England where he marries his wealthy childhood sweetheart, inherits the property of his uncle, Captain Bayley, "an old and very wealthy retired officer of the East India Company's Service,"[15] and eventually successfully stands for Parliament.

As should be evident by now, the West in the English Western stands not for some kind of complex of values opposed to society but rather for a field of opportunity from which the hero can, if he is sufficiently determined, wrest a good living which he may put to use upon his eventual return to society. The West may be a fine place to visit, but no self-respecting Englishman would want to live there. One of E. R. Suffling's heroes resigns himself to exile in Oregon by reflecting that it will only be "temporary," and moreover that "if all [goes] well we should return in two or three years

[14]"The Golden Cañon," in *Peril and Prowess* (London, 1899), p. 133.
[15]*Captain Bayley's Heir*, p. 25.

with ample means to live once more in dear old England," and an older and presumably wiser man tells one of Henty's youthful characters that a "fancy for hunting and shooting" is "well enough for a time,...but it leads to nothing."[16]

The English Western's profoundly affirmative attitude toward society and social values in contrast to the American Western's endemic distrust explains another great difference between the two. The American Western has a strong ascetic streak. The hero in American Westerns is quite often someone who has made a clear choice to renounce the devil and all his works, uniformly presented under the guise of social evil; and indeed the West of the American Western is quite often a symbol of renunciation, to be enjoyed only by those who have resolutely turned their backs on the temptations of society. The hero of an English Western, in contrast, is usually a person in a position to enjoy the best of both worlds, who can use the opportunities of one as a means to make his way in the other.

Nowhere is this more evident than in the English Westerns about the search for gold. It is a startling fact, first off, that most English Westerns concern themselves with this theme, in striking contrast to American Westerns, in which the theme is a relatively minor one. In English Westerns as well almost everyone strikes it rich. The gold fields in these stories represent a fantastic material opportunity which is offered to just about everyone, of which he can take advantage if he has sufficient intelligence to see where his best interests lie and enough of a Christian upbringing to avoid at least the grosser temptations of the flesh. The American Western about mining, in contrast, is almost uniformly a study in one of two related ironies. The first is the story of the prospector who spends his life in a futile search for a fabulously rich strike which he never finds. The second is the story of the man who "strikes it rich," only to find that all his wealth cannot buy him the happiness he seeks. Both these ironies are at least implicitly renunciatory, making the point that the single-minded pursuit of wealth is self-defeating.[17] One can imagine Natty Bumppo's comment on the heroes of Henty's *In the Heart of the Rockies* who succeed in making 35,000 apiece out of their claim by the typically English expedient

---

[16] *The Fur Traders of the West*, p. 29; "On an Indian Trail," in *Brains and Bravery* (London, 1903), p. 54.

[17] For a more detailed analysis of these plots in the American Western, see my *The American Western Novel* (New Haven, 1966), pp. 75-80.

of capitalizing their venture and forming a joint-stock corporation in order to buy the expensive machinery necessary for profitable large-scale mining.

This last example may also serve to emphasize a very real difference between the English Western and another possible American analogue with which it superficially seems to have much in common, the didactic American juvenile story of self-improvement in the Horatio Alger tradition. Again, however, a significant difference emerges. The Horatio Alger tradition, with all its ostentatious moralizing about the value of clean living and Christian morality, generally concerns itself with the fortunes of a young man who is incredibly lucky. Juvenile stories in the Horatio Alger tradition typically tell of someone who capitalizes on an unexpected stroke of good fortune. The Horatio Alger hero rarely forms a joint-stock corporation in order to make a fortune on his own; more usually his worth is recognized because of some signal service he does for someone who is wealthy and of high social position and is able to reward the moral worth he perceives beneath the young man's unpromising exterior.

Once again we are brought back to the essential difference between the English and the American Western, probably emblematic of a real difference in cultural attitudes. The American in his heart is profoundly suspicious of society, so much so in fact that his own stories for the education of the young make the veiled point that society's rewards cannot be depended upon, and that material success is best symbolized by chance happenings. Fortune favors not the bold but the lucky, and a moral man will regard its rewards not only with distrust but contempt. The American Western, a close spiritual descendant of *Walden*, is about how to get away; the English, in contrast, is about how to get ahead. And this is probably why the English Western seems so profoundly unsatisfying to an American, who asks from Western themes something more than an instruction manual in the art of success. With all their concern for the facts of Western life English Westerns care nothing about the West; they, rather than their often accused American counterparts, are pure escape.

PART FOUR

Interpretations

The American Literary West and Its Interpreters: The Rise of a New Historiography

by Richard W. Etulain

Two significant books published in 1950 illustrate the major trends in the historiography of the American literary West. Franklin Walker's *A Literary History of Southern California* exemplifies the most popular approach to western literature before 1950, and Henry Nash Smith's *Virgin Land: The American West as Symbol and Myth* became the major paradigm for studies of western writing undertaken after 1950. Taken together these two books and the methods of research they utilize provide important keys to understanding interpretations of the literary West during the present century.[1]

"The American Literary West and Its Interpreters: The Rise of a New Historiography" by Richard W. Etulain. From *Pacific Historical Review, Vol.* 45, No. 4, 311-47, © 1976 by the Pacific Coast Branch, American Historical Association. Reprinted by permission of the Branch and the author.

Research for this essay was made possible by grants from the Idaho State University Faculty Research Committee and the American Philosophical Society.

[1]The intent of this essay is to give a brief glimpse of the historical development of commentary on the American literary West. Emphasis is placed on book-length studies that illustrate major trends of interpretation and that have exerted the most influence on scholars. Discussions are primarily descriptive in nature, although some evaluative comments are included. Most footnotes list further examples of the trends discussed in the text. To give sharper focus to a subject that threatens to overflow its frontiers, discussion is limited to works published in the United States in the present century and to research dealing with the trans-Mississippi West, although also included is commentary on some books that focus on eastern frontiers and that have influenced scholars of western literature. I have not dealt with materials that treat western humor, folklore, or western films as literature.

For additional bibliographical listings, see Richard W. Etulain, *Western American Literature: A Bibliography of Interpretive Books and Articles* (Vermillion, S.D., 1972); and Etulain, "Western American Literature: A Selective Annotated Bibliography," *Interpretive Approaches to Western American Literature* (Pocatello, Idaho, 1972), 67-78. Also, consult the annual listings in the winter issues of *Western American Literature*.

In the first two decades of the twentieth century, analysis of western American literature lagged behind the study of western history. Though Frederick Jackson Turner announced his frontier hypothesis in 1893 and published several important essays before 1920, American literary historians paid little attention to the literary West before the late 1920s. This pattern continued throughout the first half of the present century: historians were several steps ahead of literary scholars in the study of the American West.

The earliest studies by literary scholars could hardly have been less promising. In 1900, Barrett Wendell, a professor of English literature at Harvard University, published his subsequently much-cited book, *A Literary History of America* (New York, 1900), in which he sought to discover what America had "so far contributed to the literature of our ancestral language" (p. 10). The contents of the thick volume and the author's point of view illustrate his strong ties to New England. Indeed, a literary historian, Fred Lewis Pattee, has suggested that Wendell's volume should have been entitled *A Literary History of Harvard University, with Incidental Glimpses of the Minor Writers of America.*[2] Wendell dismissed Herman Melville as a writer who "began a career of literary promise, which never came to fruition" (p. 229), and he criticized Walt Whitman for his "decadent eccentricity" (p. 477).

Because Wendell chose to discuss only deceased writers, his brief chapter entitled "The West" omitted mention of Bret Harte, Joaquin Miller, Mark Twain, Hamlin Garland, and Frank Norris. The attitude of the Harvard professor toward the West was an ambivalent one that mixed much condescension with a small amount of mild praise. "Amid the relaxed inexperience of Western life," he wrote, "the lower sort of Americans had tended to revert towards a social state ancestrally extinct centuries before America was discovered" (p. 504). Moreover, observed Wendell, an obnoxious materialistic bent accompanied the atavistic tendency in the "great confused West" (p. 505).

Yet after condemning the region for its social and cultural backwardness and its materialistic spirit, Wendell argued that the West held promise of important literary development. The rich variety of experience in the West — its vitality, its good humor, and its "eager-

---

[2]Pattee, "A Call for a Literary Historian," in *The Reinterpretation of American Literature* (New York, 1928), 5. For an important discussion of the development of American literary interpretations, see Richard Ruland, *The Rediscovery of American Literature: Premises of Critical Taste, 1900-1940* (Cambridge, Mass., 1967).

ness to delight in excellence"—could lead to lively forms of literary expression. The most significant of these literary types were local color stories, popular journalism, and newspaper humor. These genres appealed to the large, "untutored public" in the West. The stories, while factual and accurate, were innocent of "lasting vitality." The newspapers were often "thoroughly vicious" in style, offensive in taste and to "civil morals as well" (p. 507), yet their directness and readability saved them. And the most important western humorists— George Horatio Derby ("John Phoenix"), Charles Farrar Browne ("Artemus Ward"), and David Ross Locke ("Petroleum V. Nasby")— represented the future possibilities of western literature. But Wendell contended that the West had not yet proven itself on the American literary scene; its "varied, swiftly changing life has not yet ripened into an experience which can possibly find lasting expression" (p. 513).

Though Wendell indicated that he would stress America's contributions to English literature, he did not emphasize the western part of those contributions. He obviously knew little about the region and seemed unaware of Turner's then recent emphasis on the significance of the frontier. And though Wendell saw promise in the literature of the region, he did not seem to care much for "the great confused West." If the views of Barrett Wendell were taken as representative of the first interpreters of the American literary West, the future of the genre looked bleak.

Wendell was not alone in his negative appraisal of western literature. Five years after the appearance of his book, he was joined by Alphonso Newcomer,[3] a professor at Stanford University, who argued in his *American Literature* that western writings were the product of unlettered men of the soil and "must be gauged by somewhat altered standards" (p. 272). His short chapter, "Prose and Poetry in the West," included a few pages on Mark Twain and Bret Harte and brief glimpses of Joaquin Miller, E. R. Sill, Eugene Field, and Helen Hunt Jackson. Newcomer was convinced that no book published before or after the work of Harte and Twain " is worth recording to-day" (p. 276), though he felt it was too early to evaluate the work of Mary Hallock Foote, Hamlin Garland, and H. B. Fuller.

Like most literary historians of his time, Newcomer was convinced that the West was too immature to produce first-rate literature. He praised the humor and the characters of Twain and the "strong realism" and "piquant dialect" of Harte, but he implied that the West

[3]*American Literature* (Chicago, 1905). A similar view is apparent in George Edward Woodberry, *America in Literature* (New York, 1903).

lacked sufficient cultural roots to nourish an impressive literature or even a distinctive regional literature. Newcomer was not yet willing to identify the San Francisco school of authors of the 1860s and 70s or such other novelists as Garland, Norris and London as western writers.

Holding a different view was Bliss Perry, the noted editor and literary interpreter. In a book published in 1912 he agreed with Turner that the settling of the West had been a major theme in American history.[4] Many Americans, he observed, were still enthralled with the winning of the West and wanted to "play Indian" (p. 148). Perry implied that the speculative, boastful, and unreflective qualities of western life had shaped the American character. Americans were addicted to adventure, to the excitement of the frontier West.

For Perry, Twain epitomized American humor. His background and experiences in the West were the raw materials for his Americanness. The West had added new ingredients to the European mix, and the writing of Twain illustrated these additions. Perry concurred with Lord Bryce that the West was the most typical part of America and the region most unlike Europe. Westerners had perceived the need for both "individualism and fellowship," and the lessons they had learned ought to be taught to others. Americans must realize that while they were custodians of tradition, they were also embracers of the new. Perry cited Jack London and Frank Norris as examples of westerners who were not tied to the past and who continually sought to front the fresh experiences and ideas of their time.

Though Perry dealt only briefly with the West, he showed more awareness of its impact on American culture than most of his contemporary interpreters. He recognized that there was a "western" literature, and in this foreshadowed the larger understanding of the literary West apparent in the 1920s. He was one of the few students of American civilization who realized as early as 1912 that a full understanding of national culture required comprehension of western culture.

Other commentators devoted more attention to western literature. In his *History of American Literature* (Chicago, 1919), Leonidas W. Payne, a professor of English at the University of Texas, emphasized the democratic spirit of the West and the impact of that spirit on western writing. In words reminiscent of those of Twain, he concluded that the "expression of pure Americanism, of the democratic

[4]*The American Mind* (Boston, 1912).

spirit in its broadest significance, is the characteristic note of our Western literature" (p. 316). Payne pushed his thesis further by suggesting that western writers were literary trailblazers; they had abandoned the well-marked paths of eastern authors and had set out to find new paths of their own. Twain, he believed, was the best example of this innovative tendency in western writing.

Payne, like most of his contemporaries, was not a close reader of the literature that he discussed. His comments were usually biographical or historical in nature. Sometimes he used brief quotes to illustrate a generalization, but there were no probing comments about the form or specific content of Harte's short stories or Twain's sketches and longer works. And had he paid closer attention to the structure and content of Miller's work, he could not have said that Miller was "no imitator of the European bards, but an original poet who was willing to put down in his own way what his eyes saw and his heart felt" (p. 338). These comments miss how much Miller owed to Byron, Browning, and other European writers. And if Payne had been more widely acquainted with western writing of the nineteenth century, especially the significant group of writers that gathered around the *Overland Monthly* in the 1870s and 80s, he would not have wrongly concluded that there were no literary coteries in the West. Though Payne argued that the culture of the West was distinct from that of the rest of America, he did not demonstrate the uniqueness of western literature. He discussed Twain, Harte, and several western poets, but the discussions were primarily plot summaries or biographical sketches, which did not explain why these men were *western* writers, how they reflected the experiences he found common to the West, or how the section had branded its regional qualities into the consciousness of its writers.[5]

The most significant illustration of the paucity of comment about the literary West in the 1900-1920 era is seen in *The Cambridge History of American Literature*, which was published in four thick volumes (1917-1921).[6] Intended as the first multi-volume study of American literature, the Cambridge history was broadly conceived as a "survey of the American people as expressed in their writings rather than a history of *belles-lettres* alone" (p. iii). These volumes, put together by the leading literary scholars of America, were designed to avoid

[5] For an example of the same problem, see Stuart P. Sherman, *Americans* (New York, 1922).

[6] William P. Trent, John Erskine, Stuart P. Sherman, Carl Van Doren, eds. *The Cambridge History of American Literature* (4 vols., New York, 1917-1921).

what the editors viewed as the narrower approach of most literary scholarship.

Several chapters in the Cambridge volumes dealt with frontier and western subjects. The first two books of the set contained a long chapter on James Fenimore Cooper, briefer discussions of the eastern frontier and such writers as James Hall and Timothy Flint, and sections on western dialect and a chapter on the short story, which included treatments of Harte, Garland, and London. The third volume had a full chapter on Twain, a short section on Miller, and a chapter entitled "Travellers and Explorers, 1846-1900," which dealt primarily with the West. The final volume contained an analysis of cowboy songs and an interesting chapter on American Indian literature by the well-known western author, Mary Austin.

In spite of the commendable intentions of the editors, their volumes offered no chapter devoted to the impact of the frontier on American literature. Nor did the editors include a chapter on western regional literature, though they did provide sections on the regional literature of the North and South. Writers like Twain, Harte, and Garland were not treated as western writers, but as recent American authors whose major interests were viewed as nonregional. The inattention to the frontier and to western literature in these prestigious volumes may have been the major reason why several scholars in the 1920s complained of the lack of scholarship on the literary West.

If literary historians before 1920 slighted the literature of the American West, a rising interest in that subject began to emerge after 1925. The new interest was not surprising in view of the intellectual currents sweeping through America during the twenties. Too often interpreters of the era after the First World War overstress the Lost Generation writers. It is now evident that the Lost Generation was a small group whose life styles garnered such inordinate attention that commentators tended to overlook others who were at work in that same period.

Reacting against the internationalism of Woodrow Wilson, many Americans in the years after Versailles turned inward to find meaning in national or regional ideas. Some, like H. L. Mencken, stressed the importance of American ideas and customs. Others, like the southerners who contributed to the significant collection, *I'll Take My Stand* (New York, 1930), emphasized regional themes. These writers were reacting much as Americans had after the War of 1812 and the Civil War. After both of these conflicts, Americans relished literature that was national or regional and avoided giving equal attention to English or Continental subjects. Especially was this true after the Civil War, when America experienced its largest outburst of local color writing. In the twenties, there was a similar reaction to the internationalism of the war, and, in turn, there was an attempt to find new meaning in regional writing.

The twenties were also torn between acceptance of an urban-industrial present and nostalgia for an agrarian past that was frequently seen as a vanishing frontier. As Roderick Nash has pointed out, many Americans in the twenties longed for the frontier as a bulwark against a rising tide of cities and industrialization. Charles A. Lindbergh and Henry Ford became symbols for their age because they accepted and used the machine, but they were also strong individuals who had roots in the rural past. While these men utilized products of industrialism, they retained their ties to the past; they held on to symbols of the agrarian frontier.[7]

Historians in the twenties accepted and emphasized the significance of Turner's frontier thesis; major criticism of his views did not appear until the thirties.[8] The ideas of Turner were a major intellectual influence upon interpreters of American literature, and thus it is not surprising that literary historians turned to the frontier and its influence in an attempt to understand the major forces shaping American writing.

No work better illustrates this new interest than the essays collected in *The Reinterpretation of American Literature* (New York, 1928).[9] Norman Foerster, editor of this path-breaking volume, called for less reference to American literature as "a mere reflection of English

[7] See Roderick Nash, *The Nervous Generation: American Thought, 1917-1930* (Chicago, 1970), esp. 78-90, for a discussion of the desire to hold on to the frontier and wilderness in the twenties and, pp. 153-63, for the role of Henry Ford. See also John William Ward, "The Meaning of Lindbergh's Flight," *American Quarterly*, X (1958), 3-16; and Lawrence W. Levine, "Progress and Nostalgia: The Self Image of the 1920's," in Malcolm Bradbury, ed., *The American Novel and the 1920's* (London, 1971).

[8] Ray A. Billington, *America's Frontier Heritage* (New York, 1966), 4-16; Gene M. Gressley, "The Turner Thesis — A Problem in Historiography," *Agricultural History*, XXXII (1958), 227-249.

[9] Subtitled *Some Contributions toward the Understanding of Its Historical Development*, the volume included nine essays, eight by literary scholars and one by historian Arthur M. Schlesinger, Sr. An appendix contained an extensive bibliography which included a section on the frontier (pp. 225-226) and a useful checklist of dissertations completed or in progress through 1927. The listing is a valuable commentary on subjects considered worthy of a dissertation in the 1920s.

literature" and more emphasis on the native influences on American writing. While comparisons between American and European literature should be continued, he argued, there must be more study of the "distinctly American" qualities of American literature, and interpreters ought to scrutinize the "local conditions of life and thought in America" that molded American literature. Foerster was convinced that literary historians must reject the views of Barrett Wendell and explore the leads suggested by such historians as Turner, Arthur M. Schlesinger, Sr., and Charles Beard.

The essayists in Foerster's volume agreed that more attention should be given to American literature, but they arrived at no consensus on how the ideal study should be undertaken. Professors Schlesinger and Harry Hayden Clark reflected the chasm of opinion that still separated many students of literature. While Schlesinger called for a full understanding of the cultural and historical milieu of a writer and his work, Clark insisted that close scrutiny of the work of art was the starting place. Schlesinger's approach, explained Clark, too often led to overemphasis on backgrounds and too little analysis of the work itself.

Taken together, the articles in Foerster's volume emphasized the need for additional study of the contributions of Puritanism, romanticism, realism, and the frontier. In regard to the last, Foerster pointed out that the "influence of the frontier has been strangely neglected" (p. 28),[10] and he expressed the belief that the frontier had a large impact on Emerson, Whittier, and Twain, even though no one had discussed this influence. Admittedly, he added, the frontier spirit tended to turn sour and to become too materialistic. While the frontier was too imitative of Europe, it also became too boastful and anti-European. In a writer like Twain, both of these qualities of the frontier spirit were evident.

One of the contributors to the volume, Jay B. Hubbell, was more emphatic in stressing the scholarly neglect of the frontier's influence on American literature. While the literature of the United States had been less American than its history, he asserted, there was still strong evidence of the impact of the frontier on writing. The frontier provided authors like Cooper and Whitman with new materials and

---

[10] At this point Foerster adds a footnote: "It would now (1928) be truer to say that the influence of the frontier has been strangely exaggerated." This change of opinion reflects, no doubt, the appearance between 1925, when no major works on frontier literature were available, and 1928 of the volumes by Ralph Leslie Rusk, Dorothy Dondore, and Lucy Lockwood Hazard.

other writers with a native point of view. Discussions of the literary frontier, Hubbell insisted, ought to emphasize three topics: the frontier as historical background for literature, the frontier as the site of new literary activity, and the frontier as but *one* of several influences that had shaped the American character. While previous commentators had overlooked the role of the frontier in American literature, future interpreters, he warned, should not redress the oversight by placing too much emphasis on the frontier.

Though the essays in *Reinterpretation* underscored the insufficient amount of research concerning the frontier in American literature, there were, in fact, three major works about the subject being prepared for publication. The three projects were completed first as doctoral dissertations and then emerged quickly as books. Their publication in 1925-1927 signaled the first appearance of book-length studies devoted to the interrelationship of the American frontier and western literature.

Ralph Leslie Rusk's two-volume study, *The Literature of the Middle Western Frontier* (New York, 1925), was the first of the triumvirate to appear. Rusk was not so much interested in arguing the artistic merits of the literature of the early nineteenth century middle western frontier as he was in demonstrating how this literary activity was "invaluable for the record it contains of the growth of civilization during a unique epoch" (p. vii). His coverage ended with 1840, when, he argued, the middle western frontier came to a close.

Rusk discussed the impact of Europe, England, and eastern sections of the United States upon the Midwest and showed how authors from those areas were received on the frontier. He devoted chapters to travelers' accounts, magazines and newspapers, and drama, poetry, and fiction. The major emphasis was on breadth, and thus Rusk gave little attention to individual works and saved more space for extensive listings of significant books, newspapers, and literary events. At times his work seemed encyclopedic, more like an annotated bibliography than a literary history. The documentation often threatened to engulf the text. The second volume, for example, contained but fifty pages of text and a bibliography of nearly 400 pages. But Rusk seemed reluctant to comment on the literary quality of the many items he cited, and sometimes his treatments of major authors were brief and fragmented. His discussions of James Hall, for example, were scattered through several chapters because Hall was an editor, novelist, and a newspaperman. Finally, Rusk did not seem much acquainted with the writings of Turner and was not interested in speculating about the impact of the frontier upon middle western literature.

Dorothy Dondore's *The Prairie and the Making of Middle America: Four Centuries of Description* (Cedar Rapids, 1926) followed an organization similar to that of Rusk, but her volume contained more of the necessary ingredients of literary history. Like Rusk, she dealt with the writings of foreign travelers, the impact of the Spanish, French, and English on the Midwest. In addition, she devoted chapters to early romantic and realistic fiction of the prairies and completed her long volume with sections on literature after 1870. Unlike Rusk, she omitted discussion of newspapers and other ephemeral literary works, and she was more willing to make judgments about the merits of the writings that she did discuss.

Dondore was intrigued with what early foreign and American writers said about the land and the Indians. She demonstrated how these early writings were products of cultural biases, and she was aware of the significant relationship between changing economic and social conditions and a maturing literary culture. Dondore also showed how the development of transportation systems and towns and the arrival of explorers and immigrant groups helped to invoke the varied voices of the midwestern frontier. Throughout her long volume, she stressed the literary treatment of Indians. In fact, she dealt more extensively with this topic than did any of her contemporaries.

More analytical than previous writers in her approach to western writing, Dondore pointed out weaknesses in syntax, diction, and style. She noted stilted descriptions and snobbish prose, and she mentioned the failure of the region's writers to pay much attention to the structure of their works. Because she was willing to criticize, her book was a significant and valuable account of the rise of midwestern literature.

In the last section of her book, Dondore argued that by the middle 1920s the emergence of such authors as Sinclair Lewis, Sherwood Anderson, Carl Sandburg, and especially Willa Cather proved that midwestern literature had matured. The region was no longer a frontier, writers were no longer tied to overly idealized descriptions, and some authors demonstrated an ability to produce first-rate literature. Like many literary historians, Dondore seemed convinced that the best proof of the civilizing of the Midwest was the maturation of its literature.

The most analytical of the three important studies to appear in the twenties was Lucy Lockwood Hazard's *The Frontier in American*

Literature (New York, 1927). Hazard was well aware of Turner's contention that the frontier was the major influence in the shaping of American history—and she agreed with him. The frontier experience, she argued, had molded American literature, and the closing of the frontier had stimulated a new burst of writing. She believed that three topics dominated the new frontier literature: "regional pioneering," "industrial pioneering," and "spiritual pioneering." The New England and southern frontiers spawned the first type of pioneering, the Gilded Age encouraged the second, and the closing frontier was ushering in the last.

Throughout her brief volume, Hazard drew parallels between the historical frontiers that Americans had experienced and the kinds of literature that those frontier experiences had inspired. Industrial pioneering of the Gilded Age, for example, allowed—if not encouraged—the excesses of Andrew Carnegie and the Robber Barons. Like Vernon Louis Parrington,[11] whose influence upon her work she acknowledged, Hazard viewed the masters of capital as logical products of the individualism of the frontier. Neither Rusk nor Dondore saw the frontier as a negative influence on American life, though Hazard was less certain on this point. She agreed with Parrington and Mark Twain that the frontier spirit of the Gilded Age allowed too much individualsim—a rampant individualism that, she implied, needed to be controlled. The pioneer spirit turned sour in the post-Civil War period; it became selfish, arrogant, and inhumane. Americans were so driven to conquer virgin land, to capture available capital, and to rush up the ladder of success that they paid scant attention to their inner needs. It was this blindness, this boosterism that Twain and later Sinclair Lewis criticized.

By the 1920s the frontier as place had vanished, although many Americans refused to admit that it was gone. Hazard felt that writers of the twenties, especially Vachel Lindsay and Sherwood Anderson, realized that the old frontier had closed and that the frontier of the present and future was the "inner frontier," the jungle of man's inward sky and the wilderness of his relationships with other men. For Hazard, Vachel Lindsay, Sherwood Anderson, Henry James, and Henry Adams were the major explorers of this new literary frontier.

[11]Parrington, unfortunately, did not live to complete his *Main Currents in American Thought*, but the outline of the third volume, covering the period from 1860 to 1920, indicates that he would have increased his emphasis on the frontier West had he finished the book. The published version of the third volume includes sections on Twain, Garland, and notes for several chapters on western writers.

Thus, of the major studies appearing in the twenties, *The Frontier in American Literature* was the boldest in its interpretations. Hazard was explicit about the impact of the frontier on the literary development of America. Though she shared with Parrington a tendency to emphasize economic and social influences on writing, she was harsher than Rusk and Dondore in her judgments about frontier literature. At the same time, she was more aware than other critics that contemporary writers were changing their minds about the frontier and its impact on literature.[12]

In the two decades after the Great Crash, a shift in opinion about the character of the frontier experience and the rise of a new approach to literary interpretation became apparent. Following Turner's death in 1932 historians began to take issue with his evaluation of the importance of the frontier in American history. Some argued that he had overemphasized the role of the frontier in shaping the American character; others contended that he overlooked the impact of cities,

[12]According to John T. Flanagan, a long-time authority on western writing, students interested in western regional literature during the twenties were indebted to the studies mentioned here and to historians Turner and Frederic L. Paxson (Flanagan to Etulain, Sept. 17, 1974). Russel B. Nye found Hazard's book helpful in his early career (Nye to Etulain, Sept. 20, 1974).

I should like to acknowledge here the help I have received from many specialists in western literature. In the fall and winter of 1974-1975, I wrote to nearly a hundred persons and raised the following queries:

(1) Please summarize your own work in progress—or the projects that you soon plan to undertake.

(2) What scholars dealing with the American literary West have most influenced your work? For example, Franklin Walker, Henry Nash Smith, John R. Milton Max Westbrook, Don D. Walker, John Cawelti, Leslie Fiedler, Wallace Stegner, or others?

(3) In what directions do you think subsequent work on western American literature ought to move? Are these directions different from what you see to be the major thrusts of previous scholarship in the field?

(4) Please indicate the projects that you believe are most needed in subsequent study of western literature.

I have gained a great deal from the more than fifty responses to my request for information. Especially helpful were letters from Richard Astro, Louie Attebery, Edwin R. Bingham, Benjamin Capps, John Cawelti, Brian Dippie, Fred Erisman, John T. Flanagan, James K. Folsom, Thomas W. Ford, Warren French, Edwin W. Gaston, Jr., W. H. Hutchinson, Robert Edson Lee, Sanford E. Marovitz, Frederick Manfred, Barbara Meldrum, John R. Milton, Russel B. Nye, Levi Peterson, Henry Nash Smith, C. L. Sonnichsen, Wallace Stegner, Gary Topping, Don D. Walker, Max Westbrook, and Delbert Wylder. I am grateful to these scholars and others not listed for allowing me to quote from their letters. Their correspondence to me is cited by name and date.

immigrants, and European backgrounds in molding American history. One would think that these historical dissenters would have altered the focus of scholars studying the literary frontier, but such was not the case.

This was the more surprising because literary scholars like Robert Penn Warren, John Crowe Ransom, Cleanth Brooks, Allen Tate, and Richard Blackmur—the New Critics—were calling for a closer scrutiny of literary works and less emphasis on historical and biographical backgrounds. Too often, they asserted, literary historians overstressed the milieu of a poem, novel, or drama and tended to underplay the significance of the work itself. The New Criticism dominated many English departments in the 1940s, the 50s, and into the early 60s. But these critics had little impact on the study of western literature. In fact, between 1930 and 1950 the practice of western literary history reached its apogee.

No writer better illustrates the achievements of western literary historians than Franklin Walker. Although Walker's first book was published in 1932 and he has written five other volumes that deal with the literature of the West, his work, especially his literary histories of San Francisco and southern California, has not received as much attention as it deserves. This oversight is unfortunate, for Walker demonstrates what first-rate literary history ought to be, particularly through the interrelated use of biography, social and cultural history, and literary criticism.

Walker's first book, *Frank Norris: A Biography* (New York, 1932), demonstrates the chief strength of his work—his abilities as a superb literary biographer. In his study of Norris, as well as in his later biographical study, *Jack London and the Klondike* (San Marino, 1966), and in his literary histories, Walker pays close attention to the lives of the writers he discusses. In addition, his work emphasizes the relationships between his subjects and their milieus. One knows how and why, for example, frontier San Francisco and Los Angeles at the turn of the century produced the kinds of writers and literature that they did.

Walker's talents are seen at their best in his second and most important book, *San Francisco's Literary Frontier* (New York, 1939). The setting is San Francisco and its hinterlands between 1850 and 1870, and the focus is on the writers—Twain, Harte, Miller, Coolbrith, and others—influenced by this exciting time and place. Walker illustrates how the magazines, newspapers, and early social, economic, and cultural organizations that sprang up in frontier San Francisco encouraged literary activity. In addition, his evaluation of the prose and poetry of the early Far West demonstrates why so little of this nascent literary activity merits continued scrutiny. By uniting historical research and literary criticism, Walker succeeds in adding to the "rapidly growing body of information dealing with the influence of the frontier on American life and letters" (p. vii).

The same high standards are maintained in Walker's *A Literary History of Southern California* (Berkeley, 1950), a volume that illustrates the methodology Walker uses to construct all his literary histories.[13] He begins by introducing the topic or theme of a section and then describing the historical origins of the theme. This is followed by an analysis of writers and books that exemplify the central idea and, finally, by an extended treatment of a single writer or work that best illuminates the theme. In a brilliant chapter entitled "Cultural Hydroponics," Walker shows that southern California, like other regions of the United States, hungered for a romantic past that it could idolize, and he illustrates how writers like George Wharton James, Helen Hunt Jackson, and Charles Fletcher Lummis played important roles in capitalizing on this need by creating an idealized past. As in his other works, Walker stresses biography and cultural history and pays least attention to literary criticism. In doing so he demonstrates his ability to probe beneath the surface of cultural activity and to see what lies hidden from casual observers, a quality that is especially apparent in his perceptive discussions of Lummis, the San Diego Exposition, and the Pacific Electric. By emphasizing the symbolic importance of authors, events, and economic development, Walker prefigures one of the techniques utilized in Henry Nash Smith's *Virgin Land.*

The work of Franklin Walker belongs on the top shelf of important writings about the American literary West. His solid and well-researched volumes are indispensable groundwork for a complete history of western American literature that is badly needed. No one has produced better western literary history than Walker, and his books are still useful models for students and scholars who wish to

---

[13]Walker has not spelled out an explicit philosophy of literary history in his books, essays, or reviews, though he acknowledges the influences of Turner, Parrington, and Bernard DeVoto upon his work (Walker, June 30, 1974). But see his essay in this issue (vol. 45, no. 4) of the *Pacific Historical Review.*

pursue western writing via the approach of the literary historian.[14]

Another example of the historical approach to western literature is found in the three-volume *Literary History of the United States,* edited by Robert Spiller and several other scholars.[15] Published thirty years after the *Cambridge History,* which paid little attention to western literature, Spiller's volumes devoted several chapters to the subject. Dixon Wecter, Henry Nash Smith, George R. Stewart, and Wallace Stegner dealt with the region in such chapters as "Literary Culture on the Frontier," "Western Chroniclers and Literary Pioneers," "The West as Seen from the East," and "Western Record and Romance," which stressed the cultural ties of the West with the East and the West's attempts to please eastern readers. Smith, for example, demonstrated how earlier writers like Cooper, H. M. Brackenridge, and Zebulon Pike wrote with one eye on the details they were accumulating and the other eye trained on what eastern literati, especially the Romantics, wanted to read. Other writers, such as Josiah Gregg and Lewis H. Garrard, were less tied to eastern literary standards, more reluctant to polish their descriptions, and hence presented more authentic accounts of life along western trails and among the mountain men. Smith adds that easterners usually saw the West as a strange and wonderful place of Indians, sylvan areas, and wilderness. The West thus became a region of wondrous settings and characters, both of which held scenic and novel implications for a thirsty reading public in the East.

Though the chapters by Wecter, Smith, Stewart, and Stegner were noteworthy contributions, the editors of the *Literary History* did not include discussions of twentieth-century western literature.

---

[14]Russel B. Nye states: "My generation was powerfully influenced by Franklin Walker, first, Henry Nash Smith, next" (Nye, Sept. 20, 1974). Edwin R. Bingham finds useful Walker's "smooth fusion of literary criticism and social cultural history" (Bingham, Sept. 18, 1974).

[15]Robert E. Spiller, Willard Thorp, Thomas H. Johnson, Henry Seidel Canby, *et al.,* eds., *Literary History of the United States* (3 vols., New York, 1948). There have been revisions of this work but none adds measurably to the discussions of the literary West. Another extensive literary history of the United States, edited by Arthur H. Quinn, *The Literature of the American People: A Historical and Critical Survey* (New York, 1951), includes a chapter on twentieth-century southern literature, but only scattered sections on such modern western writers as Willa Cather, Robinson Jeffers, Ole Rölvaag, Conrad Richter, and John Steinbeck.

There were sections on Willa Cather and Sinclair Lewis and brief mention of Steinbeck and Jeffers, but these authors were not treated as western writers. By 1950, then, many literary historians were inclined to treat some nineteenth-century writers as western authors, but they were still reluctant to classify any writers writing after 1900 as *western* authors.

The publication of Henry Nash Smith's *Virgin Land: The American West as Symbol and Myth* (Cambridge, Mass., 1950) has proven to be a major turning point in the historiography of the American literary West. *Virgin Land* increased interest in western literature, helped place western writing in a new perspective, and provided students with new research techniques for their studies of the literary West. Smith's stimulating book has influenced interpretations of western literature more than any other study. In the twenty-five years since its publication, specialists in the field place it at the top of the list of books that have shaped their thinking and writing.

Portions of *Virgin Land*, which was completed at Harvard University in 1940 as the first dissertation in the new field of American Studies, appeared initially as a series of journal articles in the 1940s. When the completed volume was published in 1950, it was hailed immediately as an important new interpretation of the West in American thought and culture.[16]

Smith opens his book with a discussion of the views of Benjamin Franklin and Thomas Jefferson about the West. He uses the ideas of these two men as examples of what many Americans thought about the frontier West as it became part of their cultural experience. These thoughts gradually clustered around three themes: "Passage to India," "The Sons of Leatherstocking," and "The Garden of the World." Smith's approach in discussing these themes is an holistic one; he emphasizes that the West as symbol and myth was just part—albeit an important part—of what Americans were thinking and experiencing in the nineteenth century. Through this holistic ap-

[16]A few writers have taken issue with some of Smith's research techniques and interpretations. Laurence R. Veysey discusses some of the dangers involved in the concepts of myth and suggests that regional stereotypes may be of more use to students of western literature than the symbolic analysis used in *Virgin Land*. See his "Myth and Reality in Approaching American Regionalism," *American Quarterly*, XII (1960), 31-43. Barry Marks, a former student of Smith, challenges his mentor in "The Concept of Myth in *Virgin Land.*" *American Quarterly*, V (1953), 71-76. The most recent discussion of Smith and other scholars in the American Studies field can be found in Cecil F. Tate, *The Search for a Method in American Studies* (Minneapolis, 1973).

proach, Smith is able to show how Turner's famous essay of 1893 was part fact and part of the mythology that had grown up about the West in the previous hundred years. The final chapter in *Virgin Land* deals with Turner and demonstrates Smith's use of symbolic analysis. He shows how the idea of the West as the Garden of the World captured Turner's imagination and caused him to link many of his views about the importance of the words *nature* and *civilization* to America's cultural history. Smith shows that Turner's use of *nature* often moved beyond social analysis into poetry, a move that reflected Turner's ties to what historians have called "the agrarian myth." Using the close-reading techniques of literary critics, Smith demonstrates that Turner's use of *nature* was frequently more metaphorical than factual. In this chapter and in several other sections of his book, Smith calls for a close study of the relationship between the facts of western history and the myths that have grown up about western experiences.[17]

Virgin Land also demonstrates that scholars need not—in fact *should* not—limit their discussions to elite authors (for example, Cooper, Whitman, and Garland) if they wish to convey a full understanding of what the West meant to nineteenth-century Americans. The two chapters in Smith's volume devoted to heroes and heroines of the dime novel illustrate the author's commitment to studying all types of writing about the West. Through close study of the characters, plots, and themes of the dime novel, Smith shows how this popular genre reflected many of the controlling assumptions of the day about the nature of the American West. Smith's use of history, literature, sociology, and cultural anthropology reveals his strong attachment to an interdisciplinary approach to his subject. The sections on the dime novel are still models for subsequent research, and, as we shall see, they have been paradigms for recent research dealing with the formula Western.

The work of Smith, then, has been instrumental in encouraging two kinds of approaches to the literary West. The first method— the one that has attracted the most followers—has been called the American Studies school. These interpreters stress (in following Smith) that what people have thought about the West has frequently been more important in molding western literature than what ac-

[17] Smith explains some of his research methods in "Can 'American Studies' Develop a Method?" *American Quarterly*, IX (1957), 197-208. Also, see his introductory comments in the twenty-year anniversary edition of *Virgin Land* (Cambridge, Mass., 1970).

tually took place in the West. These writers have consistently played up the differences between what has been termed the real and the mythic West. For them, the West as state of mind is a concept that warrants continued study.

Other scholars have been influenced more by Smith's treatment of popular culture, particularly his analysis of the dime novel. These writers have recently shown a great deal of interest in the Western, a genre of formula literature that has arisen in the twentieth century. There is considerable overlap between the American Studies and popular culture schools, but the differences between the two groups are emphasized in order to plot the larger impact of *Virgin Land* upon western literary studies.

In the quarter century since the publication of *Virgin Land*, numerous scholars have relied on Smith's book for research methods and for insights into the American literary West. Kent L. Steckmesser, in his *The Western Hero in History and Legend* (Norman, 1965), acknowledges large "intellectual debts" to Smith. For example, he utilizes some of Smith's techniques in trying to separate fact from fiction in accounts of Kit Carson, Billy the Kid, Wild Bill Hickok, and George Armstrong Custer. In the only book-length study published on the western novel, James K. Folsom also admits that he owes a "great deal" to the work of Smith.[18] Folsom is interested in the "myth of the West" and the manner in which popular concepts about the West have spilled over into novels written about Indians, farmers, and frontier society. Smith's point of view and his methodology are particularly apparent in Folsom's chapter on Cooper. In his first-rate monograph on *The Middle Western Farm Novel in the Twentieth Century* (Lincoln, 1965), Roy Meyer draws upon Smith's treatment of farmers in nineteenth-century imaginative literature.

Several historians have utilized Smith's findings. Earl Pomeroy, in his study of tourism in the West.[19] employs some of Smith's discussions of western travelers to show how their views shaped subsequent ideas about the West. Joseph G. Rosa, without acknowledging the influence of *Virgin Land*, nevertheless adopts Smith's

[18]Folsom, *The American Western Novel* (New Haven, 1966); Folsom, Oct. 6, 1974. I have tried to detail some of the influences of Smith on Steckmesser, Folsom, and Robert Edson Lee in "Recent Views of the American Literary West," *Journal of Popular Culture*, III (1969), 144-53.

[19]Pomeroy, *In Search of the Golden West: The Tourist in Western America* (New York, 1957).

methods in his analysis of western gunfighters.[20] Even some of the recent western history texts testify to the influence of Smith's approach to the West. The best of these is Robert V. Hine's beautifully written *The American West: An Interpretive History* (Boston, 1973), which contains chapters on farmers, western heroes, and "The Frontier Experience" that reflect Smith's point of view.

During the last decade, two books have appeared that illustrate the American Studies approach so evident in *Virgin Land*. Both are wide-ranging studies, both advance controversial theses, and although both deal with literature of the eastern United States, they have already left their marks on the field of western literary studies.

Edwin Fussell's *Frontier: American Literature and the American West* (Princeton, N. J., 1965) is a reinterpretation of American literature from 1800 to the Civil War. The book deals primarily with Cooper, Hawthorne, Poe, Thoreau, Melville, and Whitman, and Fussell argues that these authors were inspired by the frontier, the meeting place between the civilized East and the barbarous West. But Fussell's frontier is not easy to define. Sometimes it is the high seas of *Moby Dick,* the dark forests of *The Scarlet Letter,* the sites of Poe's conflicts between nightmare and reality, and the locations of Thoreau's clashing Essential West and Real West. On other occasions the frontier is Poe's South, or Hawthorne's Salem, or Thoreau's Walden Pond. For Fussell, these frontiers are not specific locations but primarily the states of mind of the authors. He repeatedly stresses that the frontier is an idea, a metaphor. The mistake of Turner and other historians who emphasized the frontier as place, he contends, was their failure to comprehend the frontier as idea. Had they understood the metaphorical possibilities of the frontier, they would have realized that it was the "real" West.

Other views about the frontier will have to be changed if Fussell's assertions are accepted. For example, consider his belief that the frontier ended at least three and possibly four decades before Turner's announcement in 1893. Fussell argues that 1855-1860 was the watershed period of the frontier. After this era, there was no longer a viable frontier; it no longer fired the imagination of writers and thus had vanished as a shaping force. Besides this dubious opinion, Fussell offers no additional proof for his closing the frontier in the 1850s.

On the other hand, in his stress on the dualities in the writings of

[20] Rosa, *The Gunfighter: Man or Myth?* (Norman, 1969).

the American Romantics, Fussell is solidly in the American Studies school. For the Romantics, the essence of the westward movement was expressed in conflicts between East and West, civilization and wilderness, past and present, head and heart, dark and light. The first three of these dichotomies are tensions that Smith stressed in *Virgin Land,* particularly in his essays on Cooper. (Fussell's section on Cooper, one of his most persuasive chapters, draws heavily upon Smith's analysis.) Fussell also shares Smith's attachment to symbolic analysis, a technique that emphasizes intensive study of diction. Throughout his book, Fussell pays close attention to symbols, but his use of the technique is particularly evident in the last part of his book where he argues that when the frontier closed American literature veered in other directions.

Fussell's *Frontier* is a provocative study. The discussions of the metaphorical qualities of "frontier" and "West" are stimulating, but more convincing are the sections on Cooper, Whitman, and Thoreau. One wonders if the author's reading of these three writers and their visions of the frontier was not the impetus for this volume. The thesis of the book fits Thoreau best—and Poe least.

But Fussell presses his thesis too hard. If all his contentions were persuasive, his book would have replaced F. O. Matthiessen's *The American Renaissance* as the best interpretation of early nineteenth century American literature. But it has not done so, and one reason is Fussell's failure to emphasize sufficiently the impact of Europe and the Far West on the writers he discusses. And surely *The Scarlet Letter, Moby Dick,* and *Leaves of Grass* have other major and more significant meanings than Fussell is willing to assign to them.

Most of all, Fussell seems discontented with historians. He is convinced that interpreters like Turner, because they overstressed the geographical frontier (which is not entirely true of Turner), sent later readers up the wrong trails. No doubt Fussell's views are a corrective for those too tied to a Turnerian interpretation of the frontier, but in an attempt to prove his thesis he distorts the evidence. To argue that the frontier was gone by 1860 is to omit much of the frontier. This termination date misses the cowboy, several of the mining rushes, some of the overland trail years, and the sod house frontier. What seems closer to the truth is that after the Civil War, industrialism and cities caught up with the West as attention-gathering subjects. But writers like Twain, Harte, several frontier humorists, and such authors as E. W. Howe, Hamlin Garland, and Owen Wister proved that the frontier West was not as moribund as Fussell suggests. Had Fussell been more willing to qualify his thesis, to say that the frontier as place and idea was one of the major influences on writers of the Romantic period, his stimulating work would occupy an even more important spot in western literary studies.[21]

Another volume that illustrates some of the strengths and limitations found in Fussell's book is Richard Slotkin's *Regeneration through Violence: The Mythology of the American Frontier, 1600-1860* (Middletown, Conn., 1973). Much longer than Fussell's study, this hefty book (nearly 700 pages) is an outgrowth of the author's doctoral dissertation in the American Civilization program at Brown University. Slotkin pursues a large goal: He is interested in discussing the ideas that emerged from the American frontier experience between 1600 and 1860. He wants to trace the impact of European views upon the New World wilderness and to describe the national myths that emerged from the conflicts between the old and new cultures.

Like Fussell, Slotkin emphasizes the contrapuntal structure of his findings: Europe and America, civilization and wilderness, white and Indian. He is much more interested in the role of the Indian than were Fussell and Smith, who have little to say about American aborigines. In fact, Slotkin's major thesis is that Europeans, especially Puritans, in their desire to make sense out of their errand into the wilderness, formulated a myth of "regeneration through violence." Gradually these newcomers, as they became Americanized, persuaded themselves that in destroying the wilderness and conquering the Indians they were saving the continent for civilization. In his final chapter, Slotkin ponders the relationship between this destructive philosophy and modern American imperialism.

In addition to the useful comments on early frontier experiences found throughout the volume, the introductory chapters in Slotkin's book on myth-making are instructive for the student of the literary West. And his discussions of the rise of the popular hunter hero like Daniel Boone and the treatments of this hero in regional literatures east of the Mississippi are well done. Moreover, Slotkin has read widely in original sources; he deals with the works of major writers

---

[21] Some of the same topics discussed in Fussell are taken up in Wilson O. Clough, *The Necessary Earth: Nature and Solitude in American Literature* (Austin, 1964). Less well known than the book by Fussell, Clough's volume is, however, frequently more persuasive on topics that both authors treat. Another little-known volume that deals with the post-frontier era is Harold P. Simonson, *The Closed Frontier: Studies in American Literary Tragedy* (New York, 1970), which is a stimulating study of several writers' reactions to the closing frontier.

like Benjamin Franklin, Cooper, Thoreau, Melville, and with the writings of a host of minor authors. No one should fault his extensive research in primary sources. But *Regeneration through Violence* should be used with caution. Slotkin's treatment of the Puritans and their relationships with Indians does not take into account the views of Alden Vaughan, Edmund S. Morgan, and Ola Winslow, all of whom are less critical than he of the Puritans. The section on Thoreau is also distorted; the author makes too much of the Indianness of Thoreau. And other readers will question Slotkin's failure to use the accounts of Lewis and Clark, Josiah Gregg, and numerous other explorers who traveled into the trans-Mississippi West and wrote important accounts of what they saw and experienced.

Slotkin's major problems are those often found in the work of historians of ideas. He moves from work to work for evidence of his thesis, but he fails to give sufficient attention to the changing milieu of what he examines. And the tone of his book reflects the point of view of a young man discontented with what he has seen and felt in the late 1960s and drawn to other popular ideas thought to be corrective: more sympathetic views of the Indian, increased interest in back-to-the-land movements, and the search for the purported causes of violence in Judeo-Christian avarice. Despite these weaknesses, the volume is a major book in the field. Slotkin is sometimes too general and simplistic, but he is always stimulating and should be read and reread by all students interested in the literary West.

Leslie Fiedler, who has influenced Slotkin a great deal, puts even more emphasis than Slotkin on the mythic nature of the West. In some of his earlier interpretive works on American literature, Fiedler discussed western literature, but it is in *The Return of the Vanishing American* (New York, 1968) that he puts major stress on the subject. In this brief volume, Fiedler completes his "venture in literary anthropology" with a study of the role of Indians in writing about the frontier and the West. For Fiedler, American geography is primarily mythological, and "it is the presence of the Indian which defines the mythological West" (p. 21). Thus, the Western is the story of the conflict between the WASP and the Indian. And, as he had in his earlier works, Fiedler stresses here the hesitancy of white Americans to write about white women and their tendency to deal with masculine worlds.

In the final sections of his book, Fiedler centers on what he calls the "New Western." His comments on this new genre are not surprising when one realizes that Fiedler believes that "to understand the West as somehow a joke comes a little closer to getting it straight" (p. 137). He is convinced that the New Western has arisen because the older Western and writers like A. B. Guthrie, Walter Van Tilburg Clark, and Frank Waters failed to deal with the Indian in a believable fashion. Hence, such writers as Thomas Berger and Ken Kesey have produced New Westerns that treat Indians as "returned" or vanished Americans whose relationships with whites are similar to the relationships found between Huck and Jim in Twain's novels and Natty Bumppo and Chingachgook in the Leatherstocking Tales. The meeting in the wilderness between the white European and the red man is *the* theme of the West, and Fiedler is convinced that writers of New Westerns have taken up this idea. These authors do not involve their protagonists in the old myths of John Smith and Pocahontas; instead the heroes are placed in male-to-male relationships like those found in the works of Cooper, Melville, and Twain. Brotherhood is the major theme of the New Western.[22]

As Henry Nash Smith pointed out in a review of *The Return of the Vanishing American,* the reader is not always certain how seriously to take Fiedler.[23] His description of the New Western does fit Ken Kesey's *One Flew Over the Cuckoo's Nest,* Thomas Berger's *Little Big Man,* and some of the work of such novelists as David Wagoner and John Seelye. But his new genre does not describe the recent novels of Wright Morris, Wallace Stegner, Vardis Fisher, or A. B. Guthrie. Contemporary western novelists have stressed historical ties between the frontier and contemporary Wests, utilized the theme of a young man's initiation into manhood, and emphasized the importance of the arid, spacious West as setting. Fiedler does not mention any of these important themes, and because he does not, anyone who has taken the time to read a large number of novels written about the West in the last twenty-five years becomes convinced of the narrowness of Fiedler's approach. His contention that writing about the contemporary West should be a journey into madness defines the central emphasis in Seelye's *The Kid* (a novel dedicated to Fiedler), but this argument does not apply to Wallace

[22]In a recent address before the Western Literature Association (Jackson Hole, Wyoming, October 1972), Fiedler argued that the New Western, which he renamed the "meta-Western," deals exclusively with violence, sex, and racism.

[23]Smith's review of *The Return of the Vanishing American* appears in *American Literature,* XI, (1969), 586-588.

Stegner's Pulitzer Prize-winning *Angle of Repose,* the novels of Richard Brautigan, and most of the writing of Larry McMurtry. *The Return of the Vanishing American* is an important aid in understanding some fiction written about the West in the last two decades, but it is not a convincing guide to most recent western writing.[24]

In addition to its large impact on American Studies scholars, *Virgin Land* has also influenced students of American popular culture. Before the publication of Smith's book, historians were reluctant to deal with the formula Western. They seem to have considered the popular genre as subliterature and hence not worthy of study. Before 1950 only a handful of notable essays had appeared that dealt with the dime novel and Western. But Smith showed that the careful scholar could learn a great deal from the study of popular literature, and in the years since the publication of his seminal study, there has been an increasing amount of attention paid to the Western.

The most penetrating of recent writing about the Western is John Cawelti's *The Six-Gun Mystique* (Bowling Green, Ohio, 1971). In his extended essay, Cawelti summarizes the views of several interpreters of the Western and then outlines his thesis, which asks readers to take seriously the conventions of the formula Western and to scrutinize carefully the components of the formula to see what they reveal about a society that produces and reads Westerns. Cawelti reminds students that the Western can and does provide valuable insights into a changing American culture. Most of all, Cawelti argues that students of American thought and culture must cast off their predispositions about the worthlessness of the Western, must comprehend the repeated patterns in the popular genre, and must realize what these formulas tell us about American society. Henry Nash Smith fulfilled some of these demands in *Virgin Land,* but Cawelti moves beyond Smith by detailing the formula that defines the Western. He shows how the ambiguities of plot and characterization apparent in the contemporary Western reflect the growing tensions in recent America. He points out that heroes in the Western are frequently caught between reaffirming civilization or "town" values and trying to escape to a wilderness that is untrammeled by coercive law and order and still open to the actions of the strong individual.

[24]Several scholars find Fiedler's book more useful than I have in dealing with recent western fiction. For example, Edwin R. Bingham, Sept. 18, 1974; John G. Cawelti, Oct. 24, 1974; and C. L. Sonnichsen, Sept. 19, 1974.

Cawelti has produced a rich, highly original essay. Throughout his book, he touches on several themes, techniques, and ideas that are evident in the Western. While he does not deal extensively with any of these topics in his brief volume, he does illustrate how his contentions may be applied to a large number of Westerns. Students have already begun to utilize the techniques of Cawelti in studying formula writing about the West. In a recent collection of essays dealing with the Western, several of the essayists use the comments of Cawelti on the nature of formula fiction as the beginning place for their articles. These writers find especially pertinent Cawelti's views about the diverse roles of the hero, heroine, and community in the Western. Judging from the initial reactions of scholars to *The Six-Gun Mystique,* subsequent research on the Western will be strongly indebted to the insights of Cawelti.[25]

The other approach to the Western that has attracted a good deal of attention in the last few years is that of the cultural historian. Before the large impact of *Virgin Land* was apparent, W. H. Hutchinson and Bernard De Voto wrote essays discussing the place of heroes, villains, and heroines in the Western, and they stressed the importance of Owen Wister, Eugene Manlove Rhodes, and Ernest Haycox in the development of the popular type.[26] Two decades ago Joe B. Frantz and Julian E. Choate attempted to show how earlier writers of Westerns utilized stereotypes more than fact in their treatment of the cowboy.[27] Also in the fifties David B. Davis and Philip Durham chronicled the rise of the cowboy in the early twentieth century and demonstrated how Wister's *The Virginian* be-

---

[25]Richard W. Etulain and Michael T. Marsden, eds., *The Popular Western: Essays toward a Definition* (Bowling Green, Ohio, 1974). Cawelti's recent book on popular literary formulas, *Adventure, Mystery and Romance* (Chicago, 1976), includes a long section on the Western (Cawelti, Jan. 11, 1976). Henry Nash Smith, who read Cawelti's book in manuscript, feels that "the most interesting pathway of advance in the study of Western literature is that being charted by Mr. Cawelti," especially his "investigation of formulas and stereotypes" (Smith, Nov. 11, 1974). Other recent works by Cawelti on formula literature are "God's Country, Las Vegas, and the Gunfighter: Differing Visions of the West," *Western American Literature,* IX (1975), 273-283; and "Myth, Symbol, and Formula," *Journal of Popular Culture,* VIII (1974), 1-9.

[26]Hutchinson, "Virgins, Villains, and Varmints," *Huntington Library Quarterly,* XVI (1953), 318-392; DeVoto, "Birth of an Art," *Harper's* CCXI (Dec. 1955), 8-9, 12, 14, 16; and "Phaëton on Gunsmoke Trail," *Harper's,* CCIX (Dec. 1954), 10-11, 14, 16.

[27]Frantz and Choate, *The American Cowboy: Myth and Reality* (Norman, 1955).

came a paradigm for later Westerns.[28] Ten years later Durham and
his colleague, Everett Jones, in their much-cited *The Negro Cowboys* (New York, 1965), argued that the strong Ánglo Saxon prej-
udices of writers like Wister, Emerson Hough, and B. M. Bower
kept them from treating black cowboys realistically. Durham and
Jones illustrated how the study of popular literature could reveal
the tensions and ambiguities of Americans in a specific period of
time.

More recently Russel B. Nye has discussed the Western as one
significant form of American popular culture.[29] His treatment is
the best brief study of the development of the Western. Another
interpreter, Richard W. Etulain, has treated various periods in the
rise of the Western and suggested other topics and writers that merit
additional attention. There are increasing signs that many historians
have overcome their initial reluctance to study the Western and that
we can expect a new series of articles and books on this popular
genre.[30]

At this point, one might ask if any scholars have attempted to
unite the historical approach of Franklin Walker with the research
methods evident in Smith's *Virgin Land*. The answer is yes, and the
products of this marriage indicate that western literary scholarship
is maturing rapidly. One of the most impressive examples is G.
Edward White's *The Eastern Establishment and the Western Experience: The West of Frederic Remington, Theodore Roosevelt, and
Owen Wister* (New Haven, 1968). White's book, which is the published version of a doctoral dissertation in the American Civilization program at Yale University, is a stimulating study based on an
interdisciplinary methodology. White centers on the pivotal period
from 1890-1910 and traces the lives of Remington, Roosevelt, and
Wister from their early twenties and their exposure to the eastern
establishment of private schools, Ivy League universities, and mem-

---

[28]Davis, "Ten-Gallon Hero," *American Quarterly*, VI (1954), 111-125; Durham,
"Riders of the Plains: American Westerns," *Neuphilologische Mitteilungen*, LVIII
(Nov. 1957), 22-38.

[29]Nye, *The Unembarrassed Muse: The Popular Arts in America* (New York, 1970),
280-304.

[30]Etulain, "Ernest Haycox: The Historical Western," *South Dakota Review*, V
(1967), 35-54; "Literary Historians and the Western," *Journal of Popular Culture*,
IV (1970), 518-526; "Origins of the Western," *Journal of Popular Culture*, VI (1972),
799-805; "The Historical Development of the Western," *Journal of Popular Culture*, VII (1973), 717-726. The Popular Press of Bowling Green University is plan-
ning a series of monographs on popular Western writers to be edited by Richard W.
Etulain and Michael T. Marsden.

bership in prestigious social clubs to their subsequent adventures in the West. In his analysis of the experiences of these three men, White demonstrates how Americans used the East and West as symbols of the present and past, of industry and agriculture, of urban and rural, and how they tried to forge a consensus from their disparate experiences.

White argues that at the turn of the century Americans wanted frontier gentlemen or gentlemanly cowboys. Or to make the oxymoron more exact, they wanted westernized easterners. The end product would be a Theodore Roosevelt who benefitted not only from his eastern upbringing and education but also from his experiences on his western ranch. White contends that comprehension of this desire to homogenize the East and West gives larger understanding of the Rough Riders and the conservationist impulse of the era of Roosevelt. He sees both of these activities as products of Americans trying to bring together the eastern establishment and western experience.

Although White should have plunged deeper and traveled more in the many manuscript materials he lists in his bibliography, he does make clear at least a part of the consensus that many Americans tried to fashion out of diverse regional and historical backgrounds. He is aware of the myths that grew up about the West in the nineteenth century, and he shows how these myths sometimes coincided with, sometimes diverged from, the actual experience of Remington, Roosevelt, and Wister in the West. Because White is able to show the relationship between the work of these men and their milieu, his book is an excellent example of what can be accomplished when western literature is studied within the broader perspective of a dynamic American culture.[31]

Even more impressive in his marriage of the historical approach of Walker and the holistic techniques of Smith is Kevin Starr, author of the important volume, *Americans and the California Dream*,

---

[31] Neal Lambert, in his articles on Wister, employs research techniques similar to those of White. See Lambert, "Owen Wister's Virginian: The Genesis of a Cultural Hero," *Western American Literature*, VI (1971), 99-107; "Owen Wister's Lin McLean: The Failure of the Vernacular Hero," *Western American Literature*, V (1970), 219-232; and "The Values of the Frontier: Owen Wister's Final Assessment," *South Dakota Review*, IX (1971), 76-87. The same approach is utilized in Richard W. Etulain, *Owen Wister* (Boise, 1973). Ben Merchant Vorpahl stresses the importance of Wister and Frederic Remington in the formation of the cowboy hero in his *My Dear Wister: The Frederic Remington-Owen Wister Letters* (Palo Alto, 1972). No full-length literary biography of Wister has been published; one is badly needed.

1850-1915 (New York, 1973). Starr, who completed an earlier draft of his book in the Harvard American Civilization program, owes a great deal to the architectonic sense of ideas developed by such men as Perry Miller and his student, Alan Heimert, who served as director of Starr's doctoral dissertation. Starr is interested in the linear development of California's cultural history, and he also wishes to show, on another level, how the ideas of residents and outsiders about the region helped to shape the history of the area. As Starr puts it, his book "seeks to integrate fact and imagination in the belief that the record of their interchange through symbolic statement is our most precious legacy from the past" (p. vii).

To illustrate what the California "dream" came to mean, Starr deals with such cultural figures as Thomas Starr King, an early Protestant minister; Henry George, social critic; Josiah Royce, philosopher; John Muir, naturalist; and David Starr Jordan, president of Stanford University. Interspersed among these discussions are sections on such literary figures as Jack London, Gertrude Atherton, Frank Norris, and the literary and artistic community at Carmel. These sections are the best and most significant portions of the volume. Not only does Starr exhibit first-rate abilities as an historian of literature, he also demonstrates a keen eye for close reading of his many first-hand sources. Some readers may quibble with a few of his comments on London and Atherton and wish that he had done more with Harte and the *Overland Monthly*, but these faults are minor compared to his brilliant analysis of the complicated fabric that made up California's early cultural history.

Americans and the California Dream is a major book in the historiography of the American literary West. Utilizing some of the research methods and the findings of Franklin Walker,[32] Starr also stresses the importance of understanding myths and symbols if one is to comprehend the full meaning of the California dream. In addition, the author is aware of the arguments among historians about the significance of the frontier in American history, and he seems to

[32]See Starr's introduction and bibliography for comments on his indebtedness to Walker.

[33]Pomeroy, "Toward a Reorientation of Western History: Continuity and Environment," *Mississippi Valley Historical Review*, XLI (1955), 579-600.

[34]Distinctions between the Romance and the Novel in Chase's *The American Novel and Its Tradition* (New York, 1957) are essential to an understanding of some of Folsom's contentions in *The American Western Novel.* Edwin W. Gaston also makes extensive use of Chase in *The Early Novel of the Southwest* (Albuquerque, 1961).

side with Earl Pomeroy in stressing the continuities between East and West more than the novel experiences of the frontier.[33] In sum, Starr's volume is well written, full of valuable insights, and replete with useful models for research on similar subjects. Indeed, it is the most important volume dealing with western literature since *Virgin Land*.

To imply, as I may have done thus far, that *Virgin Land* has influenced directly all research completed on the literary West in the last twenty-five years would be misleading. Other books have made a significant impact on the field. During the 1960s and 70s, "myth critics," like Northrop Frye and Richard Chase,[34] and specialists in American cultural history, such as Leo Marx and R. W. B. Lewis,[35] have influenced students of western literature, especially those who completed graduate work in departments of English or American Studies. Scholars living in the Southwest or studying the literature of that region frequently cite the work of Walter P. Webb, J. Frank Dobie, and Mody Boatright as crucial in their research and writing.[36] In addition, the solid and stimulating work of Wallace Stegner, who is committed to the fruitful marriage of western literature and history, has placed its mark on several students.[37]

Another point of view that owes much to Bernard DeVoto has made its impact felt in the last two or three decades. In the early

[35]Students of the literary West swayed by Smith's *Virgin Land* usually cite the works of Marx (a student of Smith) and Lewis as major influences on their thinking and writing. As Richard Astro says, Marx's *The Machine in the Garden* (New York, 1964) "has implications which opened my eyes to certain features of Western literature" (Sept. 19, 1974). Glen Love finds Smith, Marx, and Lewis helpful because their research is "both eclectic and sound in its use of history, myth, and formal literary analysis" (Sept. 24, 1974). Another scholar adds: "It's R. W. B. Lewis, and his book *The American Adam*, who's had more effect upon my thoughts and work than almost anyone else" (L. L. Lee, Oct. 28, 1974).

[36]Orlan Sawey and Edwin W. Gaston cite Dobie, Boatright, and Webb as strong influences on their work (Sept. 20, 1974; Sept. 24, 1974). Southwestern novelist Benjamin Capps writes that "The only scholar who directly influenced my work was Mody Boatright, under whom I studied in the '40s" (Dec. 23, 1974).

[37]Thomas W. Ford writes: "I find Wallace Stegner always perceptive, especially from the standpoint of someone who is close to the West, dearly loves it, yet is able to temper his love with critical perception" (Oct. 4, 1974). Stegner's provocative essays, particularly "Born a Square" and "History, Myth, and the Western Writer," are cited frequently in general essays about the West. These articles, plus his other pieces on western literature and conservation, are collected in *The Sound of Mountain Water* (Garden City, 1969). As one advanced graduate student in American history puts it, "I soundly disagree with some of his central contentions [in *The Sound of Mountain Water*] but I have never read a book on the West and its litera-

years of the twentieth century, western novelist Eugene Manlove
Rhodes complained that eastern publishers and readers knew little
about the West and its writing and that they tended to classify all
novels written about the region as "just another Western." In the
twenties and thirties De Voto began his argument with Van Wyck
Brooks and others who, DeVoto thought, misread the western influences at work on Mark Twain. DeVoto, and many of those who
followed his outspoken views, argued that there was a continuing
conflict between the East and West in which the latter was the under-
dog. When commentators have applied this viewpoint to western
writing, as Vardis Fisher and Robert Edson Lee have done,[38] they
have asserted that the West has produced some first-rate literature,
but it has not been recognized as such by eastern, effete critics; or,
as another line of this argument runs, western writing has not been
consistently better because the East has dominated American culture and has not allowed or encouraged the truth to be written about
the West. These antieastern commentators have gained several
followers among current students of western literature.[39]

In the 1960s there was a sharp increase in the amount of material
written about the literary West. For the first time, those adventurous
scholars who wished to study western writing found several markets
open to their work. Previously, editors of literary journals seemed
convinced that nearly all writing about the West was of an inferior
sort and not worthy of scholarly attention. Historical magazines
were willing to accept biographical articles about well-known authors

---

ture that lifted my own sights higher" (Gary Topping, Oct. 14, 1974). Other specialists in western literature who admit to Stegner's influence on their work are John R.
Milton and Richard W. Etulain.

[38] The fullest account of DeVoto's battles with Van Wyck Brooks, the Lost Generation writers, and Marxist interpreters can be found in Wallace Stegner's brilliant
The Uneasy Chair: A Biography of Bernard DeVoto (Garden City, 1974). Stegner's
book proves that western history and biography can also be first-rate literature,
Stegner has edited some of DeVoto's lively correspondence in *The Letters of Bernard DeVoto* (Garden City, 1975). Orlan Sawey deals with DeVoto's literary artis-
try in *Bernard DeVoto* (New York, 1969). Fisher's position is explicit in "The Western Writer and the Eastern Establishment," *Western American Literature*, I (1967),
244-259. Lee's provocative comments are included in his well-written book, *From
West to East: Studies in the Literature of the American West* (Urbana, 1966).

[39] The West as colony of the East is dealt with in Gene Gressley, "Colonialism: A
Western Complaint," *Pacific Northwest Quarterly*, I,IV (1963), 1-8; and in the eleven
essays collected in "The American West as an Underdeveloped Region," *Journal of
Economic History*, XVI (Dec. 1956). The same subject is treated generally in Gerald
D. Nash, *The American West in the Twentieth Century: A Short History of an
Urban Oasis* (Englewood Cliffs, N. J., 1973). These writers stress economic and po-

like Cooper, Twain, and Harte, but reluctant to publish essays dealing with twentieth-century western writers.

In 1962, the *South Dakota Review* was the first journal to declare its primary interest to be western literature. Edited by John R. Milton, the quarterly has been one of the few magazines known for its encouragement of writings by and about western authors. Milton, a talented poet and writer of fiction, has devoted at least one or two issues each year to western literature. In addition to his editorial work, Milton has turned out a series of essays dealing with western writers that have gained him a substantial following.[40] He emphasizes the form, rhythm, and setting of western literature and contends that western fiction owes much to the patterns of man-land experience in the region. Milton's interpretations have been continued and amplified in the work of Max Westbrook, who stresses the Jungian and mythic quality of western literature.[41]

An even more widely known journal is *Western American Literature*, which first appeared in 1966. Sponsored by the Western Literature Association, this review has been the most available outlet in the last decade for research about western writing. Included in each year's winter issue is a useful annual bibliography of books, articles, and unpublished theses and dissertations. Thus far, most of the articles accepted for publication in the journal have been competent essays centering on specific works or authors; few contributors have ventured comprehensive views of western writing.[42] As scholarship on the subject matures and critics become acquainted with more of the literature of the West, the editorial staff of the journal should be able to demand more wide-ranging essays.

---

litical history; I have tried to point out briefly the dangers of this theory when it is applied to western literature in "Research Opportunities in Western Literary History," *Western Historical Quarterly*, IV (1973), 263-272.

[40]See, for example, Milton, "The Western Novel: Sources and Forms," *Chicago Review*, XVI (1963), 74-100; "The Novel in the American West," *South Dakota Review*, II (1964), 56-76; "The American West: A Challenge to the Literary Imagination," *Western American Literature*, I (1967), 267-284; and "The Western Novel: Whence and What?" *Interpretive Approaches to Western American Literature* (Pocatello, Idaho, 1972), 7-21.

[41]Westbrook, "Conservative, Liberal, and Western: Three Modes of American Realism," *South Dakota Review*, IV (1966), 3-19; "The Practical Spirit: Sacrality and the American West," *Western American Literature*, III (1968), 193-205. The ideas in these essays and several others are summarized in Westbrook's stimulating *Walter Van Tilburg Clark* (New York, 1969).

[42]The essays of John R. Milton, Don D. Walker, Max Westbrook, and John Cawelti are exceptions.

Other magazines have been open to essays about the literary West. *Southwestern American Literature*, published by the Southwestern American Literature Association, reflects the interests of that region. Until its demise in 1973, *Western Review* published contributions on all aspects of the literary West. Two journals representing the Western History Association, *The American West* and *Western Historical Quarterly*, have accepted a few significant essays about western literature.[43] On occasion, *The Roundup*, the house organ of the Western Writers of America, includes a surprisingly good article on the popular Western. But the journal that has been most receptive to research on the Western is the *Journal of Popular Culture*. Dedicated to the idea that the culture of all Americans deserves study, this magazine has devoted considerable space to popular literature and has published two special issues dealing with the Western.[44]

Other evidence of the increased interest in western literature is found in two recent pamphlet collections, the Steck-Vaughn Southwest Writers Series and the Boise State Western Writers Series. More than thirty pamphlets were published in the former group, and by the end of 1975 twenty had appeared in the latter collection. Intended as fifty-page introductions for students and scholars, these pamphlets seem to have fulfilled their modest purpose.[45] Major authors like Clark, Fisher, Guthrie, Stegner, and Jeffers have been dealt with as well as such lesser known writers as Charles A. Siringo, Emerson Hough, and J. Mason Brewer. The voluminous Twayne United States Authors series contains several volumes on western writers. Notable Twayne volumes are those by Max Westbrook on Walter Van Tilburg Clark, Edwin W. Gaston, Jr., on Conrad Richter, Frederic I. Carpenter on Robinson Jeffers, David Madden on Wright Morris, Warren French on John Steinbeck and Frank

---

[43]See "Writers and the West: A Special Issue," *The American West*, X (Nov. 1973). Three broad-based articles in *Western Historical Quarterly* are Richard West Sellars, "The Interrelationship of Literature, History, and Geography in Western Writing," IV (1973), 171-185; Etulain, "Research Opportunities in Western Literary History," IV (1973), 263-272; and Don D. Walker, "The Mountain Man Journal: Its Significance in a Literary History of the Fur Trade," V (1974), 307-318.

[44]The two special issues are IV (Fall 1970), 455-526; and VII (Winter 1973), 647-753. The latter was reprinted in Etulain and Marsden, eds., *The Popular Western: Essays toward a Definition.*

[45]See the brief review of the Boise State series in *The New Republic*, CLXXII (March 1, 1975), 32, and the longer estimate in *Western American Literature*, IX (1975), 312-314.

Norris, Joseph M. Flora on Vardis Fisher, Thomas J. Lyon on Frank Waters, and Earle Labor on Jack London. In addition to the numerous books, journals, series, and organizations noted thus far, several persons have also influenced the historiography of western literature through their teaching and their direction of theses and dissertations. John Flanagan has given courses in midwestern and western literature for several decades at the University of Illinois, and some of his students have produced first-rate dissertations and books.[46] The students of Henry Nash Smith at the universities of Minnesota and California, Berkeley, have contributed much to our understanding of Mark Twain and the literary West. And those who have studied with Russel B. Nye (Michigan State University)[47] and John Cawelti (University of Chicago) have turned out notable contributions in the areas of American cultural and literary history. John R. Milton (University of South Dakota) has directed several graduate projects and served as consultant for many others. As director of creative writing for many years at Stanford before his recent retirement, Wallace Stegner worked with such talented novelists as Ken Kesey and Larry McMurtry and inspired other students to study carefully the literary West.

But in the last decade Don D. Walker of the University of Utah has had the largest impact on students of western literature, particularly on those scholars who have been active in the Western Literature Association. Both editors of *Western American Literature* studied with Walker, and several members of the journal's editorial board are his former students.[48] Walker especially encourages students to study the relationships between western history and literature, and he practices well what he preaches in his stimulating essays. His willingness to utilize techniques and findings from several disciplines and his use at times of the close reading methods of formalist critics reveal his training in American Studies.

[46]Flanagan estimates that "over half of the some sixty dissertations" he has directed "bear a direct relation to the middle or far west" (Sept. 17, 1974).

[47]A student of Nye has written one of the best general studies of western literature. Unfortunately, it remains unpublished. See Francis E. Hodgins, Jr., "The Literary Emancipation of a Region: The Changing Image of the American West in Fiction" (Ph.D. dissertation, Michigan State University, 1957).

[48]J. Golden Taylor was the founding editor of *Western American Literature*. Thomas J. Lyon now serves as editor. Alan Crooks, Levi Peterson, L. L. Lee, Neal Lambert, Richard Cracroft, Merrill Lewis, Ernest Bulow, and Gary Topping are a few of Walker's many students.

Beyond this, Walker writes with the humor and verve of a frustrated novelist, and his essays demonstrate that western literary studies can be both entertaining and intellectually stimulating.[49] It is increasingly apparent that as teacher and writer Walker has had as much impact in the 1970s on the study of western literature as his mentor Henry Nash Smith.

In the last decade the historiography of the American literary West has come of age. The premier contributions to this development have been the works of Franklin Walker and Henry Nash Smith. Walker laid the earlier foundation of solid historical studies, and Smith, through his emphasis on symbol and myth and on the importance of studying popular literature, broadened interpretive approaches to western literature. Finally, within the last five years the writings of such talented commentators as Richard Slotkin, John Cawelti, Kevin Starr, and Don Walker have demonstrated that first-rate scholars are turning their attention to the literary West and producing provocative books and essays about the subject.[50]

---

[49] Few writers can match the liveliness of Walker's "The Rise and Fall of Barney Tullus," *Western American Literature*, III (1968), 93-102, which should be required reading for all students of western literature. Besides the articles mentioned previously, other notable essays by Walker include: "The Mountain Man as Literary Hero," *Western American Literature*, I (1966), 15-25; "Can the Western Tell What Happens?" *Interpretive Approaches to Western American Literature*, 33-47; Philosophical and Literary Implications in the Historiography of the Fur Trade," *Western American Literature*, IX (1974), 79-104; and "Notes toward a Literary Criticism of the Western," *The Popular Western*, 86-99. Walker edits and publishes *The Possible Sack*, a journal devoted to western literature which is distributed free from the Department of English, University of Utah, Salt Lake City.

[50] In addition to the authors and books mentioned here, one might read two collections of essays to gauge the current status of western literary studies: *Interpretive Approaches to Western American Literature*, which contains essays by John Milton, Delbert E. Wylder, Don Walker, and Max Westbrook and an annotated bibliography of other recent works; and Etulain and Marsden, eds., *The Popular Western*, which is a handy guide to contemporary evaluations of the popular Western and includes eight essays and a selective bibliography. *Western Writing* (Albuquerque, 1974), edited by Gerald Haslam, contains a dozen of the best essays that have been written on the subject during the last twenty years. The most recent study of western literature is Jay Gurian's *Western American Writing: Tradition and Promise* (Deland, Fla., 1975), which analyzes what the author considers the major themes and styles in western writing. Haslam has also edited a series of lecture-tapes on western American literature for Everett/Edwards, Deland, Florida (1974-1975). Another illustration of the growing interest in western literature is the competition among several university presses—New Mexico, Oklahoma, Nebraska, Brigham Young, and Utah, for example—for manuscripts dealing with the literary West.

Western literary studies are no longer in their adolescent stage; they have taken on a new maturity.

Chronology of Important Dates

1682   Publication of Mary Rowlandson, *A Narrative of the Captivity and Restoration of Mrs. Mary Rowlandson*. This, the first and best of the narratives of Indian captivity, details Mrs. Rowlandson's tribulations as an Indian prisoner during King Philip's War (1675-76).

1782   Publication of J. Hector St. John de Crevecoeur, *Letters from an American Farmer*, an important and influential statement of late eighteenth-century attitudes toward the West.

1784   Publication of John Filson, *The Discovery, Settlement and Present State of Kentucky*. Contains in an appendix the first major literary treatment of Daniel Boone.

1804-06   Lewis and Clark expedition to the Pacific. Important literarily as the basis for many poems, novels, and stories.

1813   Publication of Daniel Bryan's *The Mountain Muse*, an epic poem about the life of Daniel Boone.

1823   Publication of James Fenimore Cooper, *The Pioneers*. The first of five Leatherstocking tales, it was followed by *The Last of the Mohicans* (1826), *The Prairie* (1827), *The Pathfinder* (1840), and *The Deerslayer* (1841). The Leatherstocking tales represent the most important nineteenth-century development of the Western story.

1826   Publication of Timothy Flint, *Francis Berrian, or the Mexican Patriot*, the first novel in English written about the American Southwest.

1833   Publication of Timothy Flint, *Biographical Memoir of Daniel Boone*, the most widely read popular American biography of the nineteenth century.

1836   Davy Crockett dies at the Alamo, March 6th. His highly fictionalized adventures become a staple of the later Western story.

1860   Appearance of the first "dime novels," published in New York by Erastus Beadle.

1865   "The Celebrated Jumping Frog of Calaveras County" marks the first appearance in print of Mark Twain.

1869   Edward Z. C. Judson ("Ned Buntline") introduces Buffalo Bill Cody to the American public with the first dime novel about him, *Buffalo Bill, the King of Border Men.*

1870   Publication of (Francis) Bret(t) Harte, *The Luck of Roaring Camp, and Other Stories,* the most important American collection of stories about the California gold fields.

1876   George Armstrong Custer and his Seventh United States Cavalry command are annihilated at the Little Big Horn, June 25th. No other single engagement of the American Indian Wars has attracted so much literary attention as this.

1890   The United States census declares the American frontier no longer exists.

1893   Frederick Jackson Turner reads "The Significance of the Frontier in American History" to the American Historical Association in Chicago. This is the most important single document in the interpretation of the American frontier.

1902   Publication of Owen Wister, *The Virginian: A Horseman of the Plains,* a novel which definitively establishes the form of the twentieth-century Western.

1912   Publication of Zane Grey, *Riders of the Purple Sage,* the most important single source of the modern "formula" Western.

1950   Publication of Henry Nash Smith, *Virgin Land: The American West as Symbol and Myth,* the most influential twentieth-century study of the literary West.

Notes on the Editor and Contributors

JAMES K. FOLSOM, the editor, is Professor of English at the University of Colorado, Boulder. He is the author of numerous books and articles about various aspects of the American West, including *The American Western Novel* (1966) and biographies of *Timothy Flint* (1965) and *Harvey Fergusson* (1969).

DAVID B. DAVIS is Farnam Professor of History at Yale University. His interests lie generally in the intellectual history of the United States and more specifically in the problems of slavery and the cultural history of the antebellum South. He is the author of many scholarly works, notably *The Slave Power Conspiracy and the Paranoid Style* (1967) as well as the editor of two collections of essays: *Antebellum Reform* (1967) and *The Fear of Conspiracy: Images of Un-American Subversion from the Revolution to the Present* (1971).

J. FRANK DOBIE, a lifelong Texan, was a writer and historian. His works include *Apache Gold and Yaqui Silver* (1939), *The Longhorns* (1941), *The Mustangs* (1952), and *Tales of Old-Time Texas* (1955), as well as a bibliography of Western American literature, *Guide to Life and Literature of the Southwest* (revised edition, 1952).

RICHARD W. ETULAIN is Professor of History at Idaho State University, Pocatello. His interests lie in Western American history and literature. He is the author of, among other works, *Western American Literature: A Bibliography of Interpretive Books and Articles* (1972) and *The Popular Western: Essays toward a Definition* (1974).

VARDIS FISHER was author of numerous historical and fictional works, most of which deal with the American West. His fiction includes a historical novel about the Mormons, *Children of God; an American Epic* (1939); and an account of the Lewis and Clark expedition, *Tale of Valor* (1958). Others of his Western novels are *Toilers of the Hills* (1928), *City of Illusion* (1941), and *The Mothers* (1943).

OPAL LAUREL HOLMES (Mrs. Vardis Fisher) collaborated with Vardis Fisher on many of his nonfictional works. A resident of Idaho, she is Vardis Fisher's literary executor and is presently engaged in editing and reissuing his works.

W. H. HUTCHINSON is Professor of History at California State University, Chico. Editor of *The Rhodes Reader* (1957), he is also the author of a bibliography of Eugene Manlove Rhodes's writings, *A Bar Cross Liar* (1959) and of a biography of Rhodes, *The Life and Personal Writings of Eugene Manlove Rhodes* (1956).

DAVID MOGEN is Assistant Professor of English at Georgia State University, Atlanta. His interests lie in popular culture, notably the literature of the American frontier and science fiction.

S. GRISWOLD MORLEY was Professor of Spanish at the University of California, Berkeley. A commentator on both Hispanic and South American literature, he was President of the Modern Language Association of America (1950). His publications include works on Lope de Vega, Cervantes, Spanish lyric poetry, and Spanish ballads.

MAX WESTBROOK is Professor of American Literature at the University of Texas, Austin. He is the author of a biographical and critical study *Walter Van Tilburg Clark* (1969) and editor of *The Modern American Novel: Essays in Criticism* (1966). He is former President (1973-74) of the Western Literature Association.

Selected Bibliography

The most useful introductory volume to the study of the American West is Howard R. Lamar, ed., *The Reader's Encyclopedia of the American West* (1977). This volume contains articles on almost every imaginable subject pertaining to the American West and useful short bibliographies as well. The most useful single bibliography of Western Americana remains J. Frank Dobie's *Guide to Life and Literature of the Southwest* (revised edition, 1952), though it should be supplemented with Richard Etulain's more recent *Western American Literature: a Bibliography of Interpretive Books and Articles* (1972) and Lawrence C. Powell's *Southwest Classics: The Creative Literature of the Arid Lands* (1974). Ramon F. Adams's *The Rampaging Herd: A Bibliography of Books and Pamphlets on Men and Events in the Cattle Industry* (1959) and *Six-Guns and Saddle Leather: A Bibliography of Books and Pamphlets on Western Outlaws and Gunmen* (1954) are excellent but more specialized bibliographies. An annual bibliography of literary studies of the West may be found in the journal, *Western American Literature*.

James K. Folsom's *The American Western Novel* (1966) offers an overview of western American fiction. It may be complemented by Gerald W. Haslam, ed., *Western Writing: Famous Western Authors Explain their Craft* (1974), a volume consisting of essays by noteworthy Western authors. Much modern scholarship has traced the relationship of the historic West to the imaginative West, attempting analysis of the cultural needs to which the American Western mystique gives expression. Frederick Jackson Turner's seminal essay, "The Significance of the Frontier in American History", (1893), remains useful today. Kent L. Steckmesser takes a sober look at distortions of Western history in *The Western Hero in History and Legend* (1965). Richard Slotkin studies the symbolic nature of the American frontier in *Regeneration through Violence: The Myth-*

ology of the American Frontier, 1600-1860 (1973), while John G. Cawelti, in *The Six-Gun Mystique* (1971) and *Adventure, Mystery, and Romance: Formula Stories as Art and Popular Culture* (1976), investigates the Western as a form of "pop" art.